AN ENGLISHMAN,
A SCOTSMAN
AND AN IRISHMAN
WALKED ONTO A
FOOTBALL PITCH

GROWING UP WITH THE TRINITY

AN ENGLISHMAN,
A SCOTSMAN
AND AN IRISHMAN
WALKED ONTO A
FOOTBALL PITCH

GROWING UP WITH THE TRINITY

BRENDON McGUIRE

First published by Pitch Publishing, 2019

Pitch Publishing
A2 Yeoman Gate
Yeoman Way
Worthing
Sussex
BN13 3QZ
www.pitchpublishing.co.uk
info@pitchpublishing.co.uk

A CIP catalogue record is available for this book from the British Library.

ISBN 978 1 78531 502 2

Typesetting and origination by Pitch Publishing

Printed and bound in Great Britain by TJ International Ltd

Contents

DEDICATION

This book is dedicated to my mother, Sheila, and to the memory of my father, Eddie

Foreword

I VIVIDLY remember the day I left school in south Manchester. It was a warm day in July 1968, and I didn't have a care in the world as I strolled to the bus stop to make the journey home. I was just 15 years old. It was only a few weeks since Manchester United had so gloriously won their first European Cup against the superstars of Portugal's Benfica, on a magical May night at Wembley Stadium. However, despite having failed to gain any formal academic qualifications, I had much to celebrate: I was about to sign as an apprentice professional for my hometown club having been spotted by Joe Armstrong (the legendary scout) playing for Stretford Boys. It was every schoolboy's dream! I proceeded to have a 16-year career in football before changing professions and becoming a social worker for the local authority (Manchester) in 1984. I returned to the club as a part-time coach in 1990, before being invited to become full-time in 1998 when the academies were established.

At the same time as I signed for the European Champions, a young Brendon McGuire, a 14-year-old schoolboy, was preparing for his final year at school in Chadderton, north Manchester, where he would sit his General Certificate of Education (GCE) exams in the summer of 1969. He would later sign for Rochdale (one of my former clubs) as an apprentice before pursuing a highly distinguished career in teaching and lecturing, combined with playing as a part-time pro for several north-west clubs. I first met Brendon in 1997 when I was studying for an MA in sociology at Manchester Metropolitan University (MMU), and he was a senior lecturer in the PE Department. Although we followed different career pathways, there were three major features of our lives that bound us together: our Mancunian roots, a 60s childhood and an abiding love of everything to do with football, and the history, culture and tradition of Manchester United Football Club. Furthermore, we both share the honour and privilege of writing books on a particular aspect of the club's wonderful history – in my case the early years of the famous youth policy in the 50s. There's a delightful symmetry about all this, don't you think?

In this his first book, Brendon is telling the story that so many Manchester United supporters from the 60s have yearned to tell, because it's autobiographical, personal, reflective and deeply nostalgic. Undoubtedly, the 60s was a very special period in the history of the club when they won four major trophies within ten years of the Munich Disaster, demonstrating amazing spirit and resilience in recovering from the horrors of that tragedy in February 1958. The author eloquently articulates the thoughts and feelings of innumerable people when he revisits society in the 60s, and the effect that three magnificent footballers had on people around the world, let alone the city of Manchester. Set against the backdrop of the myriad of cultural influences impacting politics, music and fashion in that decade, Brendon reminds us just how electrifying this particular era was and the various personalities who dominated it, such as Matt Busby, The Beatles, Mary Quant and, not least, our three heroes Best, Law and Charlton. We are also reminded of the iconic landmarks of Manchester that meant so much to people (and still do) such as the Central Library, the Free Trade Hall, the Twisted Wheel and, dare I say, George Best Edwardia.

For many of us, childhood was an exceedingly sensitive, delicate and precious period of our lives and Brendon's was difficult at times. However, he tells how he had the good fortune to be 'left with United' after he and his brother (at his mother's prompting) 'tossed a coin' to see which of them would support City or United – his brother won and thus supported City. Little did Brendon know that losing that toss was a supremely life-changing event – the beginning of a lifetime's devotion to his beloved club, and his fascination with Best, Law and Charlton. Indeed, watching these titans play at Old Trafford became the highlight of his week as he stood on the Stretford End in the company of his dear mother. It was a chance to escape into a wonderland of joy, peace and happiness, seeing his idols performing miracles in the flesh. To him, they embodied all that was good about life and humanity. It made him want to go out to play for hour after hour with his mates, seeking to emulate their feats in the street, park, school playground or whatever space they could find to play the beautiful game. Perhaps you, too, have similar memories. I know I do, and they came flooding back in wave after wave as I turned the pages of this splendid tome.

So what is it about George Best, Denis Law and Bobby Charlton that makes a sixty-something retiree want to spend a considerable amount of his time writing about them, when many other folk of the same age are happy to sit by the fire in slippers, whiling away the hours? May I remind you that that all three players finished playing together over 40 years ago, but they still have a huge impact on both Brendon's life as well as countless others? I think part of the answer lies in their personality, the way they expressed themselves as footballers in a unique way. All three were enthralling to watch: charismatic, magnetic and magisterial. In short, they encapsulate everything that was good about football in the 60s – the icing on the cake of a truly extraordinary epoch.

In this book, Brendon McGuire will take you back, once again, to your childhood days of outdoor life, fun, play, joy, excitement, friends, music, pleasure and contentment against a milieu of football and society in the 1960s. It also has the added bonus of being a 'crash' course (if you need one), on the history of Manchester United Football Club. You will also hear the important voices of players who were actually at the club when these players were at their peak. It is certainly an outstanding and distinctive addition to the plethora of literature that already exists about the swashbuckling trinity, the sublime, compelling, incomparable: Best, Law and Charlton.

Dr Tony Whelan,
Manchester United FC, Academy Programme Advisor
Aon Training Complex
Manchester
February 2019

Introduction

PROBABLY like every other youngster who saw George Best, Denis Law and Bobby Charlton perform, I grew up hoping to emulate their brilliance without ever achieving it. But also, through watching them week in, week out, I saw three very different types of person I might become, even if I could never hope to match their football ability. The composure and sportsmanship of Charlton, an icon for all that was good in the game and in life, I perceived, was my ideal choice. Law was the scarier option, someone I didn't think I wanted to be like or could even comprehend: blond-haired, sharp-featured, Viking-like with a volcanic temper that could erupt at any moment, but who also mesmerised me. George Best was someone who I maybe wanted to be like when I got older. His was a world that I could never have dreamed about entering as a child. It took me a long time to realise that, actually, being like George Best could be a whole load of fun, but in the 60s, as a young boy, I only saw the genius play, the long hair and the cool clothes. It was enough just to stand in the Stretford End and admire him. It still is.

This book has distinct chapters pinpointing the achievements of these revered legends: Best, Law and Charlton. However, the United Trinity did not just suddenly arrive at

Manchester United as some sort of golden gift to a Manchester public, coming out of the austere, impoverished 1950s. The book tells the back-story, involving the legacy of the Busby Babes, the devastating Munich air crash and a scarlet thread of talent development that links the generations. By the early 1960s, Manchester was a city that was exploding with music, fashion and creativity. Then, enter a skinny, dark-haired boy from Belfast who wasn't too sure about Manchester or the club when he first arrived. Next, there's a brilliant goalscorer who was longing to exit Italian football and sign for Manchester United. There is, too, a survivor from the horrors of Munich in 1958, who went on to become the enduring symbol of English football in a career spanning three decades. They all had something rather special in common: they were all European Footballers of the Year in the 1960s, and they all played together in the same Manchester United team. Normal? Don't even go there.

I was raised in a loving home, but one where my father's complicated past came to light in an unfolding drama. Since my dad had no interest in football, it was left to my mother to take me to watch Manchester United play. Not the usual type of father/son football story then. Initially keen to pursue a career in football, I became an apprentice professional before moving into the non-league game. This enabled me to combine football with study, which suited me well. I trained as a physical education (PE) teacher, eventually working in five schools over a period of 19 years. I then became a university lecturer, when someone decided to pay me good money to train PE teachers and research sport (especially football) issues. It was my dream job, where I very happily stayed for 21 years until retirement.

This book is a recollection of a colourful, 1960s childhood spent supporting Manchester United, in a fast-changing city that was hooked on football, music and fashion. It is also an examination of the period from the creation of the Busby Babes, through to the club's first European Cup win, showcasing the impact and legacy of Best, Law and Charlton. I am indebted to the ex-players and their other colleagues at Manchester United who agreed to interviews, providing the unique, personal insights that inform my childhood memories.

Chapter 1

The North – Brilliant!

I HAD one of those wonderfully rich, 1960s Manchester childhoods that many children these days might only dream about. We were not constricted by parental fears about 'playing out' and disappeared for hours on end, coming home only at dinner time, tea time and bedtime. Dinner time was 12 o'clock and tea time was 5 o'clock ... every day. We jumped across rivers, climbed tall trees, rode homemade go-carts down steep hills, kept numerous pets, built dens inside bonfires (not recommended), raided other gangs' bonfires, ate organic food before we knew it was called organic (and the price inflated) and played football every day. A 15-a-side, informal game lasting three hours was not unusual. The term 'screen time' had yet to be invented.

We always used a certain style of plastic football, known as a Frido. Here there were two types, with different price points. The superior Frido A had large dimples that you couldn't resist running your hand over. Something about the intoxicating smell of this shiny, white plastic ball tells me it would fail environmental tests these days. The Frido B was cheaper and lighter, enabling a swerve without even trying and of which

Ronaldo would have been proud. The trouble with it was that it swerved every time and passing in a straight line was impossible.

If one particular lad called Gary was playing, his presence was always welcome because he owned a leather football, a case-ball, which was referred to as a 'casey'. This set him apart from the rest of us who could only afford plastic. Sometimes I would call for Gary simply because he had a casey. He was no great friend. 'Is Gary coming out to play?' I would ask his mum politely. If the answer was 'No', and Gary had a bad cold or was doing his homework, I always felt like saying, 'Well, is his casey coming out to play then?' Such a prized possession was wasted on a boy like Gary, who gave in to colds and bothered with homework when he could have been out kicking a ball around. I didn't do the football-sticker book stuff either. My idea of football was to play the game myself and watch Manchester United, not collect cards featuring players' faces from packets of sweet cigarettes. (What was that piece of confectionary ever about?)

Each day we thumped a ball against the dark red, metal gates of the local mill. The gates were about 14ft wide by 7ft high. If you skied a shot, the culprit's challenge was to climb over the gates and retrieve the ball without being savaged by the mill's two resident, completely evil, Alsatian guard dogs. Of course, as soon as someone went over the gates and landed, the other kids would start barking and making a racket so the dogs would come out and chase the trespasser. When the dogs did appear, the unlucky intruder desperately scrambled up the gates to escape, with everyone else convulsed with laughter. It certainly made you focus on hitting the target, but I cannot see any football academy using the practice these days.

As kids, we did some other more dangerous things too, which always prompted my grandfather to issue stern warnings about impending doom, saying things like, 'If you do that, you'll know about it!' Then there was, 'You haven't got the sense you were born with!' Finally, there was the ultimate threat, 'It'll take your eye out!' Thankfully 'it' never did. If falling asleep at the dinner table after double maths (who wouldn't?), he would put his teaspoon into his pint mug of hot tea and touch it on the back of my hand. It always woke me up and he chuckled loudly. As a soldier who fought at Ypres (which he always pronounced as 'Wipers') and had a bullet put through his knee, I don't think he viewed it as the biggest jolt a body might take. It made me laugh too … after the initial shock.

Then there was my dad. My dad was a character. A character's character. I loved my dad, but if they had awarded international caps for whisky-drinking, he would have represented Ireland long before his 18th birthday, and later they would probably have retired the shirt. That was the problem.

I was football mad, but he didn't take me to a single match, probably because back in the 1960s, kick-off times were always at 3pm on a Saturday, which was way too close to pub closing times. In fact, he never took me anywhere, save for a four-day trip to Blackpool where he turned up on day three, much to the amazement of my mother and displeasure of my grandfather. I am told there was another family holiday to Llandudno (of which I have no recollection) when my dad insisted on driving my grandad's little Morris 1000 to the top of Great Orme. My grandfather advised that the car would not make it up the steep incline. He was right. The ensuing argument was shared with most of Snowdonia. My grandfather, Arthur, was a no-nonsense, teetotal Lancastrian who had worked his way up in the local cotton mill to become a much-respected foreman. My father, Eddie, was a freewheeling, Irish plasterer who liked to drink, gamble and tell tall stories, usually in that order. It was a family relationship that was never going to end well.

But looking back now, with my father long passed, I choose to see only the good times and the laughter. We know now that alcohol dependency is a problem that changes personality, and so it was with my dad. Without booze, he was a kind, gentle giant with a good heart and engaging sense of the ridiculous. With it, he was someone whose drunken rages terrified me as a child. But I can now separate the father from the drink: the latter did what it did, but the father did his best to look after his family, working in the tough building industry of the time when unemployment was just around every corner. He may not have ever taken me to a match or played any games with me, or at least that I can remember, and he occasionally frightened me, but I still loved him, then and now.

My dad's education ended abruptly at the age of ten: unsurprisingly, since he had flung the slate on which he was writing (this was rural Ireland in the early 1900s) at the head of a Catholic Brother teacher in a strictly religious school in County Mayo. By 1916 he was marching to Dublin to take part in the Easter Uprising with nothing more than fiery, romantic rhetoric in his heart and a sandwich and spare pair of socks in his pockets. By the 1920s (the historical accuracy is sketchy, as was everything in my dad's life story), he was aboard the Liverpool ferry planning to make his fortune in England. This Irish Diaspora led to my family being scattered east and west throughout most of the 20th century, with numerous relations now in many parts of the UK and US. Then, as now, the pathway of young Irish men and women continues, often not noticed among the many other immigrants who have moved to these soils, complete with their dreams, needs and aspirations.

From Liverpool we think that he moved to the Midlands, spending time in Birmingham, before finishing up in Coventry during the Second World War years. He often told the story of how, as a fireman, he left his engine and mate onboard to answer a call of nature. When he returned, the vehicle and friend had been blown to pieces. Was he telling another tall story? I shall never know. My mother's take on the accuracy of my dad's stories amounts to a brusque one-liner: 'If you cut everything in half that he ever told you, that's about right.' Continuing his colourful life journey, my dad somehow ended up in Manchester. Since most of his stories were exaggerated, usually helped along by half a bottle of Bell's, his pathway to the city was never authenticated by a proven route or timeline. Why he always drank Scotch whisky and not Irish is another contradiction that I have often pondered, although it was probably as simple as Bell's being much cheaper at the time.

What was clear, though, was that by the late 1940s my father had reached Manchester, living somewhere in the poorer part of the city near Strangeways prison, in a cultural environment that still advertised its boarding houses with signs that read: 'No Irish, no blacks, no dogs'. He made friends with other outsiders. Thus, the two most loved 'aunties' of my youth (beyond my immediate kin) were Aunty Lena, a short, gregarious German woman who had married a British serviceman during the war and lived in Oldham, and Aunty Minnie, whose Jewish family worked the markets in the Cheetham Hill area of the city and who made wonderful Kosher fishcakes. My father lodged there when he first arrived in the city. Peter Kay sums up the habit of northern kids having aunts and uncles with no blood ties when he jokes that to acquire such a 'relative' all you had to do was borrow that person's Black & Decker drill. Thus, my dad did plastering jobs on the cheap for Lena and Minnie and they automatically became my 'aunties'. I was sent next door to borrow a cup of sugar (which never ever got paid back, let me tell you) and suddenly neighbour Sybil became Aunty Sybil.

Looking back now though, I wonder what life must have been like when my Aunty Lena came over to Oldham in the late 40s, to live among families who had lost loved ones in the war a few years earlier. Her German accent must have stood out so strongly as she queued for meat in the butcher's shop, or vegetables at the local market. To her credit, and that of the townsfolk, when she died in the 1980s her funeral was overwhelmed by local people who had come to know and love her. How was it for my Aunty Minnie at a time when Antisemitism was rife and family hardship and hunger was the norm? Minnie and Shulem, her husband, were both very small in stature but had kind, warm personalities that made them grow as human beings. And what had been my father's experience when he came to England and eventually ended up in Manchester? Like so many years in his life, there are things now I shall never know anything about. What I can recall as a child, though, was wondering what it was he was running from. He never talked about the past. To me, his life began and ended in Manchester, and yet there were secrets I felt he alone knew.

The past troubled my dad. I see him now, sitting in his armchair, sucking edgily on a cigarette and dressed in his bib and brace white overalls, which look spotless from a distance but which are spattered with plaster. It is 6.20am and soon he will get up and walk to the bus stop for the 6.30 bus. 'I'm going, Sheila,' he calls as he leaves, flicking the cigarette into the coal fire, not turning to look at either my brother Gerry or me. He doesn't kiss Mum, or ruffle my hair, or say any farewells to us, and yet he is okay, my dad. He has issues. I don't know what they are, but I can feel them, I can feel them even though I am just seven years old.

My father had given way on insisting that my brother, Gerry, and I should be raised as Catholics, primarily because the local Catholic school was sited on a dangerous main road that my mother did not want us to cross. However, my father was so lapsed as a believer that I don't imagine there would have been much of a disagreement over the arrangement. We did both attend Anglican confirmation classes as kids, but on the day of the ceremony, while I was confirmed, my brother would not attend as he had a hole in his shoe, which he knew would be seen when he knelt at the altar. That's how it was. Wherever money was, my family wasn't.

What was of far more importance to my dad than religion, though, was that we should inherit some of his Irishness, such as the wearing of shamrock on St Patrick's Day. It made me feel proud to wear it, knowing that it said a little about my family roots, but in another sense, when you are the only kid in high school with a little green leaf pinned to your blazer it was a bit unnerving too. When he was drunk, my father would rant about Eamon de Valera: at the time I knew not whether Eamon de Valera was a person, place or plant. All I sensed was that it was a very Irish thing and that my father had enormous respect for him/it. Some boys I knew grew up with fathers passing on nostalgic football stories, about 'Wor' Jackie Milburn, Duncan Edwards or Tom Finney: for me it was Eamon de Valera, or sometimes Michael Collins too. The only footballer I think my dad knew anything about was Johnny Carey, Gentleman John as he was known, the wonderfully talented United skipper of Busby's first, great 1948 team. Naturally, he was Irish otherwise my dad would have had no interest in him whatsoever.

Of all my father's tall stories, though, the one which was true was that he eventually met my mother in 1950, when he came to plaster the local library in Middleton, Manchester, where she worked. As he did the plastering on a small extension to the rear of the building, she heard the strains of 'Danny Boy' drifting into her office, delivered in a soft, southern Irish accent. The truth about his trade was one of the few things about my dad that was never in doubt. Dad was a plasterer and a damn fine one, having served a seven-year apprenticeship, as was the norm in those days. Tall, youthful in appearance, handsome and with a powerful motorbike propped against the library wall, he soon charmed a 20-year-old, never-been-kissed librarian. He told her he was 37. She believed him. He was 47. They married quickly. My brother Gerry arrived a year later in 1951, and I was born in 1953: a special year for a football man.

In 1953 England were handed a football lesson by Hungary in a 6-3 humiliation at Wembley, altering how we perceived our global worth in our national game. In the FA Cup, there was the so-called Matthews Final too, when Stanley Matthews outplayed the Bolton defence in a memorable Blackpool comeback to win the game 4-3. Some years previously, Stan's father, on his deathbed, made Stan promise two things: to look after his mother and to make sure he won an FA Cup winner's medal.

Of course, even for the great Stan Matthews he knew the task was huge and by no means certain. How Stan must have had tears in his eyes as his teammates held him aloft after the game and he proudly clutched his winner's medal. For Stan Matthews, the father/son connection was a hugely powerful driver in terms of enjoyment and participation in the game throughout his career.

Such father/son relationships are, quite understandably, much vaunted in football biographies and autobiographies, involving stories concerning both playing and watching. In terms of the professional footballer being an influence on his children, the relationship is expertly discussed in works by both Imlach (*My Father and Other Working Class Football Heroes*) and Shindler (*Fathers, Sons and Football*). Elsewhere, as a poignant commentary on how a son can have a disconnect with his father on any subject other than watching football, Duncan Hamilton's *The Footballer Who Could Fly* describes it beautifully. Of his relationship with his father, Hamilton says,

on both teams, intense rivalry, blood-curdling tackles and a whiff of danger; a heady cocktail. United were my beginning, middle and end, and derby matches meant being enveloped inside one glorious, all-consuming golden moment. As the years began to pass, I came to realise that Manchester had not one but two great teams: Manchester United and Manchester United Reserves. With such tribalism, my football pathway was sketched out before me.

By the time of the Reds' first European triumph on a beautiful, balmy May evening in 1968, my brother was experiencing a Jim Bowen, *Bullseye* moment, 'Well Gerry, you chose City but let's look at what you could have won with United in the 60s: the FA Cup, two league titles, the European Cup and Youth Cup thrown in for good measure.' There was, too, the thrill of watching Best, Law and Charlton perform week in, week out. The old joke in Manchester pubs at the time of United's trophy gathering was that when City eventually won the league title in 1968, their manager, Joe Mercer, called at Old Trafford to collect the cup from Matt Busby (United having won it the season before). Matt showed Joe the stairs to the trophy room and up he went. Matt stayed at his desk puffing his pipe. A couple of hours later, a curious Matt heard Joe's footsteps coming down the stairs, whereupon he appeared and asked, 'Matt, which one is it exactly?' the room being swamped with silverware.

As the Reds rebuilt after the Munich air disaster in 1958 and the trophies started to pile up, Manchester as a city was trying to emerge from its dark, industrial past. However, in the early 60s, the city centre was certainly not the buzzy, good-looking place it has since become. Whilst the magnificent Town Hall, Central Library, Free Trade Hall and Corn Exchange stood as fine monuments to Cottonopolis, it was also still possible to see the occasional dead dog or broken pram washed up on the banks of the River Irwell. This diseased waterway flowed, hesitatingly, over the driftwood and past the back of posh Deansgate on its journey to the Mersey. The shop buildings and banks were still largely covered in sooty deposits from the cotton mills, which were breathing still but heading for life support in an economically ravaged north-west. A government sell-out drained them of the last gasp of air.

My grandfather, feeling privileged to have more than a little inside track on why his own mill had to close in 1965, would often repeat what the mill owner told him: 'Arthur, they just made me an offer that was too good to refuse.' And so, the vast Accrington-brick, Baytree Mill, where my grandad had spent all his working life, spun its last piece of cloth and the huge, well-oiled machines were shipped off to India in giant crates, to be replaced by .... well, nothing. These fine buildings then stood still for more than 30 years like rotting dinosaurs, existing mainly as target practice for disaffected youths with air rifles and stones. The fact that town planners have since brought flat dwellers back into the city centre to occupy many of these historic buildings says much about the enterprise and grit of Manchester people. The irony behind the fact that we now buy back our cotton from India in the form of T-shirts and tops, often produced in legalised sweatshops, perhaps says rather more about wider, government policy.

But even during recession, Manchester was still a wonderful place to live. It was friendly, oh so northern and I would not have wanted to spend my teenage years anywhere else in the world. The music, the football, the humour, everything about the city filled my senses. However, not everyone in my family always shared my love of the region. Around this time, my wife, Cathy, a Sussex girl with impeccable Home Counties diction, stood at a bus stop in Rochdale and was astonished that she felt obliged to divulge her whole life story to a total stranger as she waited for the number 17. I tried to explain that such inquisitive behaviour passed for friendliness in these parts, but she would have none of it and called it outright nosiness.

What really reinforced her doubts about ever venturing north of Milton Keynes again, though, was when she later called at our local hardware shop seeking a new tea-towel holder. She desired one of those quintessentially 1960s kitsch, dinky devices where you pushed the top of the towel into a small round base and four flimsy pieces of plastic grabbed it like a Rottweiler's teeth. Having never heard of such a trendy piece of kitchenware, our wonderfully broad, local shopkeeper replied (in all seriousness): 'Nay, 'ave nor 'eard o' that. I 'ave a six-inch nail though. Will that do?' Gasping for breath, she summoned me to fill up the Beetle and point it in any southerly direction. Had I given in to this pressure, we would have passed my favourite road sign, near an undistinguished entry to the M1, for traffic heading the opposite way: 'The North' it says. Underneath this, an exiled Mancunian has added the word, 'Brilliant!' Quite.

But who would want to live in the south anyway? In Manchester we had George Best, Denis Law and Bobby Charlton. We had The Hollies, Herman's Hermits, Freddie and The Dreamers, Wayne Fontana and The Mindbenders, and the Twisted Wheel; the centre of the world was Manchester and the city was on fast forward. From the Peterloo Massacre in 1819 to Hitler's missiles in 1940, from the IRA bomb in 1996 through to the Arena atrocity in 2017, the city would always take whatever adversity was thrown at it and bounce back with love, pride and defiance. It's what Manchester does, and the United team of the 1960s absolutely symbolised that never-say-die spirit.

Chapter 2
Decent Dependable Men

ON a cold February day in 1994 I went to a funeral. It was in my hometown of Middleton. I call at the cemetery there from time to time to put flowers on my father's grave. Whilst parking is never usually a problem, on this day I struggled to find a space, causing me to be a little late for the ceremony. I walked hurriedly to the chapel in the centre of the cemetery. In the distance I could see a large crowd huddled outside, predominantly young men, hundreds of them, their collars upturned to keep out the atrocious weather. There was sleet in the air and the temperature was exceptionally low. As I got closer, I recognised many of the faces. They were accompanied by expanded waistlines, pronounced limps and a shortage of hair, but I knew them still. They were the local kids I grew up with, the amateur/semi-professional footballers I had played alongside in a bargain-basement career.

The funeral of Harvey Elliott was very important to us all. For me, he was the person who had the most effect upon my football ambitions, and too my memories of the great United players of the 1950s and early 60s. Harvey was our window cleaner and half of Middleton's by the look of the crowd. It was by far and away the largest funeral I had ever attended, with at least 300 mourners I would think. For Harvey, cleaning windows was merely a distraction from the main preoccupations in his life, which were playing and coaching football. He was football mad in the zany, old-fashioned sense of the term. The game defined his life, and a more cheerful life I have yet to see.

'Alright, Bren?' one old friend in the crowd asked me as I reached the throng, using the flat vowels of a Middleton accent. He accentuated the greeting with a typical Manchester nod: a sharp forward movement of the head, delivered in a curmudgeonly fashion. If you don't recognise it, the action could be mistaken for unfriendliness, but in fact the opposite is true. 'Poor old 'arvey', said another. I nodded solemnly. When Harvey coached me, I thought I was the only boy who he made feel special, made me feel I could play for Arsenal or Manchester United. I was wrong, he had cast the same spell over many others. I smiled gently. If my mum had guided me towards Manchester United with the tossing of a coin, it was Harvey who had led me into the world of trying to play the game well and understand its beauty. Harvey typified the unsung, lovely local heroes of the beautiful game.

Eamon Dunphy, in his splendidly candid biography of Matt Busby, *A Strange Kind of Glory*, described such supporting figures at Manchester United when he said, 'Busby sought to surround himself with decent dependable men, no matter what their religious convictions were.' Matt had his own trusted colleagues and in my own limited and ultimately unsuccessful attempt to secure a serious, professional playing career, Harvey was one of my own decent, dependable men. They were of particular importance to me since my father was often a distant figure. Harvey would take me for one-to-one coaching sessions on Tonge Field in Middleton. In these sessions he would work me incredibly hard (too hard by today's sport science guidelines for children) doing different types of running involving endurance and speed. As soon as I got home, I headed for the cold tap and stuck my head underneath it, sucking at the water as quickly as I could. Harvey had once turned out for Hull City before the Second World War interrupted his progress, as it did with so many other players.

In Matt Busby's world of decent dependable men, chosen when he was rebuilding Manchester United in the 1950s, this centred around Jimmy Murphy, Bert Whalley, Joe Armstrong and other key figures. Together they were preparing the club for two decades of exceptional growth. The hard times from earlier decades when wages were never certain to be paid and the banks were reluctant to lend to a struggling Second Division side, were now being put aside and the building blocks of progress were in place.

No one comes better equipped to chart the journey Manchester United were on in the 50s and 60s than the incomparably experienced former United player, coach and manager Wilf McGuinness, always defined to me back in my youth, naively, as the man who was lucky to miss the Munich flight because of a knee injury. He makes clear that three figures dominated the 1950s day-to-day experience for young players at the club:

'We had Matt Busby the boss, Jimmy Murphy, second in command, and who was as hard as nails, and then Bert Whalley. They were all great men to us. We had experienced school teachers who were wonderful to us, but these men were just football, football, football; they were very special people. When the young players died it was a terrible feeling but being at United was a fantastic life. You couldn't sign until you left school but when I did I just thought, "What a great club this is!" It was a wonderful romance and it was hard to believe I was being looked after in a tremendous way like this. Bobby was a survivor of course and I was lucky in that I missed the crash through injury. There will never be better players or better lads than the ones who I grew up with at United. It was Jimmy and Bert who cracked us on the head and said, "Come on, do this and do that!" We were knocked into shape, but we had a wonderful life. People like Walter Crickmer and Les Olive, Joe Armstrong, the scout, were all around in the 50s, but the main ones really, from our point of view, were Matt Busby, Jimmy Murphy and Bert Whalley.

'These three were special, very special. They taught us how to behave and I learned a lot from them. Brilliant people. You listened to every word they said and then wanted to try out what they had told you. You just wanted one of them to speak to you and tell you what to do. Matt's team talks were great before a game and then sometimes Jimmy and Bert told you things too. Jimmy was the number-one coach and Bert was the number two. I think they must have got together beforehand to decide who was saying what and to whom. When Matt said something, you thought you were the most important person in the world. Jimmy Murphy was great, but he was a hard man and you did exactly what he said. While Jimmy was hard, Bert would put his arm around you and pat you on the back. They were tremendous and we were very lucky to have them.'

Sharing common beliefs in the worth of players as people and the development of youth, Busby and his team set about reviving the fortunes of an underachieving club, far removed from the exceptional success they would enjoy in later years. The establishment of the scouting system and the progress of the Manchester United Junior Athletic Club (MUJAC), which had been started in 1938 for the development of young players, were key factors in this ascent. However, also central to this progress was the pastoral care of boys who were to join

Manchester United. This mattered hugely to Matt Busby, who had a father's love for the youngsters he brought to the club. After all, Busby had lost his own father early in life, cut down by a sniper's bullet at the Somme.

Busby's idea of running Manchester United through having decent dependable men around him clearly followed through into the next decade. It was still a hugely impressive model for 15-year-old local boy Tony Whelan when he joined United as a technically gifted, outside-left in July 1968, two months after their landmark European Cup triumph. A United player into the early 70s, he is now the Manchester United FC Academy programme advisor, having had an association with the club that exceeds 30 years. Whelan is also author of *Birth of the Babes*, which expertly covers the Manchester United youth policy of 1950–57.

When Tony Whelan signed for United, the coaching team was tiny compared with the high number of staff employed at elite-level clubs nowadays. And yet, although small in number, this group of men had the qualities Busby wanted and their worth was immense. Whelan remembers each one of them with great clarity:

'I came to United in 1967 after playing for Stretford Boys. I think I'd been to Stockport and Bolton on trial. For Stretford Boys we played Manchester Boys at Christies playing fields opposite Nell Lane. I think they beat us either four or five goals to one. After that, I came home one day and my mother said that Joe Armstrong had been on the phone, asking whether I'd be interested in going to The Cliff the following Tuesday night. It took me completely by surprise because I was a big City fan. Anyway, I went to The Cliff and I'll never forget it, I went upstairs and Joe Armstrong saw me and asked me how much my expenses were. I think it was one and six in old money. Joe said, "Did you not stop at the corner shop?" I said, "I did actually" and he then said, "Well here's two and six!" So, I trained two nights a week that winter and it was amazing. Fantastic. After that they offered me an apprentice professional contract when I left school at age 15 in 1968, just after they had won the European Cup. I came at an amazing time in the club's history, because those three giants, Best, Law and Charlton, were in their prime. So, I'd gone from associated schoolboy, to apprentice-professional, to signing as a full-time professional in December 1969.

'We were always at The Cliff and it was so tight, because the first team were there, the reserves and the youth team, and it was all so intimate. Matt Busby would drive his car in maybe a couple of times a week and it was like the Pope had arrived. He had this aura about him. He drove a really nice car, a mustard-coloured Jenson that looked more like a sports car and I didn't really think it suited him. I saw him more likely to drive a Rolls Royce, or a saloon of some description, not a sports car. But people just had such immense respect for him. So these were the people I first met. I especially remember Joe Armstrong, such a genial, lovely man, a charming human being. Then there was Wilf McGuinness, he was the main coach. There was also John Aston Snr, another coach, and it was just a great time to join the club. We'd just won the European Cup in May and I bowl up in July for my first day at work. I got on the bus at Wythenshawe, one into town and one out, walked down the Priory and it's my first day at work … at Man United! I even remember the day, it was an overcast and dull summer's day, a bit drizzly. I can't remember being nervous, I was just excited I think, just going into a wonderland as I had imagined it. Of course in those days, there were only seven or eight apprentices each year so it was quite an achievement. It was the talk of the block that I'd signed for United. That's how big a deal it was.'

In my own, comparatively tiny, provincial arena, one of Harvey's great friends (his funeral demonstrated that he clearly had so many) was another fine football man, Tommy Walker, who ran a small newsagents in Boarshaw, Middleton. The sign above the shop always made me look up in admiration each time I passed by: 'Tommy Walker, Newcastle United and Oldham Athletic', it said. I was always in awe of this sign. Outside once, on the first day of the 1963/64 season, I knelt on the pavement and spread out the *Football Pink*. United had gained a respectable 3-3 draw away at Sheffield Wednesday. Being just nine years old, I was naive enough to believe that the poor finish in the 1962/63 season carried over into the new season. When I discovered that it did not and that league places began afresh, it was almost a spiritual moment. Past sins and errors had been forgiven, the slate was wiped clean and we could begin again. Oh, joy!

When I got to know Tommy a little better, later in life, playing for an amateur team with his son, he was always smiling, always kindly. The modest Tommy had two Newcastle FA Cup winners' medals to his name (1950/51 and 1951/52). That impressed me enormously. Some years later still, when lecturing a group of professional footballers on a part-time degree course, I brought Tommy into the university to meet the players. He spoke movingly about his Newcastle United cup final appearances and the players warmed to him. His health had been failing running up to the occasion and his wife Lillian had been worried about him doing the session. She need not have been concerned. Tommy loved being among professional footballers again. It turned out to be one of the sweetest moments in my teaching career of 40 years, as the old man proudly showed his medals to the interested young players without an ounce of arrogance. The players in turn were incredibly respectful.

In Harvey and Tommy, then, I had around me two of the nicest football men anyone could ever hope to meet. In Tommy's case, of course, he had played against so many of them, as a 50s star himself, including the famous Busby Babes.

Through their colourful accounts and those of others (since so many Middletonians recalled the Babes) I drew pictures in my mind of the Adonis-like Tommy Taylor rising to head the ball, and the flying, handsome David Pegg with chalk on his boots. Of him, Wilf McGuinness simply says, 'He was a dribbler, he could go past you as if you weren't there. He would drop his shoulder and you'd think, "How does he do that?"'

Then there was the majestic Duncan Edwards powering his way forward with ease. I had never seen them, or played with them as McGuinness had, and yet I knew them. They were so real to me. When I once asked dear old Tommy Walker who was the greatest player he had ever played against, he replied without thinking: 'Duncan Edwards'. When I asked him about the greatest player he had ever seen, he said, just as sharply, 'George Best'. This from a man who had played alongside Milburn and encountered Matthews and Finney.

My third decent, dependable, local football man was Tom Nicholl, the part-time trainer for Rochdale FC who ran the reserve team, the point at which my under-achieving football career peaked (save for one first-team 'friendly' game). Tom was another thoroughly good, kind man, a point not lost on Tony Whelan who also came across him some years later, after his career at both United and City had ended:

'I met Tom Nicholl at Rochdale, who did everything for them, head-cook and bottle-washer. I don't think I really appreciated Tom until I left. He was a lovely man, a kindly man. I had a dispute with the club when I wanted to leave and go and play in the US. I had to take my case to a tribunal in Manchester and who was on the panel but Sir Matt Busby! Then I had to go to London for the second meeting, arguing that Rochdale should let me go for no money – a free transfer, then I could get to the States. Sir Matt assured me it would all be sorted out and it was, but Rochdale still owed me some money. They owed me four or five hundred pounds, the signing-on fee. I always remember Tom coming to the training ground. In those old days they gave you your wages in a little brown envelope. Tom took me out of the changing room and he gave me two envelopes: one was my wages and the other was the signing-on fee. But it was the way he did it that was good. He said, "I'm so sorry it's been so long, but I managed to get it for you." A touch of class. A lovely man, the "schoolteacher" type. I have very fond memories of Tom, although I only really appreciated him after I left. He would always be panicking on a Friday because the wages were late. He'd been on the phone to the bank. We used to wait for the wages to come; that's what it was like!'

Yet another person whose words I utterly relied on as a child in the 60s, whilst sadly never actually meeting him, was David Meek, who penned just about everything that involved Manchester United for the *Manchester Evening News* (*MEN*) and sister paper, the wonderful, definitive *Football Pink*. Peter Gardner had the tremendously sad task of covering everything about Manchester City, while David Meek had clearly secured the top job as far as I could see. Inside the club too, it seems, the status of David Meek was clearly immense, as Whelan notes:

'I didn't really come across Peter Gardener at City. He was a distant figure for me, but I knew David Meek. Really, he was the journalist Godfather of Man United. Everything that was written about Man United he did, and he wrote some very complimentary articles about me in my youth-team days. I got to know him after I returned to the club. He was an honest man, showing the highest reporting standards. His death is such a sad loss to journalism and football. Back in the day he was "the one". He wrote articles on the youth team, on the reserves, on the first team. He did the lot and was always such a perceptive journalist. If a player did not play well he would write the article in such a way that you got the message, without him slaughtering the player. Sir Matt had had journalists before like Alf Clarke and Henry Rose, and he was maybe a little wary of David Meek at the beginning. Suddenly, after Munich, David was the new kid on the block.

'He was brave too. I remember him writing an article in praise of O'Farrell, urging the board to give him more time. It went belly-up, but he was brave. He also supported Sir Alex when there had been some sort of poll. I remember when Paul McGuinness was leaving and he rang me up to get some of Paul's background. He was that sort of man, always did his homework. Then he wrote a really nice piece on Paul for the menu for the occasion. A thoroughly decent human being and in the 60s he was Mr Man United. A huge figure as far as I was concerned. In the photo of him in the *Evening News* he always had that hat on. He was the voice of the club, the eyes and ears too. You just wouldn't miss reading the *Evening News*. You bought it every night and the *Football Pink* was like gold dust, people standing on the pavement outside the newsagent on Saturday night waiting for it. The games finished at 4.45pm, and by 5.30 to 5.45pm there it was. The driver would just throw the bundle from the van on to the pavement, and someone would take it into the shop for the newsagent to dole out the papers to the waiting assembly – amazing memories, priceless!'

When David Meek died, aged 88, in 2018, it caused me to think how much I owed this man, not just in terms of enhancing my understanding of Manchester United but also in improving my literacy level. As a child and beyond, I read just about everything he wrote about Manchester United, and he seemed to write everything that was written (certainly within Manchester) at that time. Enid Blyton, Anna Sewell and George Orwell may have played their part in helping me increase my early reading ability, but I read much more by the man who wore the little trilby hat and smiled gently out at me on the back pages of the iconic *MEN*. A wonderful journalist and so much the people's voice of the club for so many years. He followed admirably in the footsteps of his predecessor Tom Jackson and those other gifted writers who tragically lost their lives at Munich. David's crisp, incisive, courteous writing style was a very real part of my childhood. He had a kind face, he did not tear into people in print even if he had a valid criticism, and he clearly loved Manchester United. He was Bobby Charlton behind a typewriter. That was good enough for me.

As a child I may have had problems in my immediate family caused by drink, but in other ways I was blessed to be surrounded by so many good people. Both my grandparents were incredibly supportive, compensating unselfishly for problems caused by my dad's drinking whilst ignoring the dwindling embers of their own lives. Neither of them drank and indeed my grandmother had 'signed the pledge' some years earlier, swearing never to touch alcohol. Thus, the juxtaposition of my father's heavy drinking and their teetotal ways was a constant source of tension within the wider family. My dad, bless him, battled with his demons and rather like an inconsistent footballer, had some good, average and poor performances, the latter always caused by drinking. I still had around me, though, a good number of people who, like me, had a love of the game and wanted to share it. The kindness and knowledge passed on by others blotted out the bad times.

And for those more skilled than I was and fortunate enough to have made the grade at Manchester United, decent dependable men surrounded their world too. A distinctive club identity that had started with the Busby Babes was still being passed on to young players like Tony Whelan in the 1960s:

'I grew up on a diet of "pass it to a red shirt" and "up together, back together" and "express yourself, don't be frightened of making mistakes, you're a talented player or else you wouldn't be here. We don't have to teach you to play, we'll give you some guidelines, some basic coaching principles and tactics, but we're not going to flood you with too much information. We want you to bring your talent out in the framework of the team. We'll do things together in the right way on the field and off it. We'll look smart. You'll have a blazer. We'll go to the Blue Stars tournament. We'll have a great time playing and we'll have a great time socially." It gives you this bonding, this shared experience. I still pass all this on to the young players today, absolutely. It's a shared experience. "We are following in the footsteps of the Busby Babes", we say to them still. We are the guardian of that tradition. It's about the Man United that goes back all these years. We want to protect it, this culture. You have to know what it is you're protecting. People talk about identity and sometimes people say the club is losing its identity, but I don't think that's ever going to happen. People know what this club's about. On the field, it's always been about flair, imagination, attacking football, about getting players through the youth system from schoolboy age. I can't see that changing. There might be periods where it doesn't happen but overall the train's still moving in the right direction. That's what people expect and that's what the club has always been about, and that's what's brought the club most of its success.

'If you look at the 50s and the Busby Babes and then the 90s when we were winning things, then it's young players who have done it. Like the Class of 92. I just can't see that changing. I don't think the fans would let it. It's what you buy into as a Man United supporter. If you asked proper, bona fide Man United supporters about the club, they will talk about Munich, about the aftermath, about Busby, about Ferguson, but also about players. They will certainly be talking about Best, Law and Charlton. Everyone knows who they are because of what they represented on the pitch. If you want to know what a top-class Man United footballer should look like, then there's three great examples. All European Footballers of the Year, with two of them home-grown, one of them a World Cup winner – astounding. How does that happen?'

How indeed? It was a question for which I just had to try to find an answer.

Chapter 3

Manchester After Munich

WHEN I pledged my allegiance to Manchester United as a nine-year-old in 1963, the importance of the Munich air disaster gradually started to impact me. I saw the crash through my child's eyes; learning how the club had been flooded with national and international tidal waves of sympathy and love. Even with neighbours City, club rivalries were placed aside and, as Bobby Charlton once put it, 'Everyone discovered a little place in their heart for Manchester United.' In more recent times, maybe some sort of parallel might be drawn with the love, support and sympathy extended to the victims and families of the horrendous Manchester Arena bombing in 2017, or even the earlier 1996 IRA bombing of the city centre.

What links these three events is summarised by newspaper headlines. On Friday 7 February 1958, the *Daily Express* headline read: 'On The Day After, One Thing Comes Through – The Spirit.' After the IRA bomb in 1996, the *Manchester Evening News* led with: 'Manchester Did What Manchester

Does – We Fought Back' (*MEN*, 1996); and now, more recently, their headline on the first anniversary of the Arena attack was: 'This Is What Love Looks Like' (*MEN*, 2018). When the tears subside, whilst acknowledging that they never truly pass, this remarkable, resilient city always bounces back; together, stronger, not with anger but with defiance. Thankfully, the reality of this unbreakable spirit is still being passed on to new generations of players. Marcus Rashford said of the Arena terror attack, 'Personally, there was a massive, massive impact on me, and I could see it affected the rest of the team as well. We were preparing for the Europa League final two days later, but even though we went to Stockholm, Manchester was on our minds.' (*i newspaper*, 2018)

As a child, I used to wonder what the immediate scene was like in Manchester on that fateful day, 6 February 1958. I could see Jimmy Murphy arriving by train at London Road Station (Piccadilly as it is known now) in Manchester. He hails a taxi to make his way to Old Trafford, carrying a box of oranges given to him by the Israeli FA, after Wales had beaten Israel in a World Cup qualifying round the day before. The gift now seems a bizarre addition to the story. Murphy had been attending the match as manager of the Welsh team, having been given permission by Matt Busby to miss the Munich trip. I see him arriving at Old Trafford and then sitting in his office, busying himself with paperwork, before Matt's secretary, Alma George, starts to break the news: 'Mr Murphy, please stop. Haven't you heard the news? The United plane has crashed at Munich.'

One by one the names of the dead start to come through, from calls made to the newspapers, the BBC and the police. Jimmy sips a whisky to numb the pain and then another. So much loss, such fine young men, so much time devoted to their progress and so unimportant the commitments facing the club: yet still they must be fulfilled. After all, didn't Matt

Busby take the team into Europe against the wishes of the FA, creating a potential fixture pile up? Not good publicity for the London boys if they were to demand business as usual, but the reality is there; fixtures will need to be fulfilled. But whatever Jimmy is thinking, he is not that far ahead right now. A priceless painting has been slashed across its centre. The great Peter Doherty once made the same analogy between Jimmy and art, saying, 'When Jimmy starts to talk about football and Manchester United with a youngster, he not only paints the lily – he fills in all the details like Michelangelo or Raphael.' So much passion, so much energy, so much love for his boys, so much work completed, and so much more that was to come. Now, more than half the United team gone and almost half the England side. His mind is in the past, in the present and in the future. He is a football man and eventually he will realise that the show must go on, somehow. And then he freezes. Murphy said later, 'The fingers of the clock on the wall pointed to four o'clock … but time now meant nothing.'

His grief is shared out on the streets around town (the term most Mancunians use to refer to the city centre). Women in headscarves standing at the bus stops around Albert Square and Cannon Street sobbing, as they read the *Manchester Evening News* account of the tragedy. My mum hearing the news on our little Bush radio in the living room, clouded in cigarette smoke. David Clayton's hugely interesting book, *Manchester Stories*, answers a question I always asked myself: 'What was life like in Manchester among the ordinary people in the immediate days following the crash?' We know very well what was going on inside the club through the plethora of books recounting the story, but how did the news trickle through in pre-internet days and how were people in the Manchester streets feeling? For the fans queueing for tickets at Old Trafford for the FA Cup tie with Sheffield Wednesday, suspension of the sale of tickets was the obvious marker. They did not argue. In Iain McCartney's hugely informative book, *Manchester United 1958–68: Rising From the Wreckage,* we learn more about how the news was slowly disseminated at Manchester United: for junior players, a hand-written message was simply pinned to a gate advising them that training was cancelled.

The grief was profound in an era when fans still lived in the same neighbourhoods as the players they watched. Manchester Council took up the mantle by soon setting up the Manchester United Disaster Fund. The crash was mentioned in the House of Commons. International football associations telegraphed their condolences and offers of support. In the Plaza ballroom in town, revellers were asked to stop dancing when the news broke. In Manchester's wonderful old Midland Hotel there was a two-minute silence that evening during a golf club dinner, a mark of respect repeated across the city that unbearably sad night of 6 February 1958. On the Sunday following the crash, church congregations mourned the dead and prayed for the injured.

Clayton adds that the most significant public display of emotion was yet to come though. This was the day the plane touched down at Ringway Airport with the coffins, and a procession of hearses made the short journey to Old Trafford. The young and the old, men and women, businessmen in suits and workers in overalls all stood in silence. In another account, *Manchester United in Europe,* the author, Ken Ferris, says that the crowd lining the route from the airport to the ground was estimated at 100,000. At Old Trafford, the largest gathering was at the grandstand housing the small gymnasium where the coffins were kept.

Later, United had to field many calls from fans asking whether they could come to the gymnasium to pay their respects. They were not allowed to enter. However, on 24 February at Belle Vue, 6,000 people got to pay their respects at the mass at King's Hall. The Church of England's memorial service at Manchester Cathedral attracted another 1,500. The *Manchester Evening News* was deluged with letters from City fans sharing the tragedy with their United neighbours.

For the United players who had not made the journey to Belgrade prior to that fateful crash, the day of Thursday, 6 February 1958 began like any other. Nobby Stiles was a young professional player at United at the time of the crash. He describes the day in sharp detail, which started as '... just another shift at the football dream factory'. The day was frosty in central Manchester as Nobby caught the 112 bus for the three-quarters-of-an-hour journey to Old Trafford. He looked forward to the 'same old brilliant routine' that young players in those days had to perform and which current youth players do not, much to the disdain of many older players: the cleaning of baths and showers, whitewashing the walls and shovelling snow from the pitch – the menial, character-building tasks. Then, for Nobby, some head tennis and a lunch of sausage and potatoes at Mrs Rimmer's red-bricked, terraced house along the Warwick Road.

News of the disaster was broken to him gently and partially by Arthur Powell, another of Matt's decent, dependable men, who advised the youngsters to go home and get their parents to phone the club to find out the rest of the details. Only when Nobby arrived back in the city centre did the full scale of the tragedy become clear, as he saw the faces of Byrne, Bent, Pegg and the others in the news headlines. Even his favourite player, little Eddie Colman ('Coly'), whose Timpson Shooting Star boots he loved to clean, was dead. Arthur Powell had told the boys little, and Nobby and the others had been laughing, saying the crash had maybe caused someone to break a leg and perhaps give them a chance to take their place. But when the extent of the tragedy was known, Nobby said, 'I felt sick'. There will indeed be gaps in the team now, but he doesn't want to be one of the players who fills them; he just wants to go back to cleaning Eddie 'Snake-hips' Colman's boots, as it was a few days ago. But it isn't going to happen. Later, little Nobby Stiles is making his way back along the Collyhurst/Moston bus route I know so well, back to the family undertaker's business. He is used to death, his family deals with it every day, but never has it been so personal, so enveloping, so grotesque. Later, Nobby's father put a car at Murphy's disposal: 'My dad ran Jimmy to all the funerals.'

The Collyhurst that Nobby grew up in is just down the road from my home town, Middleton. Even though I now live out of the city, I often still drive along Oldham Road and feel I have been seeing the 'C.Stiles, Funeral Director' sign all my life (although the business is now re-branded 'Stiles and Kennedy, Funeral Directors'). Either way, the sign is where I leave the Oldham Road, turn left and cut through Anthony Crolla's New Moston, to reach Middleton Junction and then Middleton town. Stiles means Nobby. Nobby means United. United means everything. That's how I always think of that sign.

I think too of Nobby growing up there, so wonderfully described in his colourful autobiography, *After the Ball*, written in 2003 the year after his heart attack. His old family house is towards the end of Rochdale Road, which was traditionally inhabited by Irish immigrants in the late 19th century and known then as Little Ireland. The other (city) end of Rochdale Road was Little Italy, where there were many Italian settlers during that same period. One notable name in this area as far as Manchester United were later concerned was the Rocca family, Louis Rocca being the son of 19th-century Italian immigrants who had arrived in Manchester to ply their ice-cream trade. Louis became a massive, central figure in the early growth of the club from its Newton Heath days, with tea boy, kit man and scout among his club roles. Rocca's house was close to where the art deco-style *Daily Express* building still stands (whilst the paper printing there is long gone) and the old newspaper office is how many Mancunians identify that little corner of town.

In later years, a well-known football song was sung in Manchester public houses, showing the mixed ethnic make-up of the city:

'Why do you wanna go to Wembley,
Worra ya wanna go to Wembley for?
Take a walk down Ancoats Lane,
and you're in Italy so grand,
Take a walk up Oldham Road
and you're in Ire-land.
China and Japan
are in Upper Brook Street;
Africa's in Moss Side so they say,
And if you wanna go further still,
Palestine's in Cheetham Hill,
Worra ya wanna go to Wembley for?'

There's a Catholic/Protestant dimension to Collyhurst and Nobby knows it: 'We marched on Friday with our saints, our virgins and bagpipes. They responded on Monday with their bugles and trumpets.' The area is steeped in the exploits of the famous St Patrick's parish, which turned out so many top players, some of whom played for United. Nobby was a talented forward in those days and scored more goals for his school than fellow pupil Brian Kidd. A small, genuine part of town, amidst the smell of Gallagher's cigarette factory and the lure of the Red Rec where games lasted for hours. So much football history, so north Manchester: poor but homely, honest and dishonest (depending on who you meet) the breeding ground for hungry fighters of all descriptions. An aspirational route out of the area through sport, as Nobby found, has become a well-trodden pathway.

Boxing, as ever, was an obvious route and those of local reputation like Jackie Brown were placed on the same pedestal as others of national renown such as Randolph Turpin, Belle Vue the go-to place for seeing these big names ply their trade. Now it's the Manchester Arena of course; the city moves on, but the tradition continues with Manchester currently acknowledged as the fight capital of the UK. The names of the fighters change, but the heritage is the same. It's Anthony Crolla now, Million Dollar Crolla, from New Moston. There is perhaps a little something of Nobby Stiles in Crolla: tough, likeable, amusing. Good Manchester lads, both.

Wilf McGuinness was born in Collyhurst, like Nobby and Brian Kidd, before moving to the new family home in Blackley as an infant, a little more than a couple of miles from Nobby's as the crow flies. They both knew Heaton Park and Bogart Hole Clough, names that meant to them what they did to me a decade later in the 60s, wonderous open places where kids from urban areas 'mucked about', played football, fed the ducks and ate ice cream. They were far removed from the drab rows of terraced housing and smoking chimneys, the engineering industry and the railways. They were places where you went for a picnic with your grandparents on a Sunday afternoon or with pals during school holidays, with tomato sandwiches and bottles of corporation pop (tap water) that always seemed to finish up with the crumbs of a Hovis loaf at the bottom. Why wouldn't you want to try to play football for a living, so that every day could be like that and you didn't have to return to the urban sprawl? Do a job you love and make a living from it? Time on the grass? Not much to argue with there. When Wilf McGuinness eventually joined United, the Manchester he knew in the 50s was conservative and restrained compared with the vast social changes that were to occur in the next decade. McGuinness says that for entertainment, 'Sometimes we would go into town, perhaps to the Plaza or the Ritz. There was also the Kardomah and Lyons Coffee House. Twenty-pound a week was the maximum wage, but we could not get that because of our age.'

My own home town, Middleton, is a little further north of either Moston or Blackley, the latter habitually referred to by BBC national presenters as 'Black-ley', rather than 'Blake-ley', although the clue this time is not in the title. Little Middleton, the middle town in between Manchester city centre and Rochdale, is not unduly pretty but is characterful nonetheless and steeped in rebellion, with the Luddites well represented during the Industrial Revolution. The 19th-century history of the place set the tone: poor people, cotton workers protesting violently about the introduction of new machinery and the loss of work. The famous Peterloo Massacre, brought to greater public attention now by Mike Leigh's timely film *Peterloo*, had its roots in places like Middleton. This poorer region of the city was where life was cheap and death came early. It has a history of cruel knights, bloody battles, the stately homes of wealthy industrialists, and ordinary people who would take the law into their own hands when pushed to do so and families needed to be fed.

Peterloo in particular is embedded into the history of this little town. The library houses the country's oldest political banner, which Middleton townsfolk held aloft as they marched into Manchester on 16 August 1819, protesting employment laws and practices that they believed harmed workers and their families. The Middleton Peterloo banner simply says, 'Unity and Strength, 1819' on one side, and 'Liberty and Fraternity' on the other. The Manchester meeting was the pinnacle of a series of protests amid rising tensions nationally, calling for parliamentary reform. The end of the Napoleonic Wars in 1815 had created famine and unemployment, made worse by the introduction of the first of the Corn Laws. Political radicalism was in the air and the Manchester Patriotic Union, a group seeking parliamentary reform, organised a demonstration featuring the radical orator Henry Hunt. Significantly, the meeting was taking place in the city that was the capital of the new factory system that the country and watching world were witnessing. One local radical, Samuel Bamford, a man who preached reform but only through orderly protest, led the Middleton march: 'With a hundred or so women at the front, and thousands of stragglers walking or dancing alongside, and under orders to maintain peace and order at all times, the column marched towards Manchester.' (Poole, 2014)

Through Oldham Street, Piccadilly and Mosley Street they went, before arriving at St Peter's Field, an area where the Radisson Blu Hotel now stands, its previous incarnation being the iconic Free Trade Hall. There is a blue plaque commemorating the events of 16 August 1819 on the side wall of the building. On that day, the marchers placed their banners before the hustings, 18 of them in total, lined up neatly. Protesters did not realise that this orderly display was in fact the feature that alarmed the authorities the most. As soon as orator Hunt began his address, troops under the control of the Lancashire and Cheshire magistrates charged into the crowd on horseback. The flag staffs were torn down and anyone who tried to save the banners was cut down, causing death and serious injury to the protesters. One man immediately had his nose cut off with a wild swing of a sabre. The Middleton banner survived and was passed down among four generations of one family, the Mathers of Middleton, before eventually ending up in the library.

The brutality of the guards on duty that day led to 15 deaths and around 650 people being seriously injured, most of them slashed by sabres and bayonets. Thus, the name The Manchester Massacre was the first given to the event, later becoming The Peterloo Massacre. Poole likens the event, in terms of being the 'bloodiest political event of the nineteenth century on English soil,' with Sharpeville (1960), Soweto (1976), and possibly even Tiananmen Square (1988). Middleton has links with The Peterloo Massacre that will remain forever. Manchester as a city will quite rightly mark the bicentenary of The Peterloo Massacre in 2019, and Mike Leigh's unique film will reinforce that message.

High above Middleton's town centre stands the grave and monument to Samuel Bamford who died in 1872. The inscription on the memorial obelisk that faces towards the site of the massacre says, 'Bamford was a reformer when to be so was unsafe, and he suffered for his faith.' Bamford was imprisoned for his protests and at one point was charged with treason. Owing to the efforts of people like Samuel Bamford, Middleton became a place of aspiration, where good people ensured that libraries flourished, and mechanics institutes attempted to help working men improve themselves and advance their families' status.

It is a long philosophical journey from Samuel Bamford to Alan Bennett, but his stance on libraries has always made me ponder the similarities. Incensed at what he sees as Tory plans to privatise libraries, he maintains that these schemes have been around since the mid-90s, with at least 'one think-tank clown,' saying they would make a 'valuable retail outlet' (in Bennett's book, *Keeping On, Keeping On*). His recollections of Armley Junior Library were like my own at Middleton Library. While he calls it 'dark and unprepossessing', it was a place where he was surrounded by books, before returning to a home where there were few. Perhaps in those post-war days there may have been more than the fair share of 'Kes librarians', made famous by their off-putting, child-unfriendly nature epitomised in that marvellously bleak, 1960s Yorkshire film *Kes*. However, this still did not detract from the ability to be able to sit among dusty volumes of old masters, or to catch the latest, wittiest thing around at the time. Also, such libraries, like my own in Middleton, were local and not positioned in municipal buildings that housed offices or shops and were out of the way. Bennett makes the point that libraries are needed as much now as they were back in his 1940s childhood, and indeed as they were needed back in Bamford's day. Bennett points to a speech in Leeds by David Cameron who called for 'Smart Education' as some sort of Big Society outreach extension. Bennett shrewdly observes that he is glad he had an 'unsmart' education, with free schools, free libraries and free university education. Quite.

While my dad's education had been cut short (through the hurled slate), meaning he never involved himself in ours, my mother and grandfather drilled into my brother and I that education mattered, a priceless gift, that included creative activities like music and sport. In our increasingly utilitarian times we seem to have rowed backwards on these ideals, led by politicians whose own schooling was privileged by money and status. I look at Middleton now and wonder whether the present library will survive, so cruel are the cuts to local services and so great the social needs in places like this. With care homes and schools to fund, levels of public literacy are collateral damage it seems to central government.

Near to the library was where we would start our journeys to Old Trafford on alternate Saturdays in the 60s. Of course, back then the 3pm kick-off times were standard across the country. The game finished at 4.40pm (plus injury time), we got the bus back into town, and soon after 5pm we were buying the *Football Pink* out on the city-centre streets, finding out how United's rivals had gone on. For the grown-ups, the Saturday evening then stretched out ahead and the pubs and clubs were ready to meet their desire for entertainment.

Former 1960s Manchester United player and later assistant manager Jimmy Ryan remembers the time well, as he explored town with his young pal, a desperately shy George Best:

'For a period, we were going into town a lot and George then was very shy. Neither of us could drink and that was what we had in common. I just couldn't drink alcohol at all, and, funnily enough, at that time neither could George. He was so shy that once, when we went on a double date one night, he never spoke almost until we saw the two girls off at the bus stop.'

Ryan explains that in those very early 60s days, it wasn't George Best who was the magnet for female football fans but the on-trend Willie Anderson: 'Willie Anderson was the one for chatting up the girls. He had the jet-black hair, the Beatles jacket and the Liverpool accent. That Mod look came in just as we were beginning at United in 62/63.'

United starlet John Cooke had been scouted playing for Sheffield and Yorkshire Schoolboys. He has fond memories of the exciting Manchester he encountered, when he signed for the Reds in 1963 as a 14-year-old schoolboy. After signing apprentice-professional forms a year later, he remained with the club until 1969:

'Manchester was a great place back in those days. We used to go out into town and we would sometimes bump into the City players. Mike Summerbee gave Carlo Sartori and I a lift home once. I always remember that he had a record player in his car, just below the dashboard in the centre console! I remember the little things like that. In Manchester the Kardomah cafe was a regular spot we would go to. I remember George giving us lifts into town. I think he had a Jag then. He would drive up King Street, off Deansgate, and pull up outside a cafe. This was downstairs in the cellar. He would buy us cheese on toast with an egg on the top.'

The generosity of George Best is a characteristic picked up on by many of his contemporaries, and the links between senior and junior professionals generally were close, whilst respectful. Cooke remembers the opening of George's boutique off King Street:

'I think we went to the opening, Carlo, Dave Sadler and me. There were lots of photographs going on. I never had a photo taken with him, but I do remember George throwing me a round-neck, striped sweater and saying, "Cookie! Try that on." I tried it on, then George said, "Go on, you can have that." I don't have it now but that was George, he was like that, generous. Malcom Wagner was next door in the Village Barber. George probably needed more friends like that and not some of the hangers-on he had later on. The players from that era all knew each other, especially with us and the City lads. Players like Tommy Booth who I still see. Manchester had a lot of Italians back then, like Carlo, especially around the Great Ancoats area. I was never homesick in Manchester. I couldn't get enough of the training and the football scene. I saw players who I wanted to emulate. I am a great believer in youth being given its chance and I think had I been pushed into the first team early on my career might have been a bit different. When Matt Busby told me I had a free transfer after I could have probably gone to any club in England at one time as a schoolboy, it was really hard to take.'

Nowadays, there is a plethora of educational and social advice given to talented young professional footballers covering such issues as: sport science, alcohol use, nutrition, athletic lifestyle and more. It is regrettable that for many players from the 1960s, this was not around during their careers, a salient and prophetic point made by George Best in one of his early autobiographies, *'Where do I go from here?'*

When the day's training was over in the 60s, young players had Manchester on their doorstep and the city's leisure time attractions were growing quickly. And if it was entertainment that you were after, no place was bigger or better to meet that demand than Belle Vue. With the possible exception of Blackpool Pleasure Beach, Belle Vue was the north's main, mega-scale entertainment park, the Alton Towers of its day perhaps being the best way to think of it. Something about Belle Vue always struck me as being slightly mad and I loved the place because of that. It was just so big, so ambitious, always adding to its attractions. It was like having Blackpool's Golden Mile around the corner from home. Ice skaters with penguins, acrobats, clowns, children riding elephants through the grounds, and lions within winking distance were just some of the attractions.

In terms of musical offerings, Belle Vue tried hard to lead the way in Manchester. In 1963, for three shillings, you could have danced in the Top Ten Club at the New Elizabethan Ballroom, seen Peter Jay and the Jaywalkers, heard a top DJ, be given free LPs (long-playing records), free EPs (extended-play records), visited 'super coffee bars' and an 'elegant powder room', drunk from a soda fountain and heard beat, rock, jive, and twist. Sadly, the decades passed and tastes changed; the zoo closed in 1977 and by 1980 the Belle Vue I had come to know and love had gone, whilst some attractions like the cinema and speedway remain.

I remember the hugely popular Belle Vue of the 60s so well. The name was magical, and the memories are huge, even if views on animal welfare have quite rightly changed over time. But as a naive youngster, Belle Vue just meant I could travel five miles from home and see apes, pythons, kangaroos, antelopes, tigers and giraffes. Additionally, I could watch wrestling, seeing big TV stars such as Masambula, Billy Two Rivers, Les Kellett and Steve Logan. My dad also wrestled and rode speedway there, he claimed. Working on my mum's 50 per cent truth meter, only one of those activities would have occurred, but I always chose to believe him implicitly since it added greatly to the romance of the place. Belle Vue? Beaux souvenirs.

Manchester United statistician/historian Cliff Butler, often referred to as the 'wise man of Old Trafford', is keenly aware of the social fabric of Manchester and sums up the city well when he says:

'The city of Manchester is fantastic. I always say, "I'm not English, I'm a Mancunian." I think we are classed as a Beta city at the moment but have ambitions to become a global city, and you can see that happening, especially with all the ongoing development in the city centre. I know we have a Metro but we will have to have an underground soon. I remember the sunken gardens in Piccadilly in the 60s too. I think they got rid of them because people were sleeping on the benches at night, but it wasn't the answer to homelessness. I like the mayor, Andy Burnham [who has made homelessness his major priority]. He's down to earth, one of us.'

With the city centre alive with enterprise and growth, the status of both Manchester clubs continues to keep pace, even if there are temporary set-backs. It's also great for the game and the city when respect is shown across the blue/red divide, as Butler points out:

'I have a lot of respect for the work Vincent Kompany is doing with the homeless at the moment. If someone has a heart I respect that, whether they are United or City, and Vincent is fast becoming one of my heroes. When I had health problems, I saw a doctor who is a City fan and we always had some banter. Well, I had this famous City programme of a match between City and Spurs, which was always known as the Ballet on Ice, in December 1967. This title was because of the conditions the game was played in. It certainly wouldn't be played now in those conditions! As a "thank you" to him, I had this picture framed of the programme, the club crests, the four goals that were scored, the lot. It's in a blue background with a white frame. When I gave it to the doctor, I said, "By the way, can I give you this?" He said, "Wow, where did you get that from?" I said, "Look, I appreciate what you've done for me and I just wanted to say thank you." I like people with a heart. I'm so proud of Manchester. It's a fantastic city.'

It is indeed. Manchester is a rainy city with a heart as big as a bucket … and with all the Pennine showers it receives, a large bucket may just come in useful. I love cities that love football. You can feel it on the streets. The taxi drivers banter about it, the advertisements scream it, and the people who live there thrive on it. Manchester is a football city. Madrid is a football city. Barcelona. Milan. Liverpool. (Did I really just say that?) But the main attraction of Manchester for me, growing up in a post-Munich era, was definitely Manchester United, with its three footballing musketeers: Best, Law and Charlton. Tony Whelan sums up the magnetic attraction of this illustrious trio, whilst rightly acknowledging the great 'supporting act' (as David Meek accurately calls it) behind the Trinity:

'All three players (Best, Law, Charlton) were just so professional and were fantastic players, whilst as a kid it was Denis Law for me. I mean, all three were different players. Bobby graceful, balletic wonderful acceleration, superb shooting ability, fantastic passing ability, fluid … but not a tackler, not a header. George could probably do everything. Denis was dynamic, great improvisation, athletic. But all three had different personalities too. It's hard to believe that all three players played on the same team. Different on the pitch and all different off the pitch. I think too that all three had a deep respect for one another. Denis and Bobby probably got frustrated with George in his prime in terms of passing the ball, but I think they all had a deep respect for each others' talents. There was recognition that the other two could do something that the one person couldn't do and vice versa. And the supporting cast with Nobby Stiles, Paddy Crerand et al. wasn't bad either, was it! Tony Dunne was one of the best full-backs the club has ever had. Alex Stepney, what a solid goalkeeper he was. People like Brian Kidd played his part as an 18-year-old kid. They weren't prima donnas. These great players had that about them. Pele was so humble, exemplified in the closing minutes of the 1970 World Cup Final in Mexico City, when he plays that famous pass into the path of Carlos Alberto to score that brilliant goal. That's teamwork, a player of his eminence and stature sacrificing self for the benefit of the team.'

Chapter 4

The Scarlet Thread

AS a young boy, like many other Mancunians in the 1960s I suspect, I grew up with one name above all others being synonymous with my beloved team: Matt Busby. Everyone I spoke to about him, be it my mother, window cleaner Harvey, or just neighbours, referred to him simply as Matt. Hopcroft explains the fact that in Manchester it was always '… "Matt," for Busby, "Denis" for Law, and "Nobby" for Stiles,' simply because of '… the deep and lasting impact made by men of extraordinary personality in the context of sport.' Exactly so. In my world, there was always endearment and reverence in reference to Matt Busby, even though the knighthood was some years off. None of us had ever met him, of course, but he was our leader taking us to the promised land of European domination, and we all respected him without reservation.

By the early 1960s, I was acutely aware that Matt Busby had been given the last rites twice and survived. I was never exactly sure what the last rites were, not being Catholic, but I knew he had heroically cheated death. That was all I needed to know. He was superhuman. He was the 'iron hand in the velvet glove'. That phrase was all around me. I thought about it over and over and concluded that this was the way to raise families, run schools and conduct business. I perceived the club as being managed by a loving but at times tough United leader, where sensitivity and affection were never allowed to become excuses for poor behaviour. The 'iron hand in the velvet glove' was, I thought, the backstory to boys learning to play winning football, in a rough, tough, cut-throat game. Indeed, in Manchester football circles, this was the image of Busby that I saw through my child's eyes; an approachable manager who you wanted to please and never to cross.

When I was eventually able to research the topic and test my theory against reality, I was pleased my childish notions about Busby's qualities had been accurate. Wilf McGuinness confirmed, 'It was unbelievable, a family, and that was down to the great Matt Busby ... and he *was* great. He was like a god to us.' My perception was accurate, too, when it came to young players who were unable to combine their talents with the right amounts of discipline and humility. At this point the club would never tolerate such character weaknesses for too long. Shades of Sir Alex Ferguson come to mind here, of course, several years later. Ferguson not only had the forethought to re-introduce the successful youth system which had been largely ignored during the 70s and 80s, but to underscore it with the pastoral care and concept of family that Matt Busby had introduced. Amongst the serial, hardcore winning mentality of both managers, there was clearly a familial warmth that was both attractive and productive.

Interestingly, in the early 60s and even including when I became a teenager in 1966, I could not have told you much about Jimmy Murphy. Matt Busby was the figurehead of the club and I think that this perception was shared by many other fans, certainly the younger ones who had not yet attempted to study the club's history. Jimmy Murphy received relatively little attention as far as I could see at that time. I knew him as simply 'the man who kept the red flag flying' after the horror of Munich. That is not to say I did not believe that this was an enormous task, I just didn't know he had done other important things before and after that moment in time. Matt Busby was the iron hand in the velvet glove, and Jimmy Murphy had kept that red flag flying. When I eventually found out the true extent of Murphy's contribution to the club in subsequent years, this was a revelation to me.

The impact and worth of Jimmy Murphy are clearly hugely significant factors in the development of Manchester United and the club's football philosophy. Manchester United, then and now, are the most storied club in Britain, and Jimmy Murphy is central to most of the main narratives. Murphy was far more than an able deputy. In reading the accounts of the management of the club during the 50s and 60s from all the associated books, one might conclude that most things come back to Jimmy Murphy. That the Jimmy Murphy Centre was eventually named so at United's Carrington training ground says much about the respect felt for the great man among those who are sensitive about the historical accuracy of the club. Support for a Jimmy Murphy statue at Old Trafford continues at the time of writing. Such recognition would be entirely appropriate, it appears, from study of the historical accounts.

That there were men of faith at the club also resonated with me as a child. At United there were people like coach Bert Whalley, a Methodist, and of whom Wilf McGuinness says respectfully, 'Bert was a lay preacher but never the sort to push his beliefs on you.' I was not a regular churchgoer, but in my part of Manchester I was always aware of the Catholic/Protestant dimension and there were still rigid divisions in terms of schooling and worship in the 50s and 60s. When I made the Middleton Boys under-11 town team, I was the only non-Catholic in the side at a time when Catholic school sport was incredibly strong. Matt Busby and Jimmy Murphy were Catholics. Putting this fact together with my town team experience, and the urban myth that United were a 'Catholic club', I remember wondering why Catholics made better footballers. Would I be a better footballer if I was one?

In Eamonn Dunphy's biography of Matt Busby he rightly points to the extreme prejudice experienced by groups such as Catholics, Jews and the Irish in Manchester during the 1930s and 40s, when the young Busby was beginning to make his mark on the city's football world. Whilst clearly not buying into the belief that United were 'a Catholic club', he does suggest that Matt's Catholic friends, like Louis Rocca and Paddy McGrath (a colourful nightclub owner, whom Busby liked greatly) were somehow brought closer together through their faith. At a time when people were openly antagonistic and prejudiced towards these minority groups (not unusually, housing and jobs were two areas of opportunity where open access was restricted), Dunphy asserts that, 'Busby was the most prominent Catholic in Manchester public life, a symbol of the faith to which he belonged, a Catholic admired and respected, around whom his co-religionists could proudly rally.' Of course, Busby's roots were Scottish/Catholic, and this group was a sizeable minority within the city. The Italian and Irish Catholics also helped to build a city that had more dwellers of minority background than almost every other city in the country, outside of London. These settlers added their unique cultures to a city that was still growing and forging its future pathway.

Some of the 19th-century Italian Catholic settlers who were ice cream traders, like Louis Rocca's family, introduced the city to the traditional flavours of their homeland. Several of these famous Italian ice cream trade names still exist today, such as Scapaticci, which can be found on Market Street in the city centre. Other Italian ice cream families were Pesagno's who traded in my home town of Middleton, and Granelli's, whose van I first saw on Oldham market in the mid-60s. Here, I always asked for a 'twist' cone, which was shorter than the usual ones and made with brown sugar.

As the early Italian migrants of the Victorian era sat outside their terraced houses in the Ancoats side streets, off Rochdale Road (the area affectionately known as Little Italy), playing their Italian folk songs, a damp Manchester must have seemed very different to the beauty of the Bay of Naples and the brooding menace of Vesuvius. In his superbly informative website, Ancoats Little Italy, Anthony Rea paints a colourful picture of a Manchester world gone by:

'During the summer nights in and around "Little Italy", one could hear accordions, tambourines, and even the occasional mandolin, well into the small hours of the morning. Men and women danced the tarantella, a dance full of expression, very popular in the southern regions of Italy. The women would stand and chat in their native costumes, or dressed in black, while their children played.'

Dunphy points out that for the Scots and Irish, too, there were similar moments of recall and sadness during the exodus to Manchester, whilst adding that for Matt Busby it was a city he was very happy to call home for the rest of his life: 'Italian charm and Irish laughter mellowed all but the fiercest adherents to Protestantism. The blood of Manchester was mixed in delightful proportion. It seemed to Matt Busby the most human of places when he contemplated going back in 1945.' Indeed, as countless settlers have found (and this has included many professional footballers, among them Bobby Charlton, George Best and Denis Law) there is something very alluring about Manchester and its people. The city centre is big enough to lose yourself in, yet small enough to get to know people. The humour is slick and observational in terms of northern life, whilst the seriousness with which the city enjoys its leisure time is clear to see.

My dad, fiercely proud of both his Irish and Catholic roots (whilst choosing neither to live in Ireland nor practise his faith) felt at home in this great city. As we were coming up the smoky Oldham Road in his beaten-up works van one day in 1965, he declared, 'I love this little shack and this smoky old town.' He was originally an outsider, like my Jewish and German 'aunties', and indeed Matt Busby had once been, but he had accepted the city, and, in time, the city had accepted him.

Busby had met Murphy (another adopted Mancunian) in wartime Bari, southern Italy. Watching an impassioned Murphy coach an army team, Busby immediately knew that he had found his right-hand man. Just before Christmas in 1944, Louis Rocca (chief scout) contacted Matt Busby and made him an offer that he hoped he could not refuse, even though United's last First Division trophy had been in the 1910/11 season:

> 37 Craigwell Road
> Prestwich
> Manchester
> 15 December 1944
>
> Dear Matt,
> No doubt you will be surprised to get this letter from your old pal Louis. Well Matt, I have been trying for the past month to find you and not having your Reg. address I could not trust a letter going to Liverpool, as what I have to say is so important. I don't know if you have considered about what you are going to do when the war is over, but I have a great job for you if you are willing to take it on. Will you get in touch with me at the above address and when you do I can explain things to you better, when I know there will be no danger of interception. Now Matt I hope this is plain to you. You see I have not forgotten my old friend

> either in my prayers or in your future welfare. I hope your good wife and family are well and please God you will soon be home to join their happy circle.
>
> Wishing you a very Happy Xmas and a lucky New Year. With all God's Blessing in you and yours.
>
> Your Old Pal
> Louis Rocca

The wording in Rocca's letter continued to fascinate me over the years. Firstly, like any self-respecting Mancunian, I always loved the idea of Manchester United snatching Matt Busby from under the nose of rivals Liverpool. When the letter was written, the unconditional surrender of Germany was still five months away, but close enough for ambitious men to start planning ahead. Rocca knew that Matt Busby would have no intention of sitting back and resting when Europe's theatres of war shut up shop. Rocca's reluctance to use Matt's Liverpool FC address is also most telling. It would seem that the drive to keep wartime secrets did not just relate to their potential impact on the battlefields, and that certain other walls had ears too … especially at Anfield. Also, Rocca's deliberate familiarity ('You see I have not forgotten my old friend …' signing off with, 'Your Old Pal') points towards Rocca's streetwise persona, something that would have played well with Busby, who enjoyed the company of colourful characters both within and outside the game of football.

Also, reading this letter in today's secular times, there are clear religious overtones: '… please God; With all God's Blessing …' However, Busby himself was quick to quash any sort of idea that a Catholic 'arrangement' was in place at United. Such an idea was nonsensical to him. In Patrick Barclay's stunningly detailed biography, *Sir Matt Busby: The Man Who Made a Football Club,* he tells of how Busby would sigh and say of the supposed Catholic link, 'It's one of those stories that get around.' Busby added that the only person who had to hold a cross at United was his goalkeeper.

However, Busby was no pushover and made strong demands to Rocca about how he wanted to run the club, without any interference from the board of directors. As Busby put it, 'Call it confidence, conceit, arrogance or ignorance, but I was unequivocal about it.' Rocca gave Matt this assurance, while Liverpool (who also tapped up Matt to manage) had failed to give him that same firm promise. No doubt, too, another attraction in Busby's mind was the fact that a youth system was already in place upon which he could build, so that it underpinned everything the club was to be about. Having already earmarked his deputy, soon after the war Jimmy Murphy was offered the assistant manager's job at struggling Manchester United.

When Busby and Murphy's conveyor belt of talent developed into the Babes of the mid-50s, a few years later I was listening to stories about these players. I was always fascinated by Eddie Colman, who I perceived as a 'proper' Salford lad, cocky, cheeky and liked by all. I learned that he was the archetypal local boy made good and one of the few players not in awe of Duncan Edwards. He was the great pal of Bobby Charlton and Wilf McGuinness, who would visit Eddie's parents' terraced house in Salford after games in the 50s. For nostalgia and humility, it is hard to beat the wonderful image of Charlton and McGuinness visiting Eddie Colman's house in Archie Street and Eddie's grandad, old Dick, fetching a jug of shandy from the corner shop off-licence. Nowadays, coaches plan how they are going to develop team spirit, primarily because they know it can aid success on the field. In Archie Street, which was the original model for early episodes of Coronation Street, team spirit was being developed more organically, brought about by friendship, northern hospitality and old-fashioned kindness. Hosted by Eddie's mother, Liz, and his father, Dick, the young players would play Sinatra records and chat long into the night. On other occasions the personnel might change with Duncan Edwards, Shay Brennan or David Pegg staying over. As McGuinness says, 'It was all very fluid.'

Colman's father was a good singer and they would have sing-songs around the piano, sharing a drink or two along with neighbours. Like most of his contemporaries, Colman did National Service, which disrupted players' progress. However, despite this, when Colman was presented with the FA Youth Cup in 1955 (the third of United's five wins during the 50s) Busby announced that he had £200,000 of talent in the reserves and youth team. Colman was captain during the first three victories. Matt Busby's vision of youth development was being realised in a big way, and Eddie Colman was a central figure in this spectacular progress. Eddie was also Nobby Stiles's hero, his death in 1958 hitting him particularly hard. I loved reading about how Bobby Charlton described these days as his happiest: a group of young boys, winning things together, all pals, sharing homes and lodgings. He was very close to Eddie Colman, even though they came from different home backgrounds, Bobby from a rural town in the north-east and Colman a real city lad, a 'townie'.

It was our window cleaner Harvey who I first heard use that phrase. Middleton is seven miles out of the city centre, and I remember thinking, as a child, that to be classed as a townie you had to live much closer to the centre of the city. This revelation made me feel like a hillbilly, living high up the long Oldham Road heading out towards the Pennines. Stand on our front doorstep and peer over the Vitafoam mill-chimney stack and I could see the Moors. I didn't think that this was possible in Salford. Eddie Colman might have been a townie, but I was sure I was not. In reality, Salfordians might claim Eddie was not a townie at all, in the sense of him not even being a Mancunian. He was a Salford lad. I was so pleased that my perception of Eddie Colman down the years had been another reasonably accurate one. Wilf McGuinness says, 'Eddie usually played right-half. A completely opposite personality to Duncan, he always had an answer but was never nasty. Little Eddie Colman was a "cheeky-chappie" Salford lad, a wonderful person. I always remember Eddie because he was my best pal at the time, loads of fun with a great personality. Eddie was just a box of tricks and he had a hell of a body swerve. He just dropped a shoulder and the defender had gone.'

Eddie's family sounded like real Salford characters, not rich in material terms but kind, friendly folk. They were the type of people my grandparents would certainly approve of: good-hearted, 'salt of the earth' people with a keen sense of humour. When Wilf McGuinness talks about the Archie Street days his eyes twinkle, his smile broadens, and the memories are as if from yesterday:

'I always remember Archie Street in Salford, not far from the ground, going there with Eddie and meeting his family. We would walk there from Old Trafford, it was so close. Eddie was an only child and he was special to the family. They thought the world of him. At United, the notion of family survived beyond the 50s and Munich, and into the 60s. But pre-Munich was just magnificent; players like David Pegg were fantastic and the friendship was great then. Someone would just say, "Are we going to such a place?" and everyone would put their hands up to go! You were just happy.

'On a Monday morning we didn't see any coaches, we just went around the back of Old Trafford and played five-a-side, sometimes ten-a-side, even 15-, 20-a-side sometimes! We played next to the railway. Then, on Mondays, we would go to Davyhulme Golf Club, where some played golf and others, like me, played cards. Shay was there, Eddie and the others. Then, in the evening, we might go to the cinema where we got in free with our passes. It was just magnificent. People like Eddie and I lived locally, of course, but for others like Bobby he had no parents with him. The team spirit was marvellous, and we won trophies galore.'

Such closeness among these young players was at the heart of the youth system at Manchester United in the 1950s, and that resonated with me. It drew me towards Manchester United like the little magnet and iron filings I used in my dreaded school science lessons, which for me always came a poor second to football. Bobby Charlton has spoken nostalgically about the hospitality of Eddie Colman's family, and also that of Wilf McGuinness's, where his parents often stayed when visiting Manchester for a game. One might conclude that this bonding was a very significant, planned part of the club's football philosophy. Certainly, it corresponds with Busby's 'team before self' ethos and construction of the Manchester United concept of family.

For while life in my own family had its highs and lows, sometimes with very few plateaus in between, what always took my mind off our troubles was the fact that in the 1960s Manchester United were very definitely rising from the ashes of Munich. That they would go on to dominate domestic and European football within a decade of that fateful air crash is indeed remarkable and was something I could not have envisaged as a child. Sadly, as the wonderful players from that 60s era pass away too (including Brennan, Best, Foulkes and Herd) so do many of their precious stories and insights. Over time, it was the humble tales like the Archie Street days which, for me, really underpinned what the club was about. Wilf McGuinness says, 'It was like being a part of a big family. When you are aged between 15 and 22 say, and you have that experience of family being together, that creates a real bond.'

That the club won the FA Youth Cup in 1964, only six years after the Munich Crash, in a tightly controlled and austere financial era, is an amazing achievement; a brisk reinstatement of the famous youth policy so cruelly shattered in the slush of a German runway. The sketchily reported, unjust guilt that Matt Busby had felt regarding Munich, when he led the club into Europe against the wishes of the FA, is then followed, within a decade, by the elation of winning four major trophies, including the European Cup. To understand that transformation and the Manchester United that I grew up watching in the early 60s, means that building blocks had been put in place in the 1950s that transcended even the Munich disaster. For, although the crash may have destroyed many of that fine team, the Manchester United way lived on within the club, a scarlet thread of talent development, laced with excellent pastoral care and a strong concept of family.

Busby and Murphy were never afraid to test their philosophies and their young stars against the best, though – a point stressed by Wilf McGuinness:

'The trips to Zurich for the Blue Stars Tournament and Germany were special. They were great experiences for young players in the 50s, very different to what we had been used to growing up. Being connected with United was very special and tours like the Swiss Blue Stars Tournament were fantastic, especially with players like Eddie Colman and Duncan. I played against players like Germany's Haller and later against Real Madrid in friendlies. The knowledge that we had won the Youth Cup when we were kids stayed with us when we came up against the same players later on. We mixed with great players, like Di Stefano at Real Madrid. Anybody who worked for Manchester United, whether they were manager, player or coach, had to be great or they left. Only "great" would do at United. You had to be a nice person too, or at least that's how I saw it at that time; personality mattered. When you got measured for the blazer with the United badge that was an amazing feeling.'

Meath County Libraries
Dunshaughlin

Customer name: Collier, Ann
Customer ID: **********3139

Items that you have borrowed

Title: Eat well live longer / Michael Van Straten with recipes by Sally van Straten.
ID: 30011004703139
Due: Tuesday 27 October 2020

Title: Growing up with the trinity : an Englishman, a Scotsman and an Irishman walked onto a football pitch
ID: 30011007334825
Due: Tuesday 27 October 2020

Title: Just my luck / Adele Parks.
ID: 30011007683650
Due: Tuesday 27 October 2020

Total items: 3
06/10/2020 14:43
Borrow 3
Overdue: 0
Hold requests: 0
Ready for collection: 0

Thank you for using the SelfCheck System.

Again, McGuinness's recollections fitted my own imagined chain of events very well. In my childhood world, listening to stories from my own team of decent, dependable men, I grew up with an image of Tommy Taylor smiling as he commits his future to Manchester United at a Barnsley Hotel. He is delighted as he signs his name on the £29,999 contract, which Matt Busby has cleverly left a pound short of £30,000 so as not to burden the young player with the price tag. The extra pound goes to the tea lady. I see Matt smiling kindly as he tips the delighted waitress, who cannot believe her good fortune and kisses him on the cheek. The craggy-faced Busby blushes and chuckles at the same time. It's a done deal, Matt Busby style.

Tommy Taylor was the player that Di Stefano had labelled 'Magnifico', and if this fabled maestro had said this, it just had to be true. I envisaged Taylor rising majestically above defenders, as Di Stefano had done, at least a foot clear of them, powering home headers. The reality, outlined by McGuinness, was very similar: 'What a player he was, great in the air. A tremendous leader of the line, not great with his feet but magnificent in the air. He climbed above the defenders, then: Bang!' The smiling executioner. Hopcroft speaks of the shining brilliance of this young team. He confirms, 'Manchester relished this fact. The old, gloomy city had a shining exuberance to acclaim.'

As a child, another Busby Babe who I often heard stories about was Roger Byrne. He always intrigued me because he was a full-back in an era when the position was defined by tough tackling and long clearances. This was the way I had been brought up to see the position. The fact that Byrne was playing in a very different way in the 50s confused me. Even in the 60s, as I tried to learn to play the game well, the golden rule as a full-back was 'never pass the ball across your own 18-yard box'. Playing for Middleton Boys under-11s at full-back, I remember that this was drilled into me. Seeing myself as a more attacking player, I did not enjoy the position, which seemed to be one where you would get scolded if you ever crossed the halfway line. Full-backs tackled, passed into midfield, were sometimes required to hoof the ball a long way forward when the defence was under pressure, and had no attacking function whatsoever. So, the fact that Roger Byrne had been playing a different role some years previously taught me that there were variations in the way tactics could be applied; light and shade in the way coaches interpreted positions and possibilities.

Roger was the captain of the 1958 side, a very stylish full-back, fast in the tackle and a good passer of the ball. He was different to the earlier generations of full-backs, quicker and smarter, dispossessing not lunging. Going forward, he was more like a winger than a full-back. Like his predecessor 'Gentleman John Carey', Byrne epitomised grace and good ball control. Facing Matthews and Finney, he was just as quick, smart and nimble as them. Roger was intelligent and qualified as a physiotherapist at night school, being a little aloof from the other players, qualities that served him well as club captain. Also, he was the star who lived around the corner from Matt Busby, and on his way to training one day he had crashed his car into the front garden of the house next door to Busby's! What a great story, so crazy that it sounds made up … except it was true, like so many tales about this legendary side. I loved that. It stirred my childhood imagination.

Matt Busby and his assistant Jimmy Murphy carefully researched players' characters to make sure they were the right choice for Manchester United. No doubt this had occurred before awarding Byrne the captaincy. The sentiment is echoed by teammate Harry Gregg's description of Byrne: 'Roger Byrne was morally one of the biggest men I ever met, both as a captain and as a person.' Wilf McGuinness confirms the high status of Byrne when he says, 'If Roger was about, we always watched what we did. He would just point a finger and say, "Hey! We're not having that. Not at United. Don't do that." We would just say, "Right" and do what he said. He was a great captain and he always made sure we behaved when he was around. He was that bit older than us.'

The stories about the great Manchester United team of the 50s that I grew up either hearing or reading about have endured throughout my life. An horrific plane crash, lost souls, a manager who twice received the last rites and a list of strong characters who dominated all the main scenes. Ray Wood was the player who warned, as the plane ran on and on and on, 'We are going to die.' Liam (Billy) Whelan was the deeply religious Irishman who said, as the plane began its final, doomed runway attempt, 'Well, if this is the time, then I'm ready.' Harry Gregg was the hero who dragged others from the wreckage, but who later admitted, 'The notoriety has come at a price, for Munich has cast a shadow over my life which I found difficult to dispel.' Some players had moved seats and escaped death because of that. Duncan Edwards was the stand-out star who joked, 'Let's have some bloody attention,' when teammates visited him in hospital, and to Jimmy Murphy who threw back his famous pre-match line, 'Get stuck in!'

Bobby Charlton was the star who had been knocked unconscious, but who escaped relatively unscathed and went back home to Northumberland to convalesce. Later he recalled, 'There was no screaming, no sounds, only the terrible shearing of metal. Something cracked my skull like a hard-boiled egg. I was hit again at the front. The salty taste of blood was in my mouth. I was afraid to put my hands to my head.' Matt Busby had defied death and his was the rich, baritone voice in the famous recording played at Old Trafford, prior to the match with West Bromwich Albion on Saturday, 8 March 1958:

> 'Ladies and gentlemen, I am speaking to you from my hospital bed in Munich, where I have been for a month

> since the tragic accident. You will be glad, I'm sure, that the remaining players here, and myself, are now considered out of danger and this can be attributed to the wonderful treatment given us by Professor Maurer and his staff, who are with you today as guests of the club.
>
> It is only in the past two or three days that I have been able to be told about football and I am delighted to hear of the success and united effort made by all at Old Trafford. Again, it is wonderful to hear that the club has reached the semi-final of the FA Cup and I extend my best wishes to everyone.'
>
> (*MEN*, 2015)

David Sadler, that most elegant of players from the great 1968 team and an eloquent club spokesman, experienced most of the Reds' triumphs in the 60s first hand. He refers to the decade spanning the Munich air crash and European success in 1968 as a story so incredible he might never have believed it, had he not lived through most of it. Personally, I also grew up with a tale so sad, so tragic, so compelling, so Manchester, that it has become a part of who I am, and what the city is today. In the 1960s, the Munich air disaster and subsequent path to glory was a main part of the Manchester I came to know so well, with a cast and story that would never be forgotten. As a child, how could I not be touched and engaged by this?

The culture and identity of the club was clearly well defined and endured beyond the tragedy of Munich, into the 60s, as Tony Whelan experienced:

'At United there was definitely an affection within the club. There was a hierarchy but there was also deep respect for senior players. If you were a youth-team player you had to knock on the first-team door. I always remember that the blazer was a big thing because it represented the values of the club. You couldn't get a blazer until you became a professional player. As soon as I signed pro I thought, "I can get that blazer now." It was special. It was a rite of passage. On the Blue Stars trip that first year all the local lads were in digs with more senior players, so they could borrow theirs. I was embarrassed and thinking how I was going to get a blazer. I don't know how I managed to pluck up the courage, but I did and asked Johnny Aston Snr. It indicated what a kind man he was that I should approach him. I said, "Look John, I need a blazer because we're going to Switzerland next week and everyone's getting one and I've not got one." He said straight away, "You can borrow our John's." When I came to ask him again a few days later he said he'd forgotten it, but it was in his case! I always remembered that, the fact that he lent me his own son's blazer to go to Switzerland. The human touch. John Jnr had been a member of the 1968 European Cup-winning team, which made this kindly gesture even more poignant.'

Like so many other youngsters in a football-mad town like Middleton, I longed to become a part of Manchester United. On many occasions when playing on Elm Street School fields, I looked over to the tall, spiked iron railings to see if Joe Armstrong was watching. I knew he was short in stature and very dapper. Anyone remotely fitting that description made me tackle a little harder and run a little faster. I dreamed that one day he would exit his sleek club car, walk slowly over to our game, pull me aside and say, 'Son, I've been watching you and you've got real promise. Would you like to come and have a trial for Manchester United?' Alas, Joe never came.

I knew that Joe was the club's most successful scout by far. I later learned how he operated. The chain of command was: first, Joe watched a boy, next the senior staff watched, Murphy and Whalley then watched and finally Busby watched. Tony Whelan calls Busby 'the central computer'. There is much romanticism written about Armstrong's 'magic eye', but while it was true that he was the procurer of talent, other parts of the system then kicked in. All the staff knew what they were looking for: ability, discipline, loyalty, clean living and enthusiasm. While small by today's standards, this scouting system yielded spectacular results. Armstrong worked at the General Post Office (GPO) during the week and used the phone to contact parents; this cutting-edge technology of the day was central to the success of the scouting system. Armstrong was able to talk to parents and arrange meetings before other clubs were on the scent of a talented youngster. He was a meticulous taker of notes. Whelan recalls that Armstrong used comments like 'fair game', which was a code for 'has potential, will watch again'. Nor was Armstrong averse to charming the boys' mothers; he occasionally gifted flowers and chocolates, recognising that the mother was the key figure who decided whether the boy left home. Not to leave out dads, he sometimes used to take them for a pint to foster good links with the family of a promising youngster. Once the bait was taken and United were chosen, he was confident that behind the scenes at the club, United had the welfare of the boys at heart, because Busby had instilled that ideal into his staff. Like Busby, Armstrong was also a principled man and would not promise parents something he felt the club could not deliver.

Being able to find difficult addresses and venues for matches because of his GPO skills, he often arrived at a match and was able to talk to the parents just before a scout from another club appeared. Once in that pole position, Armstrong's personality usually sealed the deal. Busby had a friendly term that he used to describe the way Armstrong operated, referring to his chief scout as 'the little ferret'. Bobby Charlton famously says, 'I signed for Manchester United Football Club, not Newcastle or anyone else, because of that wonderful little man, Joe Armstrong.' The reputation of Manchester United in giving youth a chance was also central to players like Duncan

Edwards signing. Incredibly, Armstrong never drove, and relied on trains and taxis to take him round the country.

When I eventually found out, many years later, that Joe Armstrong never drove in his life, I realised that I had wasted much of my youth on Elm Street field, looking for a big car from which United's main talent spotter would surreptitiously emerge. Or could it be that Joe had missed me because the bus route was poor in our area? Sadly, I cannot claim that either as we lived on the main Oldham to Manchester road. The answer probably had more to do with football ability and not quite having enough of it. Manchester United did not miss many local starlets.

Whether you played for the club or not, though, to be born in Manchester and raised in the 50s/60s meant that the crash (as it is often simply referred to in Manchester football circles) was a sorrow of unbelievable proportions. Is there another city in the country where you can simply say 'the crash' and most people (and certainly those with any football knowledge) will understand the reference, even though the event happened over 60 years ago? It is part of Manchester. Knowing about it but living elsewhere was never the same to me. Coming from Manchester and knowing about Munich meant you owned a part of the club, albeit just in your heart but maybe even your soul. Manchester is forever linked to Munich, to Belgrade, to Madrid, who played fundraising friendlies and sold memorial pennants to raise funds for United, and to small outposts like Bishop Auckland, who loaned players in the immediate aftermath of the air disaster. It is linked also to places where the dead came from, such as Duncan Edwards's home town of Dudley.

Cliff Butler elaborates on how this respect for the dead and injured continues to be shown:

'With these special places like Munich and Belgrade, we still do things to keep the links. With Bishop Aukland recently, when we played an under-23 game up there, they unveiled a plaque that day to recognise the links we have; we got players from them to help out after Munich, especially Warren Bradley, who made his name with United. He was an amateur international when he came, and then went on to win a full international cap. I remember on his ankles he always had padding, his socks always looked padded out. So, yes, we still have strong links with Bishop Aukland, even though they don't play at the same ground now.

'With Belgrade, and with 2018 being the 60th anniversary, Tony Whelan, myself and a few others were invited to go there, and it was one of the most terrific things that has ever happened to me. Those three days were just about football, about remembering the disaster and those players. Two of the greatest players from that Red Star team stood on the very spot where the famous "last line up" photo was taken. It was very emotional. People were so warm and so hospitable. It was fantastic. We have very strong links with Red Star, and with Partizan, because of course it was their stadium where the game was played.

'When we were in Belgrade, we met one of the Red Star players, Dragoslav Šekularac, who played in the match, and we presented him with a photograph of the lads [the Babes]. What a moment that was. We were sat talking to him, about four of us, and he said, through an interpreter, "Would these people like to come back to the Red Star stadium with me?" So, we went up there. Dragoslav was like their Bobby Charlton, a wonderful player. He made the call to the ground and arranged it and we went there; they showed us the stadium, took us into the president's office and we had Serbian liqueur and coffee, and then they gave us gifts, it was fantastic. With Munich, links will never be broken, and people still make the pilgrimage to the old airport site every year for the memorial. So, the Munich association will always be strong. We've got the tunnel named after it and memorials all over the ground.'

Sadly, the great Dragoslav Šekularac passed away in January 2019, another important link to that era now gone. Reassuringly, though, work to raise awareness about the Munich legacy continues in the Manchester United academy with the stars of tomorrow. Tony Whelan adds:

'Being there and being privileged to be representing the club at that particular event [in Belgrade] was profoundly moving. What struck me too was how the 18- and 20-year-old players "got it", they understood what it was about. They conducted themselves in a wonderfully respectful way, an honourable way. When we lined up there was a minute or minute and a half's gap between blowing the whistle and you thought maybe someone wasn't going to stand poised, but they did. There was no crowd there and then they had to walk off the pitch in an orderly fashion and I just thought how they had "got it", they had understood the significance of the occasion. It was all enormously respectful. So, in terms of education, you just knew that those kids realised what it meant to the club and the respect they had for those players who had lost their lives. And it reinforced to me that there had been some good work done in the education prior to that, because you don't get to that level without understanding it. Even some of the staff commented on how they realised how deeply ingrained on the club's psyche and memory was that sad, tragic event. It still resonates.

'Munich is an unbelievable story. With the First World War how can you really understand what it was like? I've read all about it but how can we actually comprehend those young lads of 17 or so living and dying in those terrible circumstances? You can't really can you? And I apply that to the Munich event. Our young lads can't fully understand it because it's generational, but I think we are just trying to explain to them that this club went through a really tragic time and lost those wonderful players in the crash, and that this has shaped the way the club is today and the values we have. The tradition of youth is part of that, and we try and say, "Why do you think the European Cup is so important to this football club?" And we tell them that the reason is that those young players died trying to win it at the beginning. Then we had a manager who suffered because of his injuries and who felt responsible for that, and then there was a little bit of redemption when we won it the first time. That's the sort of conversation we have with the young lads and that can never go away. We try to explain it in a simple way and then ask those young players to go and find out about those events themselves. It's not top-down. We'll give them a list of players, and they can go on to Google and type in "Duncan Edwards" and see what it says about him. When we do it this way they are more likely to have a look and come back and tell us what they found out. It works better than just sitting in a classroom and saying, "Right, we're going to tell you about Munich." We drip-feed it in. We want them to know about it. There's no question about that.

'I think even at senior level if they know about what they are buying into, it would help them while they were here, in terms of loyalty, having a feel for the club, not in a heavy way but making sure they know enough. They might have heard about it but do they know enough, that's the thing? It is all generational. I even find it hard to understand how people in the 50s lived their lives, in that era where there was no money. There wasn't a lot in the 60s but there was even less in the 50s. So, that intimacy, that camaraderie was what made those 50s boys so special. When Bobby tells the story about going up to Ashington (in Northumberland) and Eddie Colman and Wilf came up on holiday, like who would go to Ashington on holiday now? It just isn't going to happen anymore, that's the thing. It's generational; we have to respect the generation we are in and the ones that came before us.

Our kids' worlds look different to ours. Now, I see some of the things players do and think, "I wouldn't do that", but they are doing it because this is the generation they have been brought up in. The way they communicate now in this digital age is just not my experience.'

Visits to the graves of the players who perished is another ritual still being observed within the club. Cliff Butler explains:

'We also went to Yorkshire to visit all the graves: David Pegg, Tommy Taylor, Mark Jones. We did the three in Manchester too: Eddie Colman, Roger Byrne and Geoff Bent. Dave Bushell [head of education and welfare] laid a wreath and I put a single red rose on each one. I never saw the Busby Babes play, a few of them afterwards, but not the ones who perished. So much has been written and so much said that you feel as if you did know them. They seemed such nice lads. Eddie Colman used to go on the bus to the match with the fans. Unbelievable.'

And on a personal level, Butler recalls what the Munich air crash still means to him, each and every year on 6 February:

'There was a time on 6 February when I would stand at the clock at Old Trafford on my own and there was nobody else there. I just stayed a minute and then went, but it's become more popular now. I don't know why, it's just a modern thing. I think after Diana's death possibly, it became more of an orchestrated thing. I just wanted to commemorate the occasion in my own way, so I went back to the very spot where I was standing when I first heard about the Munich air disaster, and I now do a minute's silence there.'

For Manchester United fans who are sensitive about the club's history and understand the significance of the Munich tragedy, Cliff Butler's recall of the minutiae of that moment will resonate strongly:

'This was on Ashton Old Road, and I remember the exact moment when I heard about the disaster. My mum was an avid knitter, loved knitting, and she had an arrangement with a wool shop on Ashton Old Road that she would buy all her wool there but on the 'drip' [paying as she went along]. She would go in each week and get a couple of balls of wool, and I was alongside her that day, aged eight years. I remember a person coming in and saying to the girl behind the counter, "Hey, have you heard about United?" My mum said, "No, what?" The woman said, "They've been in some sort of plane crash, there's been an accident or something." It's never left me, that moment. That shop's gone now but when I go there each time on 6 February, I'm reasonably sure I am within a few yards of that spot. I just go and stand there for a minute.'

The national outpouring of grief after Munich did indeed cause the nation to have a place in their heart for Manchester United. But to come from Manchester, to have lived amongst people who remembered the crash, to understand the culture of the city, perhaps meant that the grief was more tangible and intense. In my own Manchester world, one childhood friend remarked that in his household the name 'Duncan Edwards' would never be allowed to stand. Upon utterance, his father would immediately change it to, 'The Great Duncan Edwards'. It is a huge part of the Manchester psyche that Duncan Edwards remains such a tragically symbolic figure.

Wilf McGuinness is very clear about the central position of Edwards in any discussion of Old Trafford greats:

'Bobby was great, and George was great, but the greatest of them all was Duncan Edwards. Those pre-Munich players were wonderful, and Duncan was the best of them. Duncan was a man-boy, a giant. He could play on the floor, was great in the air, he could do everything. He was a wonderful, quiet lad, just did what he was told and did it well. He was never cocky or nasty. He was like the others who were aged around 20 or 21 when they died. Duncan was special. I got a lot of games, largely because Duncan was so good that he could play anywhere. I always thought that Duncan was the best player I had ever seen. With Duncan it was just a case of "Let him play where he wants, don't spoil him!" because he could play anywhere: defence, midfield or attack.'

Nor is the significance of Duncan Edwards lost on David Sadler, who had heard much talk of him during his early Old Trafford days:

'There just wasn't the film being made back in Duncan's days. I went down to Aston Villa in the 1980s to celebrate the 30th anniversary of the cup final with United in 1957; they had invited me down as secretary of the Old Boys' Association. I helped them get in touch with Alec Dawson and one or two of the other United boys, like Harry Gregg, who had played. I went down to one of the hotels near the NEC, and they had big screens up all the way around a huge room. They showed the whole of the 1957 final. Well, I couldn't recall much of Duncan Edwards [from my own experience] but when you looked at the screen, there seemed to be these little men running about and there was this giant strolling around, and it was Duncan! We don't think there is much footage of George but there's even less of Duncan. I watched this film having heard Bobby talk about this colossus of a man and I had lapped all that up. Then I saw Duncan and it looked exactly like that: an adult playing in a children's match!'

What Matt Busby and Jimmy Murphy had produced prior to Munich, ably assisted by a wider team of decent, dependable men, was a scarlet thread that was strong enough to link together the generations that had passed and those to come. In the next decade, there was still respect, direct communication and honesty in the day-to-day running of the club, as Tony Whelan discovered:

'A different era of football, in some ways better. You certainly had to work for things and there was always a strong work ethic at the club. The fact that it was so intimate made communication easier and helped solidify friendships and everyone loved the club. I was a proper City fan, saw them play home and away, but I had a Damascus Road experience if you like; you couldn't help but fall in love with the place when you saw the manager and the players, the whole place. You knew all about Munich, it was never mentioned but you were aware of it. This was a special club and you got treated properly. Little things like receiving a tour itinerary and getting the club blazer which made you feel immensely proud. Just playing at Old Trafford was a special feeling. You thought, "Wow!" when you played there. You'd eat in the canteen with the first-team players at The Cliff. It wouldn't matter who you were. You might sit next to Denis Law one day and Joe Bloggs the next.'

Even the Munich air disaster had not broken the scarlet thread of talent development. There was still a philosophy of play that encouraged freedom of expression juxtaposed 'team before self', underpinned by sound pastoral care, passion and compassion.

Chapter 5
Cup Final Day Shock

FA Cup Final, Manchester United v Leicester City, 25 May 1963

I stared hard at the grainy, black-and-white image of a youthful David Coleman explaining how Manchester United might struggle to bring the FA Cup back to Manchester, playing against a talented Leicester City side who had done the league double over the Reds. Kick-off time, 3pm, was approaching as Coleman handed over to Kenneth Wolstenholme, who was about to preside over his 11th FA Cup Final. The smell of ham-shank and cabbage was wafting in from the kitchen as Mum drained the water from the potatoes into the old, cracked Belfast sink. She was singing along to 'Nobody's Darlin' But Mine' by Frank Ifield, one of her favourite singers, on our small, cream Bush radio. Her face was beaded in droplets of sweat, which she tried to remove by protruding her bottom lip and blowing strongly upwards. I sat on the plastic, black-and-white checked couch, a recent purchase from the catalogue on the 'never-never'. The Gus catalogue was on the table, which Gerry and I always looked forward to choosing our birthday and Christmas presents from. I was glued to the football while my brother, two years older than me at 11, fiddled furiously with a Meccano model of a crane. I never understood why. Only a football interested me.

David Coleman may have had his doubts about United lifting the cup, but I did not share his pessimistic view. We had Bobby Charlton and Denis Law playing, alongside other big-name players like Paddy Crerand, who I was sure would rise to the occasion. Leicester had no one of that quality as far as I could see. We may have had a poor season but when it came to the important matches, I always believed the big stars would turn up. Not a bad piece of game analysis for a nine-year-old, when I look back now. After an edgy start by United, with keeper Gaskell clearly nervous, the Reds settled and after half an hour Denis Law opened the scoring. Leicester continued to miss chances, and soon after the restart Herd doubled the score with an easy goal, after good work by Giles and Charlton. Ten minutes from time, Keyworth pulled one back for the Foxes against the run of play, before Herd wrapped up the match, seizing on a rare error from Gordon Banks. Later that afternoon, I was out on the school field reliving the match with my mates, taking it in turns to be Denis Law or Bobby Charlton. What a great feeling. FA Cup winners after an otherwise poor season. We had cheated the drop and now won the (then) hugely important FA Cup.

When I returned home, though, the mood was soon to change. A hard knock at the front door suddenly soared above the noise of the TV in the living room, demanding attention. Wiping her hands on her gravy-stained pinny, Mum sighed heavily but sweetly, saying, 'Now, who's that at this time?' At the door stood two heavily built men, wearing crumpled raincoats and life-weary faces. One looked thoroughly dishevelled, with bushy ginger sideburns and a Senior Service cigarette flopping precariously from his mouth. The other appeared more self-aware and had an air of gravitas about him. I automatically assumed it was someone wanting money, either for the rent, the catalogue or else hawkers who were selling something. If it was the expensive *Encyclopedia Britannica*, they would get no sales here.

'Mrs McGuire?' the more presentable man said as he reached inside his raincoat pocket for an identity card, flashing it quickly and then returning it to his chest.'

'Yes, that's right,' said my mum, anxiously but defiantly, since she was well used to dealing with suits, be they bailiffs, travelling salesmen, Jehovah's Witnesses or the occasional court official.

'Manchester CID. Could we come in, please?'

Without answering and keeping her eyes fixed hard on the men, my mother turned and pushed the heavy front door back so the two men could enter.

'Mrs McGuire, I am sorry to report this, but we have reason to believe that your husband, Eddie, was in fact already married when he married you, therefore making your marriage illegal.'

'Well, give it to me straight then, why don't you?' laughed my mother, throwing her head back in mock anger.

Realising by their scowls that the men were entirely serious about the allegation, my mother tried again to defuse the situation:

'Well, wouldn't that be the best news I've heard this week, if the old devil wasn't really my husband!'

'Mrs McGuire, did you know about the existence of Bridget O'Riley when your husband married you?' asked the policemen.

'Bridget O'Riley? No, I never heard of her for sure ... but I know about Old Mother Riley. Could it be her you're looking for?'

My mother was Manchester born and bred, but her marriage to my father and his large County Mayo family had brought a new range of Irish phrases into her everyday language, which always made Gerry and me giggle. Through the gap in the door, I saw the other detective take the cigarette from his mouth and lean forward so that he was only inches from my mother's face:

'Let's put it another way, love,' he said. 'If you knew that he was already married when you got wed, he's a bigamist and you're involved too. Does that help?'

At this point my brother opened the door abruptly, sensing that there was about to be either an explosion of rage from my mother or more belligerence from the police.

'It's okay, Bren and Gerry. Here, take half a crown and go and get yourselves fish and chips. I'll handle this,' my mother said.

'I'm not leavin' you,' said Gerry, and I stood my ground with him.

In truth, nothing was unusual for our family. It wasn't a Janet and John, middle-class existence, like I read about at school. 'Who lives like that?' I used to think. Our garden was a back yard with a coal hole and toilet. Dad didn't work in an office or drive a company car: he had a decrepit old, white van with 'McGuire – Plasterer' written on the side in bright red letters. Life was sometimes scary but never boring; whether it was the rental firm repossessing the telly, or news that my father had missed the coach back from Blackpool on the pub outing. Here, he was last seen spreadeagled on North Beach, drunk, with his false teeth washed out to sea and probably nearing the Dublin coast. But even by our own family standards this seemed a serious event.

'Okay, now, but just go back and do what you're doing. Okay? Gerry turn the pans off,' Mum said.

At this we went back into the sitting room and closed the door just enough so that we could hear most of what was being said, but we were there if we were needed.

'Mrs McGuire,' said the smarter detective, 'this is very serious, very serious indeed. Did you know anything at all about your husband's earlier wedding?'

'Listen now. The best thing to come out of my marriage is those two kids in there. After we married, I found out many things, like he was 47 not 37, like he didn't descend from the Irish aristocracy but from a poor farm in the west of Ireland, all sorts of things. But did I know the eejit was already married? I certainly did not.'

'Well, it looks very much like he was, to Bridget, in Birmingham in 1948 – two years before he married you in Manchester.'

There was a pause that stated acceptance of the fact and begged a moment to digest the information.

'I want you to go now,' said my mum, in a voice that suggested any other course of action was not an option, deliberately casting her gaze over their heads and out of the window on to the busy Oldham Road, which flowed like the Nile past our small, Accrington-brick terraced house.

'We understand,' said the smart detective.

'Don't fret. We'll be in touch again soon, flower,' said the other in a menacing tone, whilst beating a hasty retreat.

As the front door closed, Gerry and I came into the room and looked at Mum's face. A tear welled in the corner of her eye and she blew her nose loudly.

'Come here you two. Listen, they can take everything from me: the house, the van, the telly … and most certainly your father, but they'll never have you two.'

Rinty, our scruffy mongrel (Dad had named him after Rinty Monaghan the famous Irish boxer), licked the backs of our legs as we formed a circle of three.

'Nor him either!' roared my Mum loudly.

Later that night, just as *Juke Box Jury* was ending and Janice Nicholls muttered her famous, funny line in her best

Brummie tones, 'I'll give it foive' (for a Rolling Stones record), I heard the key turn in the lock. As my father entered the living room, and without a word, my mother flung the pan of cold cabbage at his head. The handle caught the side of his skull, with most of the weight deflected by his shoulder, the slimy shoots slithering one by one down his shiny, light-grey suit. As he lay on the ragged Axminster, he muttered threateningly, 'What the hell is this?' and attempted to raise his head in a drunken stupor. The effort tired him, though, and soon he dozed off, his breathing loud and laboured. My mother hooked out his dentures and tossed them across the table, the saliva leaving a trace of small red globules on the light-green cloth, twisting gently like the trail of a slug.

'Gerry, fetch the bottle of Bell's from the cabinet.'

At this, my mother poured small amounts of whisky for Gerry and me, and then deftly delivered her own more generous measure into an old tumbler, blowing the dust from it first.

'Here, throw it back in one go,' she demanded. 'All grown-ups do it when they've had a nasty shock.'

First, the back of my throat burned and then I started to feel all squishy, like I wasn't there, while part of me knew that I was, but it wasn't a bad feeling and there was a sickly, sweetness about the taste that sat still on my lips and made me want more. Besides, it felt like the drink was acknowledging that I was 'coming of age', a good sort of feeling.

Chapter 6

Joining the United Family

THE pastoral care of boys in the exciting days of Manchester United's youth development programme of the 1950s and 1960s was outstanding, even when compared with today's highly structured, checklist-driven standards approach. For example, the 'digs' where the boys stayed and the sharp attention to detail in ensuring homesickness was understood and allowed for characterised the experience of so many youngsters who came to Manchester United. Where it was local boys who were able to stay at home, and for exceptional young players like Wilf McGuinness the pathway he followed from excelling at schools' level to Old Trafford was well defined. He attended Mount Carmel School, Blackley, where he became head boy and met a sports teacher who was a great influence on his career, in an era when school sport was the all-important step towards elite-player development:

'My sport teacher was called Mr Mulligan, who had played a few games at Manchester City. He was a great help to me, very firm, very strong. Schoolboy football was good for me because I played for England Schoolboys two years running and Manchester Boys too. For Manchester Boys we played at Ten Acres Lane or Princess Parkway and we trained at a school near Southern Cemetery, in Chorlton-cum-Hardy.

'At school, I was a City fan. United were playing at Maine Road as Old Trafford had been bombed, so I went one week to Maine Road to watch City and one week to watch United. United looked better for young players, and so I signed at 15 and it was a great decision. I was a wing-half, although, of course, United already had two great wing-halves: Eddie Colman and Duncan Edwards. Eddie and Duncan were a year older than me. Duncan was so good that he could play anywhere, and so that made room for me. There were so many good lads.

'United were the best in the country at getting young players in. They got the system going and they came from all over the country. It was just great being associated with them. I was a junior when I came, but young players got in the first team at 17 or 18 quite regularly at United, and some of them were magnificent. They kept winning the Youth Cup year after year and to be part of that was fantastic. We felt we were growing up with this great club. Unfortunately then, for everyone, the crash happened. I had been there for five years and the crash just rocked everybody.'

For Wilf McGuinness, the club certainly lived up to his expectations, and the reputation United enjoyed for developing talented youngsters was well deserved. Even a decade later, whilst tragedy might have understandably disturbed the flow of hugely talented young players coming through the doors of Old Trafford, by no means did it quash it. Proving that a deeply held philosophy can endure even such horrors as the Munich air disaster, the experience for young boys joining United was as positive and caring in the 60s as it had been in the 50s. The end of Matt Busby's personal rainbow was the winning of the European Cup in 1968, ten years after the tragedy of Munich. Tony Whelan speaks of the victory as having a redemptive quality. When Busby had reached that goal, looking back over the arduous process he and his team had endured, he noted, significantly, that a part of what had eventually carried Manchester United over the line in Europe was 'affection'. It is a small word used in his 1973 autobiography, *Soccer at the Top: My Life in Football,* and yet it speaks volumes about how players felt about Matt Busby, Jimmy Murphy and their assistants, and the way Busby and his team felt about their proteges:

'It takes a great team to win the European Cup. It was my third great team in more than a score of years. Others created one great team: rare ones, like Bill Shankly, at Liverpool, two great teams. I am grateful to have been blessed with the energy to survive the strain of creating three. It could not have been done merely by gaining respect. To respect must be added affection – mutual affection. That's what we at Manchester United had.'

As for Wilf McGuinness a decade earlier, Jimmy Ryan was introduced to a similarly well-structured, secure environment when he entered Manchester United in 1962:

'I first arrived at United with Willie Anderson and we shared a room in digs. We have stayed in touch since. He lives in Portland, Oregon, now and I have visited him there. He got into the first team before George I think, certainly before me. It was an intentionally family atmosphere at Old Trafford and you never heard anyone complaining about the digs we lived in. Sometimes you got a bit of a scolding from the landlady for coming in late. "What time did you come in last night?" my landlady would say. "You'll have to start coming in earlier than that if you want to be a footballer."

'I used to play pitch and putt in Stretford with John Fitzpatrick and a young guy from Huddersfield called Terry

Poole, a goalkeeper. We would go across Longford Park and there was the pitch and putt. Terry turned out to be pretty good and we used to have a small bet. Terry would say to Fitzy, "Let's have a bet!" So, Fitzy says, "Aye, alright. Let's play for a fiver," trying to make Terry think he was a good player, fancying his chances. Terry says, "Okay." Within a short period of time, we were four-nil up and Terry's taking the mickey by now. Then Willie Anderson starts chipping in saying, "What are you doing, Fitzy?" winding him up. Sometimes you would see people jump over the fence with the two clubs they had loaned you! It was all great fun.'

David Sadler, describing his entry to United as a 17-year-old, had a similarly good experience. Big for his age, he had gained a fast-growing reputation for scoring goals. This had been achieved with progress from county to international schoolboys, through to Maidstone United and England Amateurs. He explains his decision to join United, despite attention from a string of top clubs, and pinpoints the staff he met at United as being key to that choice:

'I remember seeing Joe Armstrong at the amateur international matches I played in, and you couldn't help but be impressed and like him. Jimmy Murphy was the next one I saw. They suggested I come up to Manchester and spend a bit of time with them in autumn 1962. I then spent a week there, travelling up by train. They put me into digs with Wilf Tranter, a centre-half, who looked to be such a good player but subsequently did not grow, which stopped him progressing, I think. He was the sort of lad they wanted others to see as he was such a good role model. He showed me Manchester and what I needed to do at the club. It was a good week. After that week, Jimmy Murphy was very keen that I sign some amateur forms because he said it would keep other clubs off my back. There had been a fair bit of attention; Tottenham and West Ham wanted to sign me, and Jimmy made sure I signed the forms for United. So, I signed these in the autumn of 1962, went back home, and on my 17th birthday in February 1963 I signed professional forms.

'I became a fully fledged pro then, without becoming an apprentice, but I had played at a good standard with Maidstone and England Amateurs. I had already met Matt Busby by this time, seeing him first in the early period. I never knew Matt when he was doing all the on-field coaching as he did before Munich. He was never the coach in the accepted meaning of the term in my time, and as he had been before the crash. I saw the set-up they had, and I felt very comfortable with that. My father was a publican, and when I signed, Jimmy and Matt came down to my dad's pub. There was a lot of interest in the village, and it was during the big freeze in 1963. When they came out of the pub, there was a crowd there. They waved because it was like having royalty in town, and then their car wouldn't start in the pub car park! It was quite funny.

'When I was doing the matchday work I was aware that I am part of the history of the place. But right back at the beginning I wasn't aware of the history, I was just a young guy away from home. There was a family atmosphere at United, and you did feel like you were joining a family.'

When Sadler's teammate John Cooke first came to Old Trafford that same year to sign for the club, the main figures he met were Matt Busby, Jimmy Murphy, Johnny Aston, Jack Crompton and Wilf McGuinness. 'That was the whole coaching staff!' he says. Crompton was the first-team coach back then. John tells of the first day he arrived at the ground and was shown around the first-team and reserves dressing rooms by Busby himself. His mother was taken upstairs for a cup of tea by that great calmer of motherly nerves, Joe Armstrong. This tour of the ground made a huge impression on John, seeing the oak-panelled walls of the snooker room and the old club offices, it was a football world he had not experienced before. The establishment of the concept of family at United began with simple guided tours like this and meeting such a small, special group of staff who had been handpicked by Busby. John was immediately surrounded by Matt's 'decent, dependable men'.

The significance of the lodgings where Matt Busby placed these young boys was hugely important. Carefully and often personally researched by Busby and Murphy themselves, these houses helped forge the friendships of players like Sadler and Best, and Ryan and Anderson. A decade earlier it had been players like Tommy Taylor and Mark Jones, but the care and attention to detail remained the same. David Sadler notes:

'They had a number of these houses for the apprentices, the trialists, the first-year pros and such. This tradition had been established with the Busby Babes. These houses were in Stretford, Urmston, Chorlton, places close to Old Trafford and The Cliff. The landladies were usually sensible, elderly people who looked after us. For many of us it was the first time we had travelled more than five or so more miles from home. I never really thought about that at the time, but I have done a little more as I've got older.'

Indeed, the fact that the transition to living in this new environment was relatively seamless speaks volumes for the way in which the landladies looked after the welfare of these young players. These ladies really provided so much that was good for the young Manchester United footballers, and for David Sadler a lifelong friendship with George Best was created at 9 Aycliffe Avenue, Chorlton:

'In my first digs, I stayed at Kings Road, Stretford. George and I were playing in the youth team, we had the odd game in the reserves, and we had become good friends. When I came back for that new season he was in digs with the now-famous Mrs Fullaway. Ronnie Briggs, a goalkeeper from Ireland, had been staying there and had been released. When I found out about the vacancy I ended up in George's digs. We were good friends even though we came from very different backgrounds.'

Even when a young player stepped outside of the normal lodgings arrangements made by the club, the new home remained a known quantity. John Cooke explains:

'When I was living in digs, there was an Italian lad, Carlo Sartori, who had a spare room at his house in Collyhurst and I went to live with him. The family had come over to England to escape the war. I was with them for nearly four and half years and it was fantastic. I have great memories of those days. Carlo was a few months older than me and went to the Blue Stars tournament the year before I played there. In 1967 we both went to the famous Swiss tournament, the first time I had ever flown. After the tournament, Carlo and I went on to Italy for a holiday. We stayed in Milan for a few days and then went into the Dolomites where Carlo came from originally. We stayed six weeks, two young men on a Vespa riding up into the mountains after haymaking during the day! More than this, we played for the village team, mostly consisting of farmers. When we played, the whole village seemed to come out and watch. After four weeks I was running out of money, but the villagers clubbed together to fly us home. We never told United about our guest appearances!'

Carlo Sartori's family lived in the Collyhurst (Little Italy) area of the city. John's trip to Italy with Carlo demonstrates the great bond of friendship that was clearly still there in the 60s, similar to the famous sense of United family present in the 50s. John returns to Italy regularly for family holidays and he has a great affinity for the country and the friendliness of the people. Carlo Sartori played for several clubs in Italy after his Manchester United career ended.

Once boys felt safe and secure in their lodgings and the club had made them welcome, their progress was often rapid, as David Sadler discovered:

'I made quick progress in 1963, playing in the A team and the youth team where you could see there was a lot of importance placed on that youth element. Of course, for the club it wasn't a particularly good season, although they did get to Wembley. In the 1963 youth team we didn't get to the final. There was concern about that because they had been so successful in the Youth Cup in the 50s, and then along came Munich. They were struggling to get back to winning ways. So, in those first few weeks of the 1963/64 season there was a lot happening; we had just survived relegation and not won the Youth Cup, even though we had won the FA Cup. I came back from Kent for pre-season training but wasn't really part of the first-team set-up. I had played a couple of reserve-team games at the back end of 1962/63 and even that was like playing an international match. There were so many top players. In 1963 there was a lot going on in professional football: the maximum wage had been abolished, they ended up abolishing the England Amateur team, and I was one of their last players. When I came back to Old Trafford for that new season, the Charity Shield was the big focus. We were the cup winners and Everton had won the league. Everton hammered United 4-0 at Wembley, so there was a call for change.'

In the next game, against Sheffield Wednesday, Sadler was one of three changes that Busby made, including Ian Moir at outside-right and Phil Chisnall at inside-right. Sadler led the line as centre-forward, recalling:

'So that was a good start for the new season because I had no thoughts at all about getting into the first team. I just aimed to get into the youth team, because that was so high profile. The reserves would be a dream beyond that, but the first game after the Charity Shield there I was in the first team. I played a dozen games or so on the trot, we had a pretty good start and I scored one or two. Funnily enough, one was against

Everton, who had beaten us in the Charity Shield. We beat them 5-1. That was my first goal. I was in and out that season, not a regular but playing perhaps when Denis Law or David Herd were injured. So really, I came into the team following that Charity Shield game.'

During training, the impromptu games, the competitive atmosphere and the banter were all part of the way young players were introduced to life at Old Trafford, and these memories remain sharp for so many ex-players. John Cooke says:

'It was all a great experience and I have terrific memories from the 1960s. I remember games involving all the players behind the Stretford End, playing on concrete. I remember Harry Gregg diving all over the place! Players like Jimmy Nicholson were a good bit older than me and they would kick you sometimes. You had to learn to protect yourself and toughen up. Great days and how wonderful for Jimmy Murphy and United to win that Youth Cup again back in 1964, just six years after the Munich crash, with Bobby Noble, Willie Anderson, Dave Sadler and so many other really good players. We even had seven home-grown players in the '68 side. Amazing.

'They only signed about eight apprentices a year back then, whilst you also had eight from the year before. As an apprentice you did all the jobs, cleaning the dressing rooms, corridors, mainly at Old Trafford. We never actually swept the terraces though. The Cliff was done a little, but we had a guy there to do that. You had to look after all the kit, but we did not have specific players. All the players had numbers. You know what, I can't remember my old number, but I can remember George's! Number 33. Denis was 10. There were only 40–45 players altogether.'

'The centrality of The Cliff both geographically and symbolically, in terms of the history and culture of Manchester

United, brings sharp recollections from United players, including John Cooke: 'The Cliff was not a great pitch in those days. We had grass in August and then by October there was no grass! I remember The Cliff so well. I remember the old stand that isn't there now and having my photo taken there just before the Swiss trip. I remember every room in the main building. That old stand opposite the changing room is still there but the other one has now gone.'

John recalls too the 'Friday Game', when matches took place in the original Cliff gymnasium, which often had condensation dripping from the light fittings. There could be anything up to 15 or 16 players on each side, with games played on a red-shale surface that developed potholes when the weather turned icy. There was no heating in the place. Players would be split into 'bibs' versus 'non-bibs' teams and two-touch would be played. He recalls that somehow Denis and George always seemed to end up on the same team! As with David Sadler's recollection, he recalls that George and Denis deliberately played the ball against opponents' shins, just to receive it straight back and begin their two touches again. Both were outstanding in these games.

Tony Whelan also recognises the historical significance of United's old training ground and remembers, too, its endearing, if at times frustrating, idiosyncrasies:

'The Cliff is a truly historic place because the Busby Babes had trained there. The pitch was always a special place. The pitch was never great but you know that those players had grown up there and that was the thing about The Cliff. I played for the town team there and it always seemed so big. I remember too, practice matches there, reserves v first team, and the barriers round the back and then the big hill. And it would always be boggy.'

The starkness of The Cliff, positioned in a hollow amongst the working-class community of Salford, is so much a part of the history of Manchester United. Could any pitch in the country possibly claim to have produced more talent than this little strip of soggy land? The players from many junior teams must have turned up there for a game in the 60s (and beyond), observed the scruffy surroundings and patchy pitch and thought, 'Are we at the right place? Is this really Manchester United's training ground?' Burnley, for instance, had Gawthorpe Hall by then, an impressive state-of-the-art complex. However, the respect for the status of The Cliff in the rise and rise of Manchester United over the decades is stressed by Cliff Butler:

'With The Cliff, it was redeveloped in the very late 60s when the modern building went up, and then they built the indoor part which has since been refurbished. We still go to The Cliff a lot now, as we play training games there. It's just astounding to think that United won the treble from there. If you think of the players who trained there, how did they make the dinners for everyone in that kitchen? The medical room was a quarter of the size of this [fairly compact] room we are in right now. It's not that long ago either. Think of the history of that place.

'It needs some refurbishment; we've just had a swarm of wasps in there! I was brushing them up the other night! The place oozes character and history. I tend to do most of the match reports on the games there, and when I'm in the room, watching the match, I sometimes turn around and think of the players who have been there: Denis Law, George Best, Bobby Charlton and all of Sir Alex's players, in those narrow corridors. What memories. Any refurbishment has to be done sensitively because of the history of that place.'

Mind you, Old Trafford itself in the 1960s was no oil painting either. Butler recalls, 'As to Old Trafford, even the Stretford End wasn't covered when I started watching United. They put the strangest cover over it because it finished before you got to the pitch; so, if you were near the front you always got wet! The paddocks were strange too because of the joints in the corners when they were added on.'

From a young player's perspective, though, Old Trafford in the 60s meant a strict routine of jobs and hard training for United footballers like Tony Whelan:

'At 60s Old Trafford, we used to train there sometimes. We had to run around the stands, up to the cantilever, then up to the scoreboard, touch the scoreboard then run through the cantilever at one tunnel, come out the other end then back on to the track, touch the wall at the Stretford End, down to the halfway line and run around the track. We just went now and again but the first team used to train at Old Trafford every Friday, so as an apprentice we used to go there to prepare the dressing rooms, put the kit out, collect it up, clean the boots. You were assigned jobs.

'One of the jobs at Old Trafford was cleaning the boots, so no-one wanted to do the Monday morning shift, because you had 20 pairs of boots to clean and you'd better do them properly! You did them pretty much by hand and you had set players. You had two or three players each week on a rota, but when it was holiday time, again, it was just down to the local lads. That was part of the job and you wanted to do them well. Denis Law wore Mitre and you wanted to make sure his were done well, and Bobby Charlton's. I always remember George had Stylo. I think Bobby had mainly Adidas. But whatever they were you had to wash them in a sink, scrub them clean, then put the dubbin on. You had to clean the dressing rooms and then you had a bumper for the hallways and corridors. Jack Crompton would not dismiss you as an apprentice (at around 4pm) until he had come and checked. He would run his fingernail along the rails to see if there was any dust. You had to send someone up for Jack so he would come and inspect everything.

'Then on a Sunday morning the injured players came in, so you had a Sunday rota as well and the players might want the apprentices to run around and do little jobs. Nobody liked doing Sunday mornings, it was the graveyard shift. For one thing the buses didn't run as for weekdays, so getting to Old Trafford for ten o'clock on a Sunday morning was difficult. I had to get off at Southern Cemetery, get a bus through Chorlton to Old Trafford, then get off at Trafford Bar and walk or get another bus to the ground. Then the same going back. I disliked Sunday mornings but it was your job. The other thing I remember about Old Trafford was that if you didn't have a seat (because you sold your ticket) you went right to the back of the stand, in what is now the South Stand, and there was a big rail and everyone would watch the game leaning against that rail. It was mandatory that you went to all the games, so you had that great feeling of belonging and camaraderie because of that. It was like a family.'

Elsewhere around Manchester United in the 60s, John Cooke recalls only three or four office staff and a handful of scouts out in the field. However, if the architecture could not necessarily be relied upon to entice young players to Old Trafford, the warmth of welcome certainly could. The feeling being conveyed to talented young players like Cooke by Manchester United was one of security and, indeed, family, no doubt peppered by adolescent excitement.

Like all families, though, as they grow, this intimacy can be lost, and Manchester United have experienced this challenge at certain stages over the years. Cliff Butler summarises the changes in staffing that have occurred:

'We had relatively few staff in the 50s and 60s compared to today, where we now have over 800 full-time staff on different sites: Hong Kong, London, Old Trafford, The Cliff. When I started full time, I introduced the club yearbook, which was perfect bound. In that first yearbook, I took a picture and included every member of staff who was working at that time. Can you imagine that now? That's 35 years ago. I worked for the Supporters' Club before that too. This was embraced by the club and that is how I became club statistician in 1977. There have been so many strands to my job over the years: club statistician, editor of the *United Review*, loads of different jobs. At one time in the 80s I had four completely different jobs that I had to do.'

In the decades immediately following the first European triumph, not until the Ferguson era was Busby's original blueprint rediscovered and the significance of unearthing young talent cast centre stage in the club's plans. John Cooke, a recipient of both managers' wisdom, draws parallels with the attention to detail shown by Busby and Ferguson alike. He recalls how Busby would ask youngsters how their parents were, saying things like, 'Is your dad still playing golf? Or to another, 'Is your dad still smoking those Hamlet cigars?' Ferguson has been similarly cited as having a photographic memory when it came to the supposed 'little things' that in effect were nothing of the kind. In essence, they were short, kindly interactions of immense importance that often made the difference between a boy choosing Manchester United over, say, Arsenal or Spurs.

The employment of ex-players by Ferguson to key roles (Brian McClair, Jimmy Ryan, Brian Kidd and others) is another repetition of what Busby did (McGuinness, Aston, Crompton et al.) in keeping the values and traditions of the club. However, Jimmy Ryan's invitation to return to United was something he certainly never expected. He had played in the US for several years after leaving Luton as a player, returning eventually to manage the club. He says:

'However, they sold so many players and eventually I got sacked, even after we had stayed up. As a manager I was not able to buy a single player. We just sold players. I came back to Manchester because of the United job really. Before the sacking, we had won the Soccer Sixes, beating United in the quarter-final, Liverpool in the semi and Charlton in the final. After the final, Alex Ferguson came up to me. I had never met him before, and he said, "You did something different there, different to what everyone else was doing." I said, "Yes, it's because I've played in America in indoor football. I knew how you could get the best out of people." With Liverpool, they just had Peter Beardsley up front in the attacking half, and near the end of the game he was shattered. A great player, but he just couldn't run any more. What we did was change players every two minutes, two on, two off, to conserve energy. Rest, play, rest, play, every two minutes; rotation, meaning the energy levels were high for the whole game. Knowing Sir Alex now, I can see how terrific he was, that he came up to me after the game like that, congratulating me for winning the competition. Maybe that's why I got the job. That was my only contact with him, and I can only think that when Brian McClair told him I had played for United, he remembered it all.

'Anyway, after I got sacked at Luton, and on the day I sorted out the settlement figure, I was at home making a nice spaghetti bolognese for Neil my son. I am a single parent. The kids came in from school and Neil was sick that I had left Luton, and then the phone goes. This voice says, "Hello, is that Jim Ryan?" I said, "Yes" but was thinking it was my mate doing a Scottish accent and I was just about to tell him where to go. Sir Alex then offered me a job. He asked me if I would come down to meet him on the Saturday morning. It was a bit like losing a tenner and finding a hundred quid! The upshot was I drove down to The Cliff, went over everything and on the way home he phoned up and offered me the job. The day, then, that I had finally settled all the arguments about my salary at Luton was the day he actually called me!

'I just think I am lucky, even when I went through some bad times, things have worked out for me. Playing for Man United, the European Cup and then coaching with Sir Alex Ferguson. I can't believe it. He turned out to be a great manager for me, always fair, always listened to what I thought, just a great manager. If I was ever in trouble, he let me know without being too fierce about it. There was never, "You shouldn't have done that!" He could give me a ticking-off without raising his voice. He was quiet but I knew when it was a ticking-off!'

John Cooke also returned to United and is still employed there, in a full-time scouting capacity. Ironically, one of John's current tasks at the club, in addition to scouting, is to show parents of prospective youth signings around the training complex at Carrington. In this respect, life has indeed gone full circle for John, who recalls his own Old Trafford 'look-around' with Busby so well, and the great characters he met at the club:

'I have great memories. Going to get measured up for my club blazer, that was a special moment. I remember having my photograph taken in it before the Blue Stars tournament. But as an apprentice you had some dirty jobs too. The players just used to throw their kit on the floor, and you had to pick it all up and hang it up. That kit never got washed for a week. Can you imagine the likes of Best, Law and Charlton wearing that now! The senior players might have got the shirts, shorts and socks they had worn the day before, but it was not clean. No wonder sweat rashes were rife in those days!

'I remember going to the 1966 World Cup game at Goodison to watch Brazil. We were just coming out of the ground and we bumped into Harry Gregg. "What are you two doing here?" Harry said. He insisted on taking us home in his little Triumph Vitesse. Me and Carlo squeezed up in the back seats. On the way home, Harry has the steering wheel between his knees, and he gets a brush out and starts brushing his hair! What a man though. Best World Cup keeper three months after Munich. Amazing. Some years ago, Paul McGuinness and I used to take the under-18s to the Milk Cup tournament in Ireland and Harry would always turn up and give the lads encouragement, especially the goalkeepers. A great guy, Harry.'

Comparing the pastoral care policy that existed (if not in name) in the 60s and the work of today, Tony Whelan says:

'With the pastoral care policy now, it's more structured than it used to be. We have a pastoral care department at the club, a player-care team, whereas in the old days it was much less organised and structured. I think you have to say that the treatment and care of injuries is much better now. Before, you had a magic sponge and people not necessarily qualified. But it was of the time and comparisons are often unfair. I think the fact that so many ex-players are still involved with this club speaks for itself. If the club were not looking after people that would not have happened. Even when there were times when the club maybe did not do things in the right way, I think overall in general they did do it the right way.

'Former players I meet up with still talk about the youth team, the players they played with, they still want to come back. They still talk about the Blue Stars tournament, they still talk about Sir Matt Busby and Jimmy Murphy. They still talk about Johnny Aston, they still talk about Wilf McGuinness. Jimmy Hall said when he came back, "How's Wilf McGuinness? I loved that man." You think why did he love him? It's because of those human qualities. Why have I been here for 25 years or more trying to pass on that feeling, that spirit? I think there's a certain soul about this club, a certain belief in the way football should be played.'

Tony's own playing career developed at United in a fairly typical fashion, where youth was allowed to flourish and the chance to shine came early, a traditional feature of Busby and Murphy's teams:

'Within 18 months I was on the first-team tour. In that second year, the youth team got to the semi-final again but got beaten by Coventry. During the first leg at Coventry we didn't play very well; I think that game coincided with the United first-team FA Cup semi-final replay against Leeds in 1970. I always remember scoring a goal against David Icke, the Coventry keeper who later became the man who claimed to be God. So I had scored a goal against God if you like! I was playing outside-left then before playing inside-forward a little later. I had a really good season and was invited on to the first-team tour to America, Bermuda and Canada, in May 1970. This was an amazing experience, as you can imagine, because I'm 17 years of age and there's George Best, Paddy Crerand, Tony Dunne, Ian Ure, Willie Morgan, Johnny Aston and the others on that trip. I played against the Bermuda national team, against Eintracht Frankfurt, in San Francisco, and played really well. So after a slow start I had really picked up and was flying. Of course, 1970 was World Cup year so we had lost Bobby, Nobby and David to England. Wilf had a great affiliation with youth, and because Tony Young and I had done well in the youth team we were invited along on the tour. It was fantastic and I still have the itinerary.

'If you compare that with tours nowadays, I think we had just 16 players on that trip. There was Wilf McGuinness, Ken Merrick the secretary, Jimmy Murphy, a director; I think there were 21 people at the most. Imagine that happening today. I turned up at Old Trafford, got on a bus, went to the airport, through the main concourse, had a photo taken and got on the plane with everyone else. Different world, so intimate, a wonderful experience.'

Unfortunate perhaps to be a developing player at the time of major managerial changes as the 70s began, after leaving United Whelan went to Bolton on trial and was about to sign a contract. However, he was then offered a trial by City's Malcolm Allison and within three weeks was making his first-team debut against West Ham, with Bobby Moore et al. Allison's coaching style was cutting edge for the time and impressed Whelan greatly. However, within a month of Whelan's arrival, Allison left for Crystal Palace and Johnny Hart took over. City were in the lower region of the table and Hart put his faith in more-established players. Ron Saunders then took over, promising Whelan a future at the club before he, too, promptly left. Tony Book was then put in charge and gave Whelan a free transfer. Tony remains one of only a handful of players to be signed by both Manchester clubs. Eventually, though, a move to lower-league Rochdale gave him the regular first-team football he craved.

Tony Whelan later moved to the US, where he played over 170 games in the North American Soccer League. He turned out for the Fort Lauderdale Sun-Sentinel 'All Strikers Team' in 1983, which included such immensely talented players as Gerd Muller, former teammate Brian Kidd, and a certain other face he had also seen before … George Best.

Now working in today's very different football environment, Tony's recall of his United playing days, and the feeling of family that existed back then, create warm-hearted memories for him:

'I look back with the fondest memories of my time at the club, particularly playing in the youth team at Old Trafford, and of playing in the Blue Stars tournament in Zurich and winning it once. I remember, too, playing in the Lancashire Leagues, the A and B leagues. And obviously I remember the personalities, like Wilf, who was just wonderful with young players. He always made you feel good, made you feel proud to be at the club but also gave you belief in yourself. There was definitely a feeling of family and of course there weren't that many players there. People don't always realise that. There were eight apprentices in the first year and then maybe another four or five from the previous year, maximum 15 apprentices. Then above that, maybe 15 reserve-team players, then the first-team squad. If you compare that with set-ups today there were far fewer players and communication was obviously a lot easier.

'On the football staff there was just Sir Matt, Jimmy Murphy, Jack Crompton, Johnny Aston, Wilf McGuinness, the physiotherapist Ted Dalton and after them I'm struggling to think of other staff! So it was all very tight, very warm and friendly. The staff who took us on Saturday for games were part-time staff, people like Jack Paulene, Harry Ablett, Joe Travis and some others, who just turned up on a Saturday and took the team. They weren't coaches in any formal sense. That's how different it all was. It was just a very different era.'

John Cooke also recognises the differences between the two eras: 'Moulding the character of the boys is massive as you have to have a big personality to play for this club. It might have been easier in the old days to get them into the values and principles of the club. Johnny Aston, Wilf McGuinness and Jack Crompton: that was the coaching staff in those early days of the 60s. Now we have around 200 staff at Carrington. It's very different.'

As the years pass, so too do the memories about the little things that went on to make Manchester United a welcoming place for the clutch of immensely talented young players of the 50s and 60s. The names of the landladies, the streets the players walked down on the way to Old Trafford or The Cliff, and the number of the buses they caught to the ground all seem to matter more now as time has elapsed, and untold stories remain, great and small, needing to be heard and recorded. It must be stated, too, that whilst Matt Busby chose decent, dependable men to help him build the culture and identity of

Manchester United, there were also women connected with the club upon whom Manchester United relied greatly. This must be stated, even if during the time of the Babes, women working in the game were few in number. In the 1950s, two main names always appear: Irene Ramsden and her sister Joan Ramsden. Cliff Butler notes: 'In terms of the women working at the ground in the 50s, there was mainly Ken Ramsden's mother and her sister, Ken's aunty. They worked in the laundry. Then there was Matt's secretary, Alma George. They were the well-known ones. I think there were some others in the office. We have a lady in reception, Kath Phipps, who is really the last of the full-time links with Sir Matt and that era.'

Back in the 50s, Irene and Joan were always referred to as Omo and Daz, their nicknames arising from the main two brands of washing powder back in those days. They washed the players' kit and bantered with the young stars, with cheeky-chappie Eddie Colman usually leading the mischief. They provided the radio where the players listened to the FA Cup draws and eventually, in the gymnasium prior to the church services, they polished the coffins of the young men who had teased them. Wilf McGuinness sums up their loss in football terms, saying, 'They were all magnificent. They would have won everything.' No doubt Irene and Joan would have seen them first through a mother's eyes though.

What, too, of the landladies in the club digs around Stretford, Urmston and Chorlton about whom a book in itself might be written? Forgotten names, except to each of the young lads who came to Manchester United and were immediately made to feel at home, in the carefully crafted network of lodgings that had been vetted by Busby and Murphy. David Sadler speaks warmly about the 'famous Mrs Fullaway' who looked after George Best and himself. She was, though, but one 'sensible, elderly woman' amongst many who accommodated the starlets of Manchester United in the 1950s and 60s. Their roles were integral to the settling in of boys like Sadler, who arrived at the club from Yalding, Kent, a very different background to the industrial city landscape of 1960s Manchester. These were women upon whom Busby and Murphy could rely and the accounts of these ex-players bear testimony to that. Times were different then and few women were employed in football, which was perceived as a 'man's world'. However, it would be churlish to think that without the contribution of these women and the likes of Lady Jean Busby, Winifred Murphy, and the partners of many United coaches and players, Manchester United would have become what it is today.

And indeed, had my mother not taken me to see George Best make his debut, I might never have witnessed that first special moment and started my own 'wonderful romance' with Manchester United.

Chapter 7

Manchester La, La, La

FOR Manchester United's young footballers, the city centre of 1960s Manchester was changing rapidly, as the post-war decade of austerity and restraint gave way to the huge social changes of the so-called swinging sixties. The developing music scene in Manchester was vibrant and far-reaching. Exciting new pop bands were bursting through and preparing the scene for the Northern Soul explosion to follow.

From my point of view, The Beatles's one and only performance in my home town of Middleton was the stand-out musical event of the decade. While I did not see the concert as I was only nine years old, the fact that the Fab Four performed in my little town was huge for me as I was already a big fan, listening to their music on my small Decca transistor radio. I had also already bought their first two hits: 'Love Me Do' and 'Please Please Me', before the Middleton gig took place on Thursday, 11 April 1963, at the Co-operative Hall, attracting a crowd of around 300 teenagers. The Beatles released 'From Me to You', their third EMI single and first number-one hit, on the same day. Danny Hardman, a local historian and musician, says of Middleton: 'There are four places in Middleton that every musician from the sixties reveres: the Co-op Hall where The Beatles played, St Dominic's (Savio School) where the bands rehearsed, the Old Boar's Head where we drank and Lily's where we ate.' (*MEN*, 2007)

Now, while the first three references in the above quote might be clear in terms of what the venues were, 'Lily's' would mean little to anyone outside of the town. In fact, Lily Kwok opened Middleton's first Chinese restaurant (the Lung Fung officially, but merely the 'Chinese chippy' to us kids back then) at Taylor Street in the late 1950s. Leaving abject poverty behind in Hong Kong, she had learned to cook her exquisite curry sauce on the long voyage to England, passing her time by helping in the ship's kitchen. Before leaving, she had experienced sadness following the death of her husband, a successful soy sauce businessman, who was murdered by a rival competitor. When Lily and her family arrived in Middleton, they were the only Chinese people in the town. The story of her remarkable life is told in a book titled *Sweet Mandarin*, an inspirational tale about the woman who in Middleton was known simply as 'The Boss'.

One memorable piece of advice from Lily to her diners was to eat anything that has its back to the heavens, except the table and chairs! Certainly, I had never tasted curry before going to the Lung Fung and the place made my diet more cosmopolitan for certain. The taste of Lily's curry sauce, infused with lashings of coconut milk, was memorable and so exotic to us kids, who marvelled at the delicious yellow paste draped over our chips, as we walked the backstreets. Mushy peas took a vacation for a while. The Lung Fung became so popular that after The Beatles had visited, so did Cliff Richard and The Shadows. The Hollies also loved the place because they were rarely recognised there. Even Lily didn't know who these regular customers were! Many other celebrities appearing in town would often make the seven-mile journey just to dine at Lily's cute little restaurant.

Her three granddaughters, Helen, Lisa and Janet Tse, now run the impressive Sweet Mandarin restaurant in the trendy Northern Quarter in Manchester city centre, and their grandmother's wonderful curry sauce recipe is still served. In 2012, twins Helen and Lisa succeeded in persuading Dragons' Den duo Duncan Bannatyne and Hilary Devey to invest £50,000 in their new Sweet Mandarin Sauces venture. In 2014, Helen and Lisa both received the MBE. A successful stage play has been written about the family story (*Mountains: The Dreams of Lily Kwok*) and performed at several venues, including Manchester's Royal Exchange Theatre. A film is currently being made too. Little Lily Kwok left quite a legacy from her life in Middleton.

On the national stage, a musical performer from the early 60s who was acquiring a huge reputation was Dusty Springfield, who had created an image of a white female vocalist who sounded more like a black soul singer. Manchester was a significant stepping stone in her evolution, and United's footballers sometimes joined the throngs at the go-to venue of Belle Vue. Jimmy Ryan recalls seeing her there:

'We used to go to the Plaza, which was a Saturday night dance sort of place. Or we would go to Belle Vue. I went there once to see Dusty Springfield. I used to look at Dusty and think there was something awkward about her. She was a lesbian, of course, and I wondered whether she felt awkward because she knew that what people were seeing wasn't necessarily who she was. If we went to Belle Vue, usually on a Sunday night, we had to get home early because we had to make the last bus, which I think was the number 53, to Stretford.'

For the sensational Dusty, her appearance in the very first *Top of the Pops* television programme on 1 January 1964 was filmed at the Rusholme Studios, Manchester. Appearing alongside her were The Rolling Stones, The Hollies, The Swinging Blue Jeans and The Beatles, who were by now way out ahead in terms of their rivals. The standard of pop music was incredibly high during this period; in August 1964, Dusty's, 'I Just Don't Know What To Do With Myself', was competing with 'It's All Over Now' by the Stones and 'A Hard Day's Night' by The Beatles. Dusty was involved in competition within her female world too, as she battled with Dionne Warwick and Cilla Black over key songs like 'Anyone Who Had a Heart', and pretty much anything else composed by the stellar Burt Bacharach.

Dusty also played her part in countering the racism of the period too, defying the South African government by having a clause written into her contract that stipulated she would only play to non-segregated audiences. Undeterred by racist protesters, she was faced down by the South African government of the day and threatened with deportation, unless she swore not to perform before mixed audiences. Showing great bravery by refusing to comply with the ultimatum, she was served with a deportation order. When she left the airport, a line of black porters donned their hats in respect of her stance, whilst to the white official who saluted her, she spat out, 'Fuck you' (Bret, 2010). In turn, the South African government banned the sale of Dusty's records, while the British government refused to intervene. She returned to Heathrow to rapturous applause from her fans and those who had followed the case. So, through its promotion of singers like Dusty, Manchester was displaying the same anti-apartheid sentiments that were growing nationally, as the beginning of the end of the pernicious South African regime started to occur. Dusty was a trailblazer in bringing the Tamla Motown sound to the UK, and Manchester certainly benefitted from her efforts, being massively on-trend with the developing musical genre.

John Cooke remembers the music and fashion scene well and suggests that Matt Busby also knew what was happening in his beloved Manchester, and where his players might be found:

'I remember the music scene clearly: Tamla Motown and The Beatles. Brilliant days. We used to go to Oscar's, Slack Alice and Annabel's, which was off Albert Square, I think. When George was with us, he was always reserved, never, ever, "Look at me. I'm George Best." He was in the corner, private always. I remember four or five years ago, and the old boys had a do at Old Trafford. It was about 7.30pm and Frank Worthington walked towards me. He was wearing a black-and-white dog-tooth check suit with big squares. And he says straight away, "John Cooke, the George Best era!" I couldn't believe he remembered me! He was a Huddersfield lad. We played them in the Youth Cup. I think we beat them 3-0. But he remembered me. Great times. Manchester had a lot of nightclubs and discotheques in the 60s, with The Beatles and all that music coming to the fore. Busby knew everything that was going on in the town, though, in the same way that Fergie never missed a trick!'

For me, like so many children who grew up in the 1960s, The Beatles were the first and best of the new wave pop musicians. At home, my mother did not understand, or when I think of the fashions or appeal of The Beatles I recall her talking disapprovingly of them. They were smart and clean-cut in an overt sense, yet there was something about them that still harboured distrust among older people. The haircuts in particular were unorthodox and maybe these created the doubts.

But with Manchester United the FA Cup winners in 1963 and The Beatles ruling the charts, it was hard to imagine there being anywhere better to live than Manchester. Maybe somewhere prettier, maybe somewhere posher, but nowhere as exciting. No wonder The Beatles performed at so many venues in our great city!

For United's footballers, too, the city and its entertainment venues were brimming with energy, innovation and musical discovery, as Tony Whelan recalls:

'As to Manchester in the 60s, I still have my player's passes, five of them. I still treasure them. I used to use them to get into matches here through the staff door. You got two complimentary tickets which you could give to your mates and family, but the pass enabled you to get in. It had the rules of the club, like not being able to smoke on a matchday! Back in the 50s that little pass could get you into the pictures in town, but those days had gone by the time I was there. But it was still the mid-60s and I was a massive Beatles fan. I loved The Rolling Stones, The Beach Boys, The Kinks, all that music of the time, the fashion, the hipsters. I grew up with all that and it coincided with my coming to the club. Of course, on the negative side you had the Vietnam War raging, the assassination of Martin Luther King and you had the Black Power episode in the Mexico Olympics a little later, Tommy Smith and John Carlos, which was shocking at the time. Then you had The Beatles with *The White Album*, so this was '68 when I am coming to the club and I am just 15. Looking back, I was signing for United before man landed on the moon a year later! There was just so much going on in the world politically and socially, and certainly in music and fashion. It's only now looking back I pinch myself and ask, "Wow, was that really me? Did that actually happen?" Certainly, the 60s was huge and it was in Manchester.

'I was too young to go to the Twisted Wheel and places like that, but I knew about them. What I do remember clearly are trips to the Free Trade Hall where acts like The Faces and Cat Stevens played. You had to queue up to get your tickets and I was there once or twice a week. I had a pal and we would take it in turns to queue. I saw The Who at Belle Vue and Santana at the Palace. Wow! I saw The Moody Blues at the Odeon; it's closed down now, sadly. I mean it wouldn't happen today. You paid your seven and sixpence, or whatever it was, it's crazy. They all played Manchester. The Hollies, The Eagles, I saw all of those bands. There were no favours because you were a footballer, you just got in the queue. I remember watching the '66 World Cup on a grainy black-and-white TV. The first World Cup game I ever saw on a big colour TV was in 1970. But it was a fantastic era to grow up in and I just remember being a happy kid.'

While The Beatles may have been the biggest thing to come out of Liverpool, with many other Merseyside acts following on behind, Manchester's ascent in terms of pop music was arguably longer lasting. By 1962, Macclesfield-born John Mayall and Hughie Flint from Manchester had become members of The Blues Syndicate. Wayne Fontana and The Mindbenders were recording successfully by 1963 and The Hollies were up and running too, having played their first gig under that new name (previously The Deltas) in the Oasis Club. Also, in 1963 the Twisted Wheel opened its doors for the first time, becoming the main venue for local Mods. In the same year, Freddie and The Dreamers had their first chart success with 'If You Gotta Make a Fool of Somebody', and The Hollies had made the charts with 'Ain't That Just Like Me'. The Dakotas too were another talented Manchester band, who joined forces with Bootle-born Billy J Kramer to record the massive-selling 'Do You Want to Know a Secret?'

In 1964, when Manchester-born Wayne Fontana and The Mindbenders reached number five in the charts with 'Um, um, um, um, um, um', they were rewarded with a tour with Brenda Lee. In the same year, Georgie Fame and The Blue Flames reached number one with 'Yeh Yeh', while the Salford songbird, Elkie Brooks, had also broken through. Another major emergence that year was a song by Herman's Hermits who recorded a Gerry Goffin and Carole King track called, 'I'm Into Something Good'. The Hermits's version reached number one in the UK charts, the popularity of the song spanning the decades with its resurgence as a latter-day United fan song. Like Herman's Hermits, The Hollies developed into another hugely successful Manchester band. Their hits included: 'Just One Look', 'Bus Stop', 'Look Through Any Window', 'He Ain't Heavy, He's My Brother', 'Jennifer Eccles', and 'Carrie Anne'. Both groups also enjoyed considerable success in the US.

By 1965, though, the influence of US music was really impacting the Manchester music scene. The Wheel had moved to Whitworth Street and started to play Detroit soul music, creating the birth of Northern Soul in the city. In terms of the latter, the Twisted Wheel was the major music venue. Long John Baldry and Alexis Korner both appeared there and tracks on the play-list for an average Saturday-nighter in the mid-60s, included: 'A Walk on the Wild Side' by Jimmy Smith; 'Boogie Woogy' by John Lee Hooker; 'Hit the Road Jack' by Ray Charles, and 'The Night' by Frankie Valli and The Four Seasons. The Wheel represented a new, adult, mysterious world where I wanted to take a peek inside. Tony Wilson, of Factory Records fame and one of Manchester's most iconic figures, later pinpointed the club as being equally as important as his own Hacienda club, the go-to venue in town for 'Madchester' clubbers in the 1980s and 90s.

Some observers put the number of nightclubs in Manchester at the height of the music explosion of the 1960s at around 200, whilst many of them were technically illegal admittedly. To fans of the Wheel this club was the birthplace of Northern Soul, playing records by obscure, black American artists, whilst London was still stuck in commercialised Tamla Motown. It was owned by the same family (Jack, Phillip and Ivor Abadi) and was the forerunner to the less-famous

Blackpool Mecca and iconic Wigan Casino, Mancunians being quick to point out this timeline to their pie-eating cousins. When some of these black artists appeared at the Manchester venue they were amazed to be feted and, in some instances, carried triumphantly on the shoulders of dancers, a world away from the racist reactions they had received in their homeland. The Wheel, originally on Brazenose Street before its move to Whitworth Street, was a magnet for working-class youths who wanted to experience all-night dance marathons and cool, soul music. Originally a coffee bar with no booze on sale, fashion styles were trialled and followed here as soul was played at a time when record shops and radio were not fronting it. Iconic acts like Wilson Pickett, The Spencer Davis Group, The Pretty Things, Edwin Starr, and Geno Washington all performed there. The Wheel eventually closed in early 1971, owing to a bylaw that stopped premises from staying open more than two hours into the following day.

The names and reputations of Manchester's nightclubs also continued to grow strongly in the 60s. These included: Oscar's, Mr Smith's, Time and Place, the Jigsaw Club, Talk of the North and the Heaven and Hell Club. The Oasis Club on Lloyd Street put on The Beatles's first professionally organised (Brian Epstein) show outside of Liverpool in 1962, with the Fab Four going on to appear there three more times. The Rolling Stones also appeared there in 1963.

Mancunian Davy Jones was another singer making a huge name for himself on the local music scene, along with appearing in *Coronation Street* and joining the American band, The Monkees. This was significant, to me at least, because the blurring of roles was new. Surely a pop singer had nothing to do with kitchen sink, northern drama. Accepting that this could be a sort of crossover job for a multi-talented individual, I remember thinking that for him then to join an American group and become part of an early reality series, well that was just fantasy. Nowadays, it has become almost the norm with the plethora of talent shows and reality programmes that followed, but back in the 60s it was a strange concept to get hold of.

For footballers of that day, the spectacular fusion of music, football and fashion in 60s Manchester affected more than just George Best. Jimmy Ryan reflects:

'When the 60s exploded I think it distracted me in some ways. These things maybe stopped me from becoming a really good player. When I lived back in my home village everything was connected to football. I was crazy about football, but in the 60s, the music, the groups, Bob Dylan, they all distracted me in some way. Chasing girls too didn't always help! I met some nice girls in the 60s, one or two I am still in touch with as friends. When I met one of them recently, she reminded me about how we used to walk into town, to The Mogambo coffee bar. We would go in and have a coffee. Even when I went to meet Willie Anderson in Oregon, Willie would remind me about two Italian girls we had met in 1962 ... in the chippy! And I had never ever thought about it until that moment!'

George Best's links with musicians started when he met Malcolm Wagner in 1965 at Le Phonographe, one of Manchester's first discotheques. Wagner had been a member of local group The Whirlwinds, along with Graham Gouldman, who later became a founder member of 10cc and who established a huge reputation as a songwriter. In 1967, Best opened his second Edwardia boutique in Bridge Street (his first shop was in fashionable Sale, Manchester) and right next door was the Village Barber, owned and run by his great friend, hairdresser Malcolm Wagner. Earlier in the decade, Wagner's Whirlwinds had been a very significant presence on the burgeoning Manchester music scene.

In Wagner's hugely entertaining book *George Best and Me: Waggy's Tale*, one senses that this was a man who knew the

Manchester music and fashion scene of the 60s particularly well, and also that he really knew and understood George Best. He points out that in 1961, a good night out in town revolved around coffee bars such as Amigo's, The Mogambo, The Bodega, The Cona and The Oasis. The Kinks were the resident band at The Oasis and Dave Lee Travis was the DJ. The Twisted Wheel was a game-changer, though, with a sudden influx of live bands and showcasing the on-trend US music pouring into the city. Wagner sums it up by saying, 'If ever the time was right for a musical explosion it was 1961 and if ever a city was ripe for a musical explosion to go bang in – it was Manchester.' The city became a main 'go-to' place nationally for a good night out and certainly rivalled the London scene. Manchester people worked hard but when work was over, they liked to let their hair down in spectacular fashion. By 1963, the coffee-bar scene was sliding into a fast-expanding world of nightclubs and other large-scale venues offering music and alcohol. The theatres were doing good business and Granada TV was becoming an increasingly important player in the fast-growing national media scene.

Michael Parkinson was making a huge name for himself in television during the mid-60s, and his Granada TV appearances inevitably brought him into contact with Best. It is hard to speak of Manchester in the 60s and the growing creative scene without mentioning the effect George Best had on fashion. The fact that George Best headed up this surge of youthful creativity is highlighted in Parkinson's 1975 biography of the great man, *Best: An Intimate Biography*, still a definitive text in terms of understanding the mercurial Irishman at this early point in his Manchester footballing life. Parkinson draws the links between Best and The Beatles in the sense that like the Fab Four he gave young people a sense of identity, creating new fashions in his wake as he drifted his way through the city's nightspots. If Best grew his hair long, people followed:, fans and fellow-players alike. If he sported a moustache or beard the trend was copied. His slim-fit clothes accentuated his slender, athletic frame and, of course, Best, at several points in his career, modelled clothes for catalogues and a range of other shops.

Tony Whelan recalls that often George would bring back clothes to the ground for young players, no doubt aware of the differences in earnings among teammates:

'When George was at the club, he used to bring clothes in. He'd just walk past the places where we used to hang out at Old Trafford and The Cliff, and he'd drop off these hipster jeans and shirts. He'd say, "There you go lads." He didn't have to do that, but he did and was always such a genial, happy-go-lucky guy. There was no airs and graces about him. Even though he was this massive superstar, he always had time for the young players and so you were never completely in awe of him.'

Even Best's Stylo football boots broke fashion conventions, with their low-cut style and side laces. Their impact on the boot market was massive, meaning that sales of Stylo boots exceeded the company's wildest dreams, whilst being a quantum leap in terms of creative significance. Best was not only sponsoring boots but having input in terms of what they should look like to enable optimum performance. This had been done before insofar as Stanley Matthews, for instance, used soft Italian leather that wore out in a few games and needed regular replacement. Denis Law had also preferred soft Italian leather for his all-black boots. However, Best's involvement in boot design had greater impact on the sport market and was done in a much more flamboyant, overtly commercial manner.

The Beatles's fame and the dramatic impact it had on British youth culture had coincided neatly with George's dramatic ascent in the game. George Best was embroiled in a youth culture that was now changing at arguably a faster pace in British society than ever before. Young people were questioning their own role in that society and the values and advice passed down by their parents, and George was leading that revolution in Manchester.

The geography of Manchester helped enormously with the growth of the city's musical scene. While out-of-town places like Talk of the North in Eccles were drawing punters, the city centre offered a discrete village where young people could move around and sample different creative offerings without walking far. Granada Studios, for instance, was only a stone's throw from George Best's Edwardia boutique and Wagner's Village Barber. The Twisted Wheel was a short walk further on at Brazenoze Street, whilst New Century Hall, in the basement of the Co-operative tower where many well-known bands performed, was also close by. There were so many other clubs, too, in the city centre at this time. The result was a fusion of local people, actors, musicians, TV presenters, designers, and businessmen; in fact, 'anyone who was anyone' in the city (or thought they were) headed for Manchester city centre. George Best's Manchester United debut in 1963 catapulted him into the midst of this fashionable world of music and celebrity, and he quickly became the biggest 'anyone' of them all in town.

Michael Parkinson gives clear, sharp focus on the status of Best within this group of aspirational young men and women: 'Whichever pub or discotheque he patronised immediately became Manchester's most popular nightspot. Whichever girl he dated, no matter how obscure, made the gossip column. He went on television and said he would never kiss a girl who smoked. Two-packs-a-day girls wrote and said they'd never touch another cigarette. So did a few men. Best's appeal was universal.'

By 1965, Wagner and Best were frequenting Le Phonographe on regular nights out, while his form at United was consistently brilliant. That same year he met Mike Summerbee and the three men would visit nightclubs like Time and Place, near Manchester Cathedral, and Annabel's. Wagner says that the idea for the positioning of his barber shop and George's boutique was down to the expert skills of Manchester architect Frazer Crane, who was seeking to develop, 'a creative village in the midst of a large bustling commercial centre.' The John Dalton Street area of town already had several upmarket shops and restaurants and the siting of the two men's businesses was inspired. Wagner sums up the fusion of creativity that was occurring in Manchester during the 1960s: 'During this period, young fashion designers, musicians and sportsmen became the heroes we venerated. By and large, they were working-class lads and lasses and I suppose that was part of the huge change we'd witnessed first-hand in Manchester.'

Another musician who helped bridge the music/football divide in Manchester was Phil Lynott, the lead vocalist from Thin Lizzy. The tragic story of Lynott had its early beginnings in Manchester when his Irish mother Philomena came to Moss Side as the single mother of a mixed-race baby, Phil's father being an immigrant from British Guiana. She speaks glowingly about the city and its welcoming nature to outsiders when she says:

'Moss Side then, 50 years ago, was beautiful – leafy avenues, Alexandra Road, the park, everything. Manchester was the warmest and loveliest city. I was down and out when I had my little black baby. In those days, to have a child out of wedlock you were spat on, battered, beaten. I'd been thrown into a home for unmarried mothers. But when I settled in Manchester, I found it the warmest place. I met wonderful people there.' (*MEN*, 2011)

Sending Phil back to Dublin when he was four, so she could earn money, Philomena worked in a dress shop near Lewis's on Market Street, then as a barmaid. On Saturdays

A typical 1960s northern scene. Pigott Street, Hulme, 1967

A fashion show in the 1960s at Manchester Polytechnic

Central Station, Manchester, mid-1960s

Disaster in Munich display at The National Football Museum, Manchester, 2019

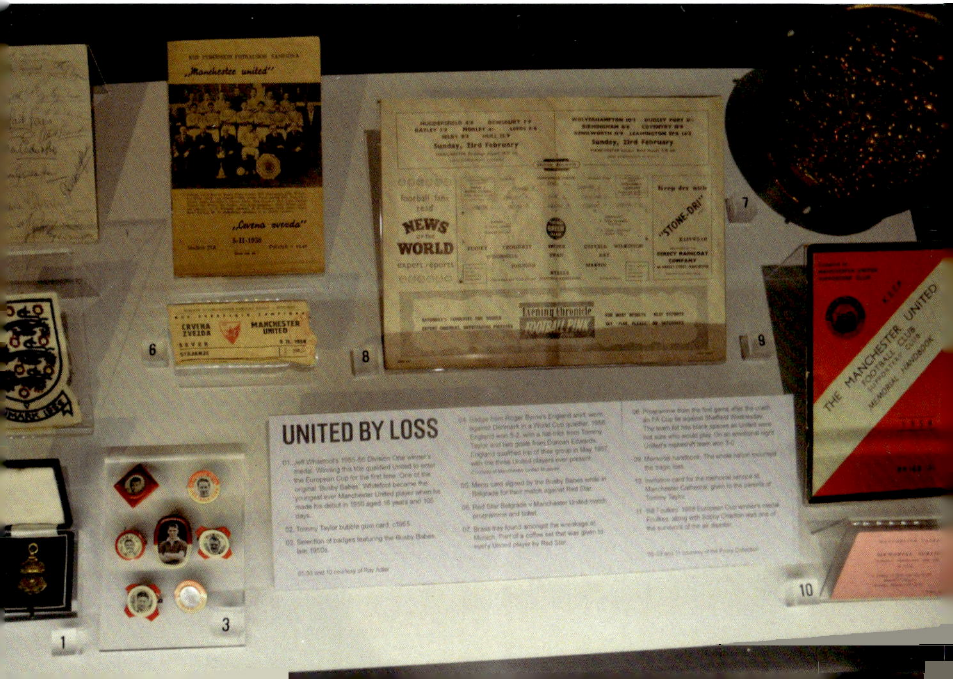

Fairground ride at Belle Vue, Manchester, in the 1960s

George Best and the iconic 1960s Mini motor car. Display items at The National Football Museum, Manchester, 2019

George Best Edwardia boutique in Manchester city centre, about 1972

George Best memorabilia at The National Football Museum, Manchester, 2019

Lily Kwok (right) with her children, Arthur and Mabel, outside The Lung Fung Restaurant, Middleton, in 1960

Manchester's famous Corn Exchange, much changed from its original function but busy as ever today, 2019

Piccadilly Gardens, Manchester 1960s

Sir Bobby Charlton and the author at the Bobby Charlton Soccer School, Hopwood Hall, Middleton, 1992

The author's mother (second right) preparing for the 1968 European Cup Final match

The 'Last Line-Up' 1958 photo, part of the Disaster in Munich display at The National Football Museum, 2019

The National Football Museum, Manchester, 2019

The Peterloo plaque on the side of the Radisson Blu Hotel's frontage, Manchester 2019

View across Piccadilly Gardens towards Piccadilly Plaza development, whilst under construction in early 1964

Worn but treasured souvenirs from the 1968 European Cup journey and the Intercontinental Cup game with Estudiantes

Bobby Charlton holds the Jules Rimet trophy aloft after England's 1966 World Cup victory. Bobby also won the European Footballer of the Year award in 1966

Bobby Charlton, Denis Law, George Best, Sir Matt Busby, Brian Kidd, Pat Crerand and David Sadler

George Best is busy checking out the merchandise at one of his Manchester boutiques

George Best turns after his stunning solo goal in the 1968 European Cup Final. George won the European Footballer of the Year award the same year

High above the opposition as usual, Denis Law powers in a header. Denis won the coveted European Footballer of the Year award in 1964

Jimmy Murphy, Bobby Charlton, Matt Busby and Jack Crompton are jubilant in Madrid, Spain, on 15 May 1968 after the European Cup semi-final, second leg against Real Madrid

Manchester pop band The Hollies in live action during the 1960s

Manchester United legends Denis Law, Bobby Charlton and George Best in August 2000

Manchester United, happy with the European Cup at Old Trafford, in July 1968

Police watch a section of the Stretford End crowd, in the 1960s

The Beatles, Dusty Springfield and Tom Jones all appeared in Manchester during the 1960s

The Kinks, the resident band at The Oasis coffee bar in Manchester during the early 1960s. The Beatles and The Rolling Stones also played there

she helped out on a market stall selling Dannimac coats that were seconds. Rather like Gannex raincoats, made famous by the Labour Prime Minister Harold Wilson, anyone who remembers the original name Dannimac gives away their age in an instant. However, whilst Dannimac products continue to sell, the Gannex fell away and the famous Elland mill used in manufacturing was demolished in 2010. Lyndon Johnson, Krushchev, Queen Elizabeth and the Duke of Edinburgh had all worn the famous coat at the height of its appeal.

Philomena went on to run the iconic Clifton Grange Hotel in Whalley Range, where celebrity lock-ins after hours were the norm, at a time when licensing laws were very different to today. Technically, Philomena only had a licence to serve residents, but the boundaries got pushed somewhat. Phil later recorded his debut album using the hotel name as its title, while the name does not feature in the actual title song. Known as the Showbiz Hotel, or The Biz, one of its most famous visitors was George Best. Phil and George struck up a close friendship, sharing their Irishness, their generous natures and their fondness for alcohol. (My dad would have fitted in well here I think, since he too displayed all three of these characteristics.) Like George, Phil's life was cut tragically short by his addictions and he died aged 36 years in 1986. Philomena says, with deep irony, 'He didn't learn how to say no. People would demand things of him, and I suppose, like dear Georgie Best, he started attracting the wrong crowd. He felt he had to keep proving himself.'

Towards the end of the 60s, traditional Manchester pop groups like Wayne Fontana and The Mindbenders started to split and new musical tastes were evolving. The city responded as it always does, not by capitulation but by innovation. Strawberry Studios opened in Stockport, the first main recording studio outside of London. The Ashton-under-Lyne group Fivepenny Piece released their first single, and Blackpool-born Graham Nash from The Hollies teamed up with Crosby and Stills. Barclay James Harvest, from Saddleworth, released their debut album, while Hotlegs, with group members from Prestwich, rose to number two in the charts with 'Neanderthal Man'. This song was out of Strawberry Studios and Hotlegs later relaunched as 10cc, going on to worldwide fame.

Another massively successful local group who led the Manchester music scene towards the end of the decade was the Bee Gees. While they are often referred to as a Manchester band, the three brothers were actually born in the Isle of Man, the family moving to Manchester in 1955. The boys' father, Hugh Gibb, came from Chorlton-cum-Hardy originally and moved his family back to the south Manchester town. From a semi-detached house in Keppel Road, Chorlton, the brothers spent countless hours working together on their famous harmonies. They formed The Rattlesnakes, a skiffle/rock and roll, five-piece group with two friends. They honed their act singing during intervals between shows at local theatres. In 1958 the family moved to Australia and their promising career was interrupted. However, spurred on by the burgeoning rock scene in England and the unparalleled success story of The Beatles, they returned to the UK in 1967, fitting comfortably into the swinging London scene. They charted with 'New York Mining Disaster 1941', and then followed up with the successful 'To Love Somebody'. However, the song that really resonated with the British public and secured their first number one in the charts, in 1967, was 'Massachusetts', which for many (maybe including George Best?) opened up the America of their dreams, the lyrics accompanied by a rich powerful melody.

The Manchester football and music scenes existed comfortably, and in many ways added to my love of Manchester United, such were the increasing connections being made between two hitherto distinct worlds. Also, the fashions of the day were starting to interest me, several of the styles catching my eye during my frequent sorties into the city centre. No style made a bigger impression on me than the Mod look of the early 60s. Buying into the culture, it seemed, as with Manchester United, another good wagon to hitch a ride on, as the country continued its transition from the grey 50s to a new decade offering greater choice and affluence. Essentially, Mods were, '... seeking a different way of being working class, one that resembled a middle-class lifestyle but in which they retained their working-class identity and maintained valued social links with older relatives and communities.' (Weight, 2013)

I suppose nowadays we would just call this being socially mobile; having the skill-set to be able to move in two very different worlds with ease. We would also consider it a desirable thing to have. My mother inadvertently taught me how to do this by use of her famous 'telephone voice'. With most callers like Aunt Minnie or maybe an Irish relative ringing from County Mayo, there was no discernible difference in her accent, with the usual hint of flat Mancunian vowel sounds. However, when anyone called who sounded remotely official, such as the local builders' merchants, usually asking about an unpaid bill and was the name really McGuire or Maguire, she became the Home Counties secretary, accentless and impeccably spoken. When the call was over, she would revert to everyday Manchester speak and ask, 'What d'ya want for yer tea?'

The idea of being a Mod, taken from the extended term modernist, began life in London 'in the late 1950s and peaked in the early-to-mid-1960s' (thescooterist, 2012). With smart, well-fitting suits (often handmade and very expensive) Mods listened to British groups like The Who, The Small Faces and The Kinks, as well as African American soul music, British beat music and R&B. With Italian motor scooters, especially

Lambrettas and Vespas, they frequented coffee bars that stayed open into the early hours, rather than pubs that had strict times of closing. The Kinks described the fashion-obsessed Mod culture brilliantly, in their definitive song, 'Dedicated Follower of Fashion':

> 'They seek him here, they seek him there,
> His clothes are loud, but never square.
> It will make or break him, so he's got to buy the best,
> 'Cause he's a dedicated follower of fashion.'
>
> (Davies, 1966)

Interpreted as either a witty observation of the British fashion scene at the time, or an aside to the trendy Carnaby Street boutique world that had emerged, or maybe just prompted by a casual conversation, the track has lyrics that convey the peculiarities and dandyism of the Mod culture particularly well. They suggest that cost was an obstacle that had to be overcome somehow, to meet these fashion desires. Chelsea or Beatle boots, desert boots, bowling shoes, Crombie overcoats and Fishtail Parka jackets were all part of cool Mod gear for men. The long Parka jackets served a practical purpose too, insofar as they kept the smart clothes that were being worn underneath immaculately clean. The fact that motor scooters' moving parts were encased in metal also helped the cause here.

For Mod women, super-slim models Jean Shrimpton and Twiggy, along with Cathy McGowan, who fronted the cult television show *Ready Steady Go!* pushed Mod fashions out to an eager female audience. Mary Quant's designs were another dominant feature of female Mod fashion in the 60s, with her first boutique in Kings Road, London, having been opened as far back as 1955. In 1961, she opened her second shop in Knightsbridge, and by 1963 she was selling her clothes to a worldwide audience. Quant's name is the one most usually associated with miniskirts and later hot pants too. When Twiggy modelled her clothes, especially the miniskirt, her slender, boyish physique was exactly right to show off Quant's designs. The masculine shirts and dress styles masked natural curves well and represented a huge change from earlier, more traditional female fashions. Mary Quant's designs were later lent to household goods, make-up and even the Mini motor car – in itself another key symbol of 1960s England. Naturally George Best drove a Mini Cooper at one point, as did Twiggy, Paul McCartney, Ringo Starr et al.

As groups like The Who then started to change their style and drift away from Mod culture, so the timespan of the Mod phenomenon became limited. By 1966, their colourful transformation was all but over. The fact that the original young men and women who were part of that first Mod generation were now getting married and raising families was another associated factor. However, the movement left a strong legacy for thousands of youths around the country, not just in London but in other major cities like Manchester. Some 'hard Mods' became skinheads, keeping clothes styles such as Ben Sherman shirts and Sta-Prest trousers, whilst combining them with Dr Martens boots and shaving their heads.

While I never actually articulated the wish to be a Mod or even knew exactly what I was pursuing, the trend seemed a desirable pathway to follow. It was a fashionable movement, girls were obviously buying into it too, so it seemed a good way to get noticed by them, and the clothes just seemed really cool. Seeing photos of George Best in trendy Mod gear in the *Manchester Evening News* added greatly to that appeal. The longer hair with heavy fringe, well-fitting suits, button-down shirt collars and crew-neck sweaters just screamed 'fashion' to my naive, younger self. When the Fred Perry white cotton polo shirt became a part of the look, that had me hooked since it combined fashion with sport, and although it took pretty much until the end of the decade until I could afford to buy one, the wait was worthwhile.

The irony behind the shirt, of course, was that Perry himself, the working-class lad from unfashionable Stockport who became Wimbledon champion, had tried and failed to break into the class-controlled culture of the English Lawn Tennis club after his singles final success in 1934. Being the son of a Labour MP did not help his cause at the All England Club of the 30s, nor did the fact that he came from the north. With his father being the secretary of the Co-operative Party, this really sealed his northern credentials, with many club members wishing that he had stayed in the 'grim north'. He also lacked a university education and played in an overtly competitive manner, which would have certainly been tolerated had his background been different. However, the event which he says remained with him forever was in the immediate aftermath of the first of his three Wimbledon title wins, after defeating Jack Crawford:

> 'Soaking in a post-match bath in the locker room, he [Perry] said he overheard the plummy tones of a committee man suggesting to Crawford that the laurels had gone to the wrong player. Crawford was handed a bottle of champagne, while the honorary All England Club member's tie that was Perry's due was left for him, draped over the back of a chair. "All my paranoia about the old-school-tie brigade surfaced with a vengeance," he said.'
>
> (Henderson, 2009)

In a move triggered by the disgust he felt at the snobbery of the tennis world in England, Perry moved to the US, taking American citizenship. When the Mods took the sales of this shirt to dizzying heights in the 1960s, for Perry it was a fitting riposte to the 'blazerati who had looked down their noses at him' (Weight, 2013). For Mods it was somewhat less complex; they liked the cool look of the shirt and once worn it enabled them to easily present as being middle class, even if coming from a working-class background. It was the garment of aspiration, whilst, co-incidentally, the backstory of Perry's reaction to English class issues fitted the narrative particularly well.

Thus, the fashion and music worlds that players like George Best, David Sadler and Jimmy Ryan were now growing up into in Manchester differed immensely from the 50s scene that McGuinness, Charlton, Edwards and Colman had experienced; the latter dripping with American influence from the crooners like Sinatra and Crosby through to the Elvis generation. Mods sought European not American influence in their fashion styles, music and films; the French and Italian styles were especially desirable to Mods, who sneered at the 'old' American fashions still being copied by Rockers. Their aspirations were rooted in the continental fashions they experimented with, from carefully snipped haircuts to the iconic Lambretta scooter. The style extended into body language, too, with Mods copying the slackened lower lip made famous by French actor Jean Paul Belmondo. To Mods this expression was known as 'throwing a noodle' (Weight, 2013).

The differences between the Manchester music scenes of the 1950s and 1960s (and which young footballers were experiencing, too) were stark. Through its affinity with US music and Northern Soul in particular, 1960s Manchester became even more cosmopolitan, its musical offerings broader than Liverpool's, where the Merseysound had been so dominant. Then, as now, some would argue, the funding of the two cities by central government had favoured Manchester and this also impacted on the entertainment available.

Finally, no summary of the Manchester music scene in the 1960s would be complete without mentioning Bob Dylan's famous concert at Manchester Free Trade Hall, on 17 May 1966. Dylan was moving, creatively, from acoustic to electric music-making and the change had aroused controversy among his fans. This dispute had begun at the Newport Music Festival in the US in 1965. Bringing this baggage with him to Manchester, one fan, annoyed by the switch and feeling he was selling out on his folk roots, vented his fury by yelling, 'Judas!' as Dylan began his final song of the set. The utterance has become one of the most famous audience interruptions in musical history, its impact heightened by its occurrence at that precise moment before the final number. A visibly disturbed Dylan muttered, 'I don't believe you! You're a liar,' before turning to his band and saying, 'Play it loud,' as they launched into 'Like a Rolling Stone'.

Jimmy Ryan didn't quite make it inside the Free Trade Hall that night, but got as far as the foyer and recalls the event in great detail:

'I got interested in rock music and remember how it just exploded with The Beatles and all the other modern music, The Rolling Stones and others, and then I heard this single, "Blowing in the Wind". Hearing this, I realised that the lyrics were deeper and actually said something. Before, I had just listened to songs like "She Loves You" and never paid any attention to the lyrics. I like reading, so when I heard Dylan's song and started to think about the lyrics and the references he made to different things, I realised he was putting across a point of view that might be completely different to what other people thought. His song "The Lonesome Death of Hattie Carroll" in 1963, about the black woman who was beaten to death by a rich, white man, spoke to me. Dylan is saying the sad thing is not just that she died but the fact his sentence of six months was so lenient, because he was white and she was black. I had to listen to lyrics like these to realise that there was a separate message behind the song itself. When people used to ask, "How come you know all the words of the songs?" that was it, I wanted to know what the singer was actually saying.

'I was just fascinated by Dylan. I went to his concert in 1966 but I couldn't get in. I think we had played a reserve-team game just before and I was late getting there, to the Free Trade Hall. So, I stood in the foyer and I could just about hear the music. Then I heard all this booing and hissing, and I wondered what on earth was going on inside. Then the fans came out and there were television cameras there. Some fans were saying, "He's betrayed us!" What they meant was that he had used an electric guitar to play folk songs and they therefore felt he had betrayed folk music. I think that he didn't want to be pigeon-holed as a folk artist, especially because he had the mind that allowed him to see different things. The papers were full of it. I just happened to be down there on that night, and it turned out to be a famous concert:, the Judas Concert as it became known.

'I think Dylan was different. He wasn't going to write songs that rhymed "moon" with "June", he wanted to write songs with a message. I have several books about Dylan. I have seen him three times. It turns out that Roy Keane is a Dylan fan and Solskjaer too. I went to a couple of Dylan concerts with them. The first concert wasn't so good. He was playing his songs but with completely different arrangements. The second concert was brilliant. I remember him doing, "Leopard-Skin, Pill-Box Hat".

As the decade pulled to a close and just beyond, the breaking up of the United Trinity, for me, coincided with the decline in joyous music from a golden era. From The Hollies to Northern Soul, Manchester had embraced the musical changes but fragmentation nationally was now occurring. The musical genres that followed in the 70s included disco, glam rock, punk rock and reggae. As ever, Manchester as a city moved with the times and catered for the different tastes emerging. For Manchester United, a team devoid of its three biggest stars would not be able to handle change so easily. By the beginning of season 1972/73, the Trinity were to play together only six more times.

Chapter 8

I See the Stretford End Arising

AS a child, Thursday nights were always happy times in our house, and even now the day evokes fond memories of childhood.

Around 7.30pm the smell of plaster from my dad's overalls and whisky on his breath would waft into the house; he would appear with a bag full of chocolate and sweets and a smile on his face. He had been paid by the site foreman, cash in hand, had enjoyed a couple of drinks, enough to put him in a good mood but not so many that he would be unable to rise for work the next day. I always looked forward to the confectionary he brought: Fry's 5 Boys chocolate bars, Turkish Delights, Walnut Whips, Picnics and packets of Spangles. My mother always received a half-pound box of Black Magic chocolates. Sometimes, too, if the work had been plentiful, he would bring home a couple of small bottles of Babycham for my mum, a sickly-sweet champagne perry that she always let me sip. Thursday nights were the best night of the week.

My dad would have his tea on a tray in front of the television, the coal fire would be burning, maybe a comedy was on TV, such as *Steptoe and Son*, and all was well with the world. He didn't say anything, gave no account of his day and just wolfed down his tea, but that was okay, he was peaceful and happy. My dad could not relate to clever, observational humour like *Hancock's Half Hour* and certainly not *Monty Python*, but he loved the toe-curling antics of the forever-impoverished Steptoe family. It's the only time I can really remember him laughing. Other times he tried to read but found it too difficult. He would stare hard at the front page headlines of the huge, broadsheet *Manchester Evening News*, hoping to recognise some of the words. But it wasn't his eyes that were at fault. He scoured the side columns to see if there were any other words or phrases that he could make out and looked for any interesting pictures. But he would soon get frustrated and fling the paper to the floor. I never saw him reach page two or write any more than his signature.

Friday nights were less predictable. Dad would always come back late, maybe around 9 or 9.30pm, having gone straight to the pub from work. Sometimes he would just doze off the drink in his chair, but other times he would enter and was argumentative from the off. Something wouldn't be right. We were making too much noise, my mother hadn't cooked his meal properly, or something else was wrong and he would belittle her in some way. I always knew it would be a long night when this happened. He had usually spent more than he should have done at the pub and when asked to tip up his wages there was not much left; that was the real reason for his wrath. My mother had to feed and clothe us, with the week and its associated costs stretching out before her like Wembley Way.

I hated the noise and just wanted it to stop. When I heard Dad's heavy footsteps coming up the stairs I was relieved, as

I knew he was retiring to sleep off the booze. I drifted off to sleep then, imagining what I would do in the football match the next day; the Nobby Stiles tackles I would make, the Bobby Charlton passes and the Denis Law headers. It rarely worked out like that, but it took my mind off the bad and on to the good.

The elation of Saturday always made me forget what had happened the night before. It was an ever-welcome new dawn, even if pouring with Manchester rain. On a typical Saturday, if fixtures allowed, I would go to watch United play at home in the afternoon, or away games at other north-west clubs like Burnley. After my mother had initially introduced me to the wonderful world of Manchester United, I would go to watch the games with her and a pal, David, travelling either on the bus or in the back of my dad's rusty old Bedford van. David and I chose to sit amidst the opened bags of sand and cement because we could see the road surface through the hole in the van floor. It was great fun dropping small stones through the hole and hearing them ricochet off the chassis. The lock on the back double-doors was faulty and every now and then one of them would fly open. We took it in turns to pull it back into place, both of us convulsed with laughter as drivers behind sounded their horns.

My own insignificant arrival as a fan of this great club coincided with a decade of regrowth and success. Although I longed to wear the famous red shirt, like most other boys from United-mad Middleton (or 'Middy' as it was known locally) I had to contend with being merely a fan. I was, though, a very colourful fan, sporting a red-and-white bowler hat with the words 'Red Devils/Man United' painted on the sides and carrying an umbrella that identified every member of the 1963 cup-winning team. We always stood in the same spot in the Stretford End, on the large stone step, in front of a red, metal crush barrier just to the side of the tunnel. You got to know the same faces and they always made a space for you. That was how it was back then.

If travelling by bus, my matchday journey to Old Trafford from Middleton was made up of a seven-mile ride on the number 59 into town, followed by the couple of miles or so on another bus to the ground. The buses in those days were huge, hulking lumps of metal, the sort of which you now only see in vintage car shows, where nostalgia dictates that you must sit on the back seats downstairs first and then the front seats upstairs. To have ridden one back in the day, though, was to have the memory ingrained forever. Aerodynamic they were not. They were large, rectangular metal boxes, ridiculously high and with around 30 windows. The radiator was visible at the front of the bus and was about the same size as a family refrigerator is now. They were noisy, dirty, slow, utterly wonderful machines with well-sprung seats (new ones at least) and numerous metal poles on which you could swing along the deck and pretend to be a monkey at Chester Zoo. In terms of health and safety, they would win no award these days. The entry platform at the rear of the bus was open, save for an upright metal pole to grab hold of. My brother and I would see who could jump off whilst the bus was slowing down for our stop but still moving, daring each other to do it at ever greater speeds. My own speciality in secondary school days was leaving my school trombone on the bus, going to my grandparents' home for lunch and then remembering about the instrument. It finished up at Victoria Bridge Bus Station in Manchester city centre on several occasions. Sadly, it said everything about my motivation and thus aptitude for music. I never left my sports bag on the bus.

Continuing our journey to Old Trafford, my mother and I would then walk across to Chorlton Street to catch the follow-on bus to the games. As we did, we passed the wonderful Piccadilly sunken gardens on our journey. Why any town planner would remove such a beautiful feature as these gardens is beyond me. From Florence to Madrid, sunken gardens are still enjoyed by city workers and tourists alike. In our country we seem to throw away that which we should value more, in our rush to the future.

I choose to think of the gardens as they were back then, with hundreds of red and yellow tulips standing to attention, endlessly watered by the famous Manchester rain and displayed in rectangular boxes of soil, cut into the lush turf. The grass slopes ran down into the garden square with four concreted pathways leading to one ornate central fountain. Perhaps at night it was a hard place to police, I don't know, but during the day it was a beautiful oasis of rural calm in a busy, bustling city.

Getting closer to Chorlton Street, five red phone boxes stood next to each other. Beautiful in the simplicity of design, they were solid, functional and so much a symbol of England as it was then. The A and B buttons may have driven people to despair and suffered many an angry thump, but it was reassuring to see them and always said to me that we were a proper city, being able to afford five of them in one place. Even then, the skyscraper buildings were going up apace, just as now. In more recent years the city centre has still enjoyed a huge building boom despite recession and austerity. Manchester is a restless, ambitious city, always.

Below ground was also of great interest in the exciting new world of 1960s Manchester, as the city planned an underground railway system linking the station at Piccadilly to Victoria. Recently the subject of renewed interest in the wake of ongoing transport concerns (*MEN*, 2018), researchers have discovered maps and drawings that show how Manchester almost had its own underground tube line 20 years before the Metrolink arrived. The remains of the 'Picc-Vic' tunnel are around 30 feet below the Arndale Centre, the Topshop branch positioned above what would have been a station at the centre of the electrified line. There is also a network of other tunnels in different directions around the city centre. How incredibly close Manchester came to this project happening is the source of considerable controversy, with the national economic slowdown of the 70s being blamed for the mothballing of the plans. However, many Mancunians feel aggrieved that London's tube system grew during that same period, while no new money headed north. It was ever so, many might say.

Back up above ground, the signs that Manchester has always enjoyed a good drink hovered over the Piccadilly Gardens square in the 60s; Mann's ales and Black & White whisky billboards stood on top of the tall, terraced buildings on the approach road to Piccadilly Station. Looking further along the rows of buildings, some businesses had found the cash to have their premises cleaned, while others had not, and shopfronts were caked in the industrial grime from decades gone by.

The cars that whizzed through the city centre on our way to Old Trafford were usually boxy affairs, like a Ford Anglia or Morris 1000 van. Sometimes more upmarket ones such as a Sunbeam Rapier of Ford Zodiac flashed by, my eye caught by their go-faster stripes and aggressive front grills of shining chrome. I loved being in the city centre. Even the increased traffic fumes added to the intensity and excitement of being somewhere bigger than my own little town. Thinking I might see a weaving Best dribble, or a thunderbolt from Bobby or some sort of explosion from Law set my pulse racing. With Denis that could have been anything from an impossible hang in the air and bullet header, to a punch up with some man-mountain centre-half. Either way it was pure theatre and I loved the excitement. Once you had paid your money (four shillings for adults and one and sixpence for kids, in the Stretford End) and pushed through the heavy, red turnstiles you were there to be entertained. That was the deal with Manchester United in the 1960s. You expected them to win and you expected the victory to be delivered in style ... and the combination happened with great regularity.

On some very rare occasions on a trip into town before a match, we might have a meal out; in such instances it was always the UCP cafe. The initials UCP stood for United Cattle Products. Young Manchester United players like Sadler and Best were still being given meal tickets for the place during the 60s. At their peak, UCP shops and cafes were a feature of most Lancashire towns of any size, offering the cheaper cuts of meat such as offal. It was a glamourous lifestyle back then. Since money was always tight in our home (a massive understatement if ever there was one) my mum used to covertly pop anything we couldn't eat, a small piece of meat or fish perhaps, into a folded napkin and drop it into her white, faux-leather handbag to take home for Rinty, our scruffy dog.

Then, since we could never afford the puddings on the menu, my mum would surreptitiously hand me a small piece of cake she had bought from 'the Co-op', thus satisfying cravings for a sweet ending to the meal whilst saving money. Had we been discovered by one of the more observant waitresses (dressed in the standard, austere UCP uniform of black tunic and white apron) carrying out such tyranny would have been the height of embarrassment, from which I for one would have never recovered. Thankfully, after a few successful attempts to conceal the dessert and surviving one or two suspicious glances, we became very adept at carrying out the manoeuvre and were never caught. All this for a slice of Battenberg.

Elsewhere in the city centre, fine buildings stood tall as priceless monuments to the history of Manchester as the world's first fully industrialised city and the growth of the Lancashire cotton industry. But whatever the attractions in the centre in the 60s, there was nothing to touch the thrill of finally reaching the Warwick Road. You could smell the football ... and also the hot dogs, greasy burgers and chips. European night games were the ultimate thrill, as the darkness brought an element of danger and excitement beyond the scale of the daytime fixtures. With street lighting so poor compared with the present day, watching the mounted police move the crowd along in the darkness was mesmerising. The fans who made their way down Warwick Road had no need to take selfies or check their mobile phones, as is done now. This was live theatre with no distractions.

Today we were going to see Paddy Crerand spray the ball around, Tony Dunne would have the winger in his pocket, Harry Gregg and later Alex Stepney would patrol their six-yard box with ferocity, and of course the golden trio of Best, Law and Charlton would do exactly what they wanted, without forewarning us. Even among their teammates the United Trinity excited and brought huge anticipation in ample measures. John Cooke confirms that inside the walls of Old Trafford, though, the main three superstars of Manchester United were just hugely professional, exemplary athletes: 'They were incredible players to be around, not only ideal role models but friendly, helpful people who encouraged youngsters. Busby and the management would not allow anyone to be a big-time Charlie, just like Fergie wouldn't years later. You see, when these big-name players came there was no problem. George, Denis and Bobby were all just really good professionals. I have great memories of them all.'

Certainly, as spectators, what terrific value for money we got in those heady days of the 1960s. Paying just one shilling and sixpence to enter Old Trafford and see these footballing wizards seemed like the bargain of a lifetime and it was relatively cheap compared with the cost of living then. Clubs still regarded the game as a working-class pursuit in the main and attracting 'dads and lads' (as it mostly tended to be then, except in families like mine) enabled them to hold on to their fan base. Certainly, even though coming from a home where money was a constant worry, I can never remember questioning admission prices back then. Like many others from such backgrounds, live entertainment took your mind off troubles at home, and for me Manchester United filled a void.

On our way down the Warwick Road, and whatever our family finances were like, the purchasing of a home programme was vital. In this publication, the back page printed a small, square token on the top, left side; once home this had to be carefully cut out and added to those from previous games. The mass then enabled you to queue and wait for the special games: the FA Cup ties and of course the frequent European night games. In these pre-internet days, and when club membership was still a far-off corporate dream, buying into this ritual was essential for all committed fans. Programme in hand, once we reached the Stretford End gates, the long queue of men dressed in drab raincoats snaked around the equally drab brick walls. Few women were attending football matches on a regular basis back in the early 60s, while United had more than most with the George Best effect developing. I can never remember my mother talking to another woman at any game though.

Once inside the ground, the climb up the steep, stone staircase led to the tunnel from which we would appear, directly in front of Harry Gregg's goal. I know he shared it with other keepers for half the game, but to us, and to Harry I suspect, it always felt like his personal space. At set pieces he made very clear that this was his area and punched his way past any beefy centre-forward who fancied his chances. If we did not get our regular spot on the low wall to the side of the tunnel, we pushed our way to the white, wooden railings at the front. When the players came out, you felt so close to the action that you could almost touch the keeper, and if you stood to the side of the goals, stray shots might take your head off, meriting a loud 'Oooohhhh!' from the crowd. Death was sometimes averted by inches after David Herd or Bobby Charlton let fly with a screamer, but if it missed your head it was all great fun. The fact that it hit someone else's, seemed not to matter to me at the time, it had missed ours and that was the main thing.

The whiff of Woodbines and Player's cigarettes drifted above, and the beery breaths of burly factory workers or dockers standing next to you epitomised the Stretford End of my youth. While the big sounds of the 60s were always playing over the tannoy (The Beatles, The Hollies, Herman's Hermits etc.) I remember too the quirky songs like 'The Letter' by the Box Tops in 1967, 'She's Not There' by The Zombies in 1965, and Heinz's 1964 hit 'Just like Eddie'. The latter might have been my dad's signature tune, whilst the crowd had their own version with rather more colourful lyrics. Whenever I hear that particular tune nowadays, I am back in the dear old Stretford End of the 60s, George Best is weaving his way down the wing, and the roar of the crowd is getting louder with each twist and turn.

With his usual great attention to detail, Cliff Butler neatly sums up the vastness of the crowds and the very basic ways in which clubs accommodated fans in decades gone by:

'I was talking to one of the office girls recently and she was saying she was a Grimsby Town supporter, so I told her about the importance of Grimsby to Old Trafford history. They played an FA Cup semi-final here against Wolves in 1939 and it was the biggest crowd ever to be in the ground: 76,962. All of it except one stand was standing-room only. When it was built they said it would hold 100,000 but it never did. Even 66,000 was tight when I started going. Can you imagine what the Grimsby game was like?

'In the 60s, I remember how the crowd used to sway and you would go down to the bottom, to the white wooden railings almost, and then you had to push your way back upwards. Once you were in the terraces you couldn't get out again, but I always felt safe in there, in the Stretford End, because you were amongst your own. The noise they made was something else; there was a real passion, with the chants and the humour.'

You were indeed amongst your own and that was the thing; most fans did come from Manchester, unlike today it might be said. Probably a lot of Stretford Enders came from homes like mine too. I knew I wouldn't be the only kid there who had a home life affected by drink. Knowing that made me feel secure. There was a strong feeling of community. You pick on one of us, you pick on all of us. The Stretford End was a family of working-class, red-or-dead followers. Probably most were anti-establishment, I suspect not well-off, straight-talking Mancunians. Judging by the number of inebriated fans at games, too, the crowd lived up to George Best's claim that Manchester had the hardest-drinking men in the world. And whilst it seemed that half of the 12,000 or so Stretford Enders, packed like sardines into its old terraces, were actually drunk, the atmosphere was nearly always good-natured. Through my dad's problems with drink, I could always spot in others the feeling of release and joie de vivre brought on by alcohol … and the moment it was about to turn into something less pleasant. I still can.

If a fight did take place in the Stretford End, it was usually settled quickly and before the army of stewards and police were needed. If they were, the policemen of the early 60s took few prisoners, and retribution was handed down in a fairly brutal manner. If the crowd thought the police had overreacted (and sometimes even if they didn't) the officers' jackets would be covered in spit by the time they had arrested the brawling drunks and dragged them to the cinder track. There were no CCTV cameras in those days, whilst the club did experiment with them later in the 60s. But for the most time, the Stretford End was a safe, happy home with brilliant humour on show ... provided you were wearing red and white. Only a fool would turn up there in another club's colours or with a Cockney or Scouse accent. Even Crewe was regarded as the soft, dodgy south and anywhere west of St Helens was definitely distrusted.

Cliff Butler's eyes sparkle when asked about his own introduction to the Stretford End of the 60s, during the glory days of Best, Law and Charlton:

'I saw my first United game in 1958 after Munich, a Boxing Day match against Aston Villa. I had travelled from Higher Openshaw where we used to live. We got off the bus at the Queens Hotel on Aytoun Street and then caught the train to the ground. I can still visualise being at the back of the terrace now. I haven't missed a game at Old Trafford since December 1965, apart from ten years ago, when I missed seven matches owing to a heart operation. I've been to every league game, every testimonial, every friendly, every cup match. Football has always meant a lot to me, but particularly Manchester United. I've always been a proper Red. I've been around the club since the early 70s. I am the club statistician officially, but most people call me the club historian because if you have the stats you have the history really. I liked the late 60s seasons, from 64 onwards let's say. When it got into the 70s it wasn't the same. It never had the same feel after the European Cup Final. It was the culmination of reaching that goal.

'The game was so simple back then. They came out three minutes before the kick off, they'd have a warm-up, kick one or two balls about, a couple of shots at Alex, then the whistle blows and off we go. Now, they're out for two hours before the game starts! It was a wonderful era. There was a humour about the chants and the Stretford End was one entity. Even the programmes were better in those days. It has to be an age thing! I used to always buy two programmes in the 60s, one for the token and one with no cutting out for the collection. I used to think I was a collector, but I have realised since that I am just a hoarder!'

The chants referred to were not orchestrated by officialdom as they seem to be nowadays, rather they arose from the pubs and terraces in a much more spontaneous fashion, as they did when the Stretford End delighted in seeing City knocked out of the European Cup early by little Fenerbahçe:

'Who's that knocking on the window
Who's that knocking on the door?
It's Joe Mercer and his mates
They've got turkey on their plates,
Cos they can't get into Europe anymore!'

Another of my other favourite chants, although a shorter one, was for John Connolly, the much-underrated winger who arrived at Old Trafford from Burnley and who turned in some highly impressive performances. At the time, there was a catchy jingle that accompanied a TV advertisement for John Collier menswear: 'John Collier, John Collier, the window to watch, John Collier.' In the Stretford End, the United fans chanted:

'John Connolly, John Connolly
The winger to watch,
John Connolly!'

On the field of play, by the mid-60s the United team was interwoven with hugely talented, home-grown young players, like Best and Sadler, and massively influential signings, such as Denis Law and Pat Crerand. The United team of 1964/65 was an outstanding outfit that might have achieved the ultimate prize before the 1968 European success, a point not lost on Reds star David Sadler, whose own career by then was progressing strongly:

'We won the league in 1965 and you had to win the league then to get into Europe. Even if it wasn't talked about directly, Europe was always in the background. Matt loved playing in Europe, and he had been so instrumental in taking them in when the FA said "No". The things they said during Munich about having to get back to play the game on the Saturday; you would have been up to your eyeballs in trouble if you didn't and the threats they would make to clubs who didn't get back in time. When you put that against going up the runway … why didn't they wait until the next day when the weather might have been better? There were so many undercurrents that were going on.

'Being in Europe was such an important part of United in those days. It was always special, we had to win the league, we had to get into Europe. We played in the Inter City Fairs Cup and we played in the European Cup Winners' Cup. In 1965, we won the league and we had a great chance in Europe that year. I was getting a few games personally, but I was really struggling for goals. Football for me all the way along had been fairly easy. When I look back, so much of it had been physical and I had scored goals regularly: schoolboys, England Amateurs, Maidstone United, youth football. I was playing centre-forward for England Youth and things had all gone pretty smoothly. Now I was starting to log up a few first-team appearances but wasn't really scoring goals. As a centre-forward, I had got to that level but I needed to score goals on a more regular basis, and it didn't happen.

'Jimmy and Johnny Aston senior, who I spent most of my time with, started to look at me playing in different positions. I remember going to the Blue Stars tournament in Switzerland; it was a nice trip because you were there for about a week. Matt would sometimes go, along with Jimmy Murphy and John Aston. They lost a centre-half and they asked me if I would play at the back, and that became the second string to my bow, which I was looking for. I was never going to be a goalscorer like Denis; I was playing okay, but as a centre-forward you have to score goals. So, gradually, I ended up going back, playing centre-half, midfield sometimes. I played a number of European games and we got to the semi-final of the European Cup. With the benefit of looking back now, that was a better team than we had in 1968. Bobby, Paddy, Denis, Billy were all two years younger and, of course, George was around in 1966. I am sure that Matt would have thought, in the quiet times, when he and Jimmy were sitting around, "We should have won that European Cup in 1966."'

Whilst those discussions were perhaps going on inside the club, back on the terraces the pressing aim was always to get tickets for the big European matches. The Stretford End then was full of larger-than-life characters, 'proper Mancs' you might say. One of the most important figures on the Stretford End terraces in the 60s was Ronny the ticket man. Ronny was probably in his late 40s, talked fast, had heavily Brylcreemed black hair and always had a 'dimp' (a half-smoked cigarette that had been relit) balanced skilfully on his bottom lip. Even allowing for Ronny's healthy profit margins, there were always plenty of takers. No one knew how he obtained the tickets and no questions were ever asked, but whatever the match Ronny could supply them. Our money was handed over, Ronny scribbled my mother's name in his little red notebook and the next home game the tickets would always appear ... until one fine day back in March 1965.

United had drawn an incredibly ugly, violent FA Cup semi-final with Leeds at Hillsborough and the replay was set for Nottingham Forest's ground. When Law walked from the field at the end of the first game, the white collar of his shirt was in place whilst the red body of the garment had been torn away and hung limply, attached to the collar by a slender thread. The other fiery players on view that day alongside Law, included Crerand, Stiles, Bremner, Collins and Jack Charlton. Few pre-match predictions saw anything less than an explosive encounter with such players and so much at stake. Certainly, having attended the first match I remember it was brutal in the extreme. But then that first feisty meeting was soon forgotten, and the bust-ups had only made the replay more enticing. The main task ahead was to get a ticket for the match.

With only a 43,000-ground capacity, tickets were even more scarce than usual. Only Ronny could solve our problem. On the last-but-one home game before the replay, the queue for Ronny the ticket man was nearly 50 deep. However, missing ten minutes of a First Division game to be able to watch the FA Cup semi-final was a price worth paying. Ronny was in full flow when we got closer: 'Worrya want? I can get two tickets for the replay at Forest. Four-bob tickets. I can do 'em both for a quid. Take it or sod off.' People laughed when they were insulted by Ronny. It was part of his attraction.

We handed over our heavily creased, precious one-pound note (which probably deprived the gas board of payment that week) and looked forward to picking up our tickets at the next Old Trafford game. However, when we got to the match and went to collect our tickets there was no Ronny. Whether he had died in the previous fortnight, been put in jail or simply cashed in his 'earnings' and moved to Palma Nova we never did find out, but somewhere there was a spiv who had watched his last game in the Stretford End.

When I look back now at the crushes and crowd sways, it makes me wonder how some of the later tragedies took so long to happen. Crowd control was poorly regulated, certainly given the huge attendances wherever Manchester United played, and compared with standards nowadays. The horrible feeling of being squeezed and squeezed again while making our way home was part and parcel of football attendance. An FA Cup tie at Barnsley in February 1964 was a stand-out game, which United won comfortably 4-0, but where the ground could not cope as easily with the 38,076 crowd. As a child, looking up at taller adults, I remember studying their faces as the crushes intensified. If they looked panicky or people were swearing, or summoning the police on horseback, I knew it was serious. Sometimes it was. Most times, though, the jostling and shoving was good natured, and at United home games relaxed faces reassured me that we would make it to the end of the Warwick Road.

Cliff Butler neatly sums up what those 60s crowds were really like:

'I remember a game up at Sunderland, at Roker Park, when I got separated from my dad in the crowd. He got in and was going frantic. The crowd was swaying outside, and he was dashing from turnstile to turnstile inside, looking for me. Anyway, when I got to the turnstile outside, I yelled, "I've got no money!" Well, this Mackem behind me said, "Don't you worry son, I'll pay for you. Go on, get in." Can you imagine that happening now? The second replay was at Leeds Road, Huddersfield, and United won 5-1 with Denis getting a hat-trick. The crowd were all mixed in those days and every goal we cheered, but we were okay. United and Sunderland was always a special game. They were a good team then: Vic Halom, Billy Hughes and some other quality players.

'The crowds could be frightening though. I was twice involved in crowd crushes at Hillsborough prior to the tragedy. Exactly the same circumstances, against Derby and against Leeds, in the Leppings Lane end. My brother and I loved the crowd sways, it was part of going to the match. At the Derby game, when Gordon Hill got both, it was so tight. The following year against Leeds, we were in the same place and again it got so unbearably tight that we both agreed to leave. We went out and moved to the old corner terrace and we then had loads of room. We looked down into the Leppings Lane end and the crowd was packed in so tightly it never moved. It was an accident waiting to happen.'

Once at the end of Warwick Road, no trip to Old Trafford would be complete without the 60s ritual of buying a rosette or lapel pin badge or some other piece of tacky merchandise, just as long as it was red and white. An 'El Beatle' shiny tin badge was a precious jewel to a 12-year-old kid in 1966. There were silky rosettes, cheap cotton baseball caps (half red, half white) noisy wooden rattles that would be classed as offensive weapons these days, and just one type of scarf with printed red and white rectangular boxes.

Another well-known ritual at the Chester Road end of the Warwick Road bridge was the sight of a thin, dour-looking old man dressed in a shabby, grey raincoat and bowler hat, holding a placard that said 'The End of the World is Nigh!' His religious fervour seemed to impact little on the jostling crowd, who would throw one-liners back, like, 'You're right there, pal. It's the end of the world if we don't beat City today!' The man always gave as good as he got, though, and might reply, 'Remember when the game finishes though!' his face breaking into a mischievous smile. I wonder if just one person stopped to reflect on his message, and whether he would have settled for that success rate given the environment in which he worked. His presence was a regular part of the marvellously atmospheric experience of following the Stretford End's advice of 'Walking down the Warwick Road ... to see Matt Busby's aces!'

On the way home, by the time we arrived at Piccadilly just a few minutes past 5pm, the *Football Pink* was already out on the streets. I often wondered how this could happen so quickly, so reliably, week in, week out. Colin Evans in his delightfully off-beat book, *Sun, Snow and Strike!* (describing a mad weekend of cricket and extreme weather in Buxton in 1975), gives an insight into the process: 'For a paper like the *Pink* you wrote it as a "runner", filing one-piece midway through the afternoon, then an hour or so later topping and tailing it, in other words adding another six paragraphs or so as well as providing an "intro" of around 100 words.' As a Manchester United game could change at any moment, with three match winners like Best, Law and Charlton playing, the tension between reporter and copy-taker must have been fraught with frustration, whilst competing for the telephones in the press box was another trial. Telephoning the match report through to a copy-taker completed the much-awaited newsprint, which greeted football fans anxious to see what other results had occurred that afternoon. By the time we had caught the bus back to 'Middy', I knew the outcome of every senior game that had been played that afternoon, having no need of a mobile phone or tablet.

I always liked to read the *Oldham Green 'un* as well, which I would buy when pocket money allowed two newspaper purchases. In it was the fondly remembered Spot the Ball competition. My grandfather was wrongly convinced that as I could play the game just a little, I must have a natural talent for this quirky challenge, and he believed my input would bring us money. Here you had to mark with an X in the exact place you thought the ball was positioned in a photograph of local game action. Just when it looked like the ball had skimmed off Oldham Athletic's Jim Fryatt's balding head and was half an inch away from his right shoulder, it turned out to be two inches away from goalkeeper Harry Dowd's left foot. It must be the most insane football competition ever devised and one only the photographer could truly be in with a chance of winning. So 1960s.

When we got home, with the thrill of seeing a fantasy moment from Best, Law or Charlton now a fading memory, reality kicked in. If my father wasn't in the house that meant he was at the pub and the evening would be a long one. If he was in the house, he had spent more than he had reckoned on the night before, and, perhaps having given a little to my mum for housekeeping, was flat broke. The next day he would have to 'borrow' money back from my mother just to be able to get to work on Monday morning. If he was broke on a Saturday, my dad would usually sit and watch the wrestling; this was where I learned about all the top wrestlers who I would then go and see fight at Belle Vue. It was so much better when he had no money and could not go out.

When the booze was out of his system he was a much kinder person, not a 'hands-on' dad by any means, but affable and highly amusing, in the sense that you never knew what unsuccessful piece of DIY he would attempt next. One such moment was when I arrived home one night to find six painted light bulbs hanging from the clothes line in the back yard. Being unable to afford bright orange, coloured glass bulbs that were fashionable, he decided to give our ordinary plain ones a coat of Johnstone's trade paint. The idea seemed both brilliant and mad in the same breath. To replace a fuse in a plug he would use a rolled-up length of Senior Service silver paper, and a tap washer would be made from any odd piece of rubber. Most of his handywork in the house was underpinned by such irrational thinking, excepting anything connected to plaster, where he was the building trade's answer to Henry Moore.

If we returned home from the Saturday match and my dad was not in the house, I used to dread his return. For a couple of hours, we would sit and watch some television and that would take the feeling of anxiety away. *Juke Box Jury* was usually on and it was great fun listening to some of the new releases in such an important pop era. The presenters were so familiar to me; David Jacobs, Pete Murray, Alan Freeman and Katie Boyle were regulars, while Jane Asher (who I had a huge crush on, along with half the nation I guess) also made several appearances.

The format for the show was extremely formal, with plummy BBC accents still carrying most weight. The ridiculously long juke box arm protruded, twisted and placed each record on the turntable and a jury of four judges decided whether a song was a hit or a miss. *Britain's Got Talent* it was not, just a moment in time that looks now as if it has been frozen in ice for over 50 years. On one programme, two of the jurors were the well-known Nina and Frederick, the Danish married couple who had considerable chart success themselves. Speaking in impeccable English and with more than a little disdain in their voices, they gave their opinions on one particular song, 'Poetry in Motion' by Johnny Tillotson. Nina made special mention of the poor pronunciation of the lyrics, so much so that she imagined she heard 'Like a tree in motion' instead of the title line. Had poor Johnny Tillotson's finishing school been bombed, I wondered?

On one occasion, my dad came through the door with my Uncle Tommy, just as the jury was reviewing the final song, a Helen Shapiro track, 'Walking Back to Happiness'. Uncle Tommy, fortified by several whiskies, marked his entry by pointing out in a loud voice, 'She sings like a fella!' He then joined in the rendition in a boisterous manner, as my mum suddenly realised there would be another meal plate to fill. My dad and Tommy were cut from the same cloth for sure, and I imagined him to be what my dad must have been like in years past. I liked Uncle Tommy as he was funny and colourful, but his visits always carried a sting in the tail. Tall and very good-looking, Tommy had a Dean Martin smile and swagger about him along with an engaging, lilting Irish accent. My dad would have been around 60 years old by then and Uncle Tommy in his early 40s. But because they were so similar, Dad and Tommy used to rub each other up the wrong way.

On a good day, it was just squabbling or disagreements about something or other, and they would sit at the small dining room table waiting to eat and grumbling at each other. However, this could lead to loud arguments as the drink kicked in and then punches started to be thrown. In under 30 minutes, listening to stiff, starchy BBC accents would be replaced by a scene that resembled a John Wayne, wild west movie. My mum would keep the peace for a while by bringing in the food, usually a large piece of boiled pork, a plate of cabbage and an enormous bowl of potatoes with a knob of Kerrygold butter on top. Nina and Frederick might have used Danish butter, but it was always Irish in our house. The whole meal was typical Irish country food, which, for both men, was their heritage. There would be no pudding as neither had a sweet tooth. Instead they would start on the whisky again to wash down the meal.

Occasionally, my Uncle Tommy would bring over home-made pocheen, an illegal, clear Irish whiskey he had made from potatoes and which he had brewed back in Galway. He used to smuggle this through customs by putting it in a pop bottle and applying a label saying 'Holy Water'. Ireland was such a Catholic country then that I suppose it was never checked. The sight of it being pulled from his case and his roguish grin always made us laugh, but the after-effects of it did not. When the pocheen appeared, I knew that the evening television entertainment was over. There would be more disagreements, sometimes about money, but other things too. I did not know what they were but recognised the rift to be very deep. The conversation always went back to Ireland and things that had happened in the past. Tommy was highly agitated about something my dad had done or not done. The voices got louder, the swearing worse and I always tried to block it out by going into the front room and standing by the window, overlooking the busy Oldham Road. I would watch the faces of the people going by, wondering where they lived and what their homes were like.

Often Tommy would storm out of the house with no farewells and my dad would let out a string of expletives, slam the door and then make the walk upstairs to sleep it all off. My mum was left to side away all the crockery and rearrange anything that had been broken or tossed about in the fighting. Often my brother missed all this as he tended to go out much more than me, being slightly older and more caught up with teenage life than I was at the time. If my dad did retire early, I would help mum put the house back together and get ready for *Match of the Day*. Manchester United with Best, Law and Charlton, were my escape route; they always helped me to look forward to happier times.

If my father liked to drink more each day from Thursday through Saturday, Sunday was always a more sober day. This had little or nothing to do with religion, more that he had work the next day, and while my father had many different selves, he took his work seriously. I respect that. He was never late, he worked hard, refused to claim any benefits and never shirked. When plastering work was scarce, he would repair roofs, striding cockily up the steep slate inclines, cigarette in his mouth, playing to the gallery of passers-by who looked up in wonder, waiting for him to fall. I knew he would not fall.

He was very aware that people were watching him, and sometimes would pause to stretch his back and whistle loudly. Other times he would wave to the watchers with a cheeky grin on his face. Up in the high places he had his stage; he was George Best with a trowel. Dad was happy-go-lucky, alive in the moment and never thinking too far ahead. He was a character and people liked him for that; capable of extremes of selfishness and kindness, foul temper and gentleness, strength and weakness. If my father was a colour he would be red. Manchester United red. Not beige. A man of contradictions, but never bland.

In some sort of parallel universe, my Saturday home life often replicated a Manchester United match: you had to be prepared for the unexpected, there were cameo performances, and, always, high drama. And even if the result was poor, you knew you were going to go back there, because it's where you belong and because family matters.

Chapter 9

A Bit Special Our Bobby

WHILE Best was the stand-out genius by the mid-60s, and Law the spiky, blond-haired assassin who would put his head inside a cement mixer if it promised a goal, Bobby Charlton was the player I most wanted to see play and try to emulate. On one occasion, I deliberately stood in the more expensive, roomier Stretford End Paddock (two and sixpence for kids) intent on following his movement for the full 90 minutes. I figured that if I ignored the overall play and just focused on what Bobby was doing, I would learn plenty to then weave into my own modest, midfield game.

The plan was wrecked at about minute nine, when Best suddenly sprang into life and the crowd went berserk at one of his weaving, jinking runs. Unable to bear the suspense of what George was doing, to my shame I took my eyes off the majestic Charlton and, like the rest of the stadium, saw the young Irishman smash in an unstoppable goal. After that, I recognised that my original plan just would not work with explosive talents like Best and Law on show. As they did things in dramatic, split seconds there was no time to be looking somewhere else. Still, everything Bobby ever did gave me ideas and encouragement to improve my own limited game.

To observe Bobby glide past opponents was like watching an Aston Martin as it accelerated through the gears. Smooth, effortless grace epitomised Bobby's movement. He would drop his shoulder in the process of a surge forward, although it was almost an unneeded arrogance as the defender was already rocking on his heels. Interestingly, many of his colleagues and opponents have likened Bobby Charlton to a racehorse over the years, a 'thoroughbred' as Wilf McGuinness called him. Franz Beckenbauer, the great German sweeper, who faced him so many times, most memorably in the 1966 World Cup Final, commented that 'he had a pair of lungs like a horse'. Whilst Charlton had sublime skill, he also had the hardest running game to underpin his great technique.

Jimmy Murphy had no doubt sown this seed in training, when Bobby would be summoned to chase and return balls that Murphy would belt out from the centre circle towards each corner flag in turn. One day Charlton asked Murphy why he always gave him such a hard time this way, making exhausting 40-yard runs. Murphy advised Bobby that there were many hopefuls at the club, some of whom would make the grade while most would not. Murphy assured Bobby that he would be an asset for the club and that this was why he 'punished' him so relentlessly in training. It certainly paid off; Bobby Charlton was a player who could run long, hard and fast all day, with supreme fitness underpinning his prodigious talents on the ball. Bobby Charlton had a fantastic physique in his prime and was a top-class athlete.

Whilst the great Charlton was never going to be a tackler or a header (these were definitely not his strengths), once allowed to run with the ball, he had his place among the gods of the attacking game. He was not perfect, though, even though I perceived him to be only a fraction away from that status; on the odd occasion even his feared shooting could let him down. David Meek, in the *Manchester Evening News* (1967), recalls one such moment: 'Bobby Charlton must have had his eye on something else when he powder-puffed a penalty at Hodgkinson.' Of course, amongst the amazing strikes and goals there was that odd shot when he mis-caught the ball. However, when it did go right, as it did more often than not, the sight of a Bobby Dazzler (the name given to Bobby's epic goals in the 50s) hitting the net and still travelling upwards, causing an impossible protrusion and terrific photo opportunity, created an indelible memory.

Ironically, one of his most memorable moments, though, was a headed goal, coming of course in the 1968 European Cup Final against Benfica, the ball skimming off his wispy hair to land in the corner of the net. But of his many other strengths, his two-footedness was just stand-out brilliant. Many match commentators nowadays declare that 'the ball came to his weaker foot' with no sense of irony. There was no such fussiness with Bobby and many fans may have to think hard to remember which foot was the better one. Bobby Charlton was immensely comfortable using either foot, although the statistics show that he scored more goals using his right foot.

To recall another glorious goal, the one for England against Mexico in the 1966 World Cup Finals, Bobby says he was surprised when no defender came towards him as he bore down on goal. Being aware of the smoothness of the Wembley turf and trusting the ball to run true, Bobby remembered one of Jimmy Murphy's golden rules: 'Just bloody shoot. Don't try to place them. Make sure you hit the goal.'

Astonishingly, in his recall of the goal in the award-winning autobiography, *The Manchester United Years*, Bobby neglects to say which foot he actually hit it with. It was a remarkable goal. Indeed, Bobby struck the heavy ball with his right foot, catching it with the side and top of the laces so sweetly from over 25 yards. Even now, looking back on the power and technique involved in the action, it seems an extraordinary strike as it crashed into the net with the Mexican keeper helpless. This, of course, was the goal that kick-started England's World Cup, after the underwhelming opening game against Uruguay, and resulted in the team's visit to Pinewood Studios with film buff Sir Alf, the meeting with Sean Connery, Yul Brynner et al., the chance to play better against little Mexico, and then … that goal.

Bobby's understated recall of the goal amounted to a wonderful one-liner, 'An important goal that …' There are so many reasons why Bobby Charlton is such a loved and respected sportsman, and his modesty is a key one. Oh, for such understatement and genuine modesty today in our noisy, self-promoting social media world where many people (including some players) tweet their lives away.

Bobby's childhood was typical of the poorer regions of the north-east in the 1930s and 40s. He says, 'One of the abiding memories is of the hunger, but then I thought it was natural to have that feeling.' Whilst food was scarce, love was in good supply and the fit between club and player when Bobby eventually came to United must have been a very natural one. He came from a loving family and joined another one in Manchester, sporting key figures like 'Uncle' Joe Armstrong, Jimmy Murphy and Matt Busby.

As a teenager, watching Bobby play, there was for me another attraction beyond his game and general demeanour, and this was the fact that he had been helped into the sport not by his father but by his mother, Cissie. This sat well with me, given that it had also been my mother who had introduced me to football, not my father. Cissie was of course related to the famous Milburn football clan, Bobby coming from an amazing four generations of players in his family. In Geoffrey

Green's illuminating text, *There's Only One United*, the writer spoke prophetically when he said, 'Nature's gentleman, one day Bobby will be remembered as the jewel of them all.' Bobby's maternal grandfather, Tanner, had been a hard man and trainer of professional sprinters. Whilst able to ruffle a few feathers both in the Charlton family and community where he lived, Tanner was adored by Bobby. In turn the old man doted on his grandson. He set him up in sprint races giving him a 70-yard start against professional sprinters and praising him hugely when he won.

Bobby had grown up besotted by the magical qualities of the attacking players of the game and one of his greatest idols was Stanley Matthews. As for Bobby, Stan's father saw similar athletic potential in his son and raced him against older boys with bets being placed by spectators. Such events often drew large crowds. Stan's fitness was underpinned by a strict regime of exercises and deep breathing, chest-expanding, skipping, walking, running and street football. Such devotion to fitness represented the world that Bobby also grew up into. Later, watching Stan play when Blackpool visited St James' Park, Bobby said of his boyhood hero, 'His movement was both mysterious and thrilling in a unique way …' Bobby had fallen deeply in love with the beauty and artistry of the game through watching players like Matthews.

The Charlton/Matthews similarity did not end there. Bobby's father, Bob, was immensely strong and nicknamed Boxer, revelling in the visiting shows of bare-knuckle boxers. This sprint/boxing combination was also the environment that Stanley Matthews experienced as a child, during his own upbringing in the Potteries. Matthews's father, Jack, had been known as the Fighting Barber of Hanley, earning his daily money cutting hair, whilst side-showing in the boxing ring. On one occasion, at the Old Liverpool Stadium, an opponent did not get up after the count and was taken to hospital. Jack

Matthews was placed in Walton Jail and informed that he could be facing a serious charge if the stricken boxer did not respond to medical attention. Fortunately for everyone concerned, the boxer made a full recovery and Matthews was released from prison at 5.30am the following morning. Jack Matthews, the last boxer in England to feature a handlebar moustache, won 342 from 350 professional fights.

These were hard times and the skill and speed of both Bobby and Stan, while neither was a fighter, were shaped in these tough working-class environments. Matthews's knees were cut to ribbons, playing among the shards of broken pottery on the scrapheap pitches of Hanley, while Charlton learned his skills in the soot-filled streets of Ashington. Both men were supremely fit and because of this played beyond the normal age for players, especially in Matthews's case.

Stan was born in 1915 and Bobby in 1937. Incredibly, Matthews represented his country across three decades: the 1930s, 40s and 50s. His league career extended further into the 1960s. Matthews and Charlton narrowly missed playing in the same England side since Matthews's international career ended in 1957, after 22 years' service to the national team, while Bobby's England days began in April 1958, just a couple of months after the Munich disaster. Despite the press clamour for Charlton's inclusion, England manager Walter Winterbottom did not use Bobby in the 1958 World Cup.

Bobby says of his dad, 'My father wasn't a football man ...' and that he had been more at home attending to the pigeons, geese and rabbits that he kept, rather than being on a football pitch. For Cissie Charlton, the goal of her sons, Bobby and Jack, pursuing a career in football was of great importance and she involved herself fully, whether it was standing on the touchline in school matches or later recalling football experiences in her own autobiography, *Cissie*. Sadly, she did not live long enough to see another son, Tommy, also go on to represent England at walking football in 2018. This latent talent was a point not lost on Bobby, though, who always believed his little brother could play the game well. Cissie's fourth son, Gordon, is the least mentioned of the four brothers. He too was a promising footballer as a youth and had trials with Leeds aged 16, but the club declined to sign him as a professional a year later.

Significantly, the first person Joe Armstrong spoke to regarding Bobby was Cissie Charlton, during a youth match between East Northumberland and Hebbun and Jarrow. Observing Bobby's two-footedness, Joe came over to Cissie, told her that he liked what he saw and invited Bobby to visit Manchester United. Cissie's involvement in Bobby's early career sometimes caused tension, with Bobby saying, 'Sometimes the enthusiasm she displayed in supporting my progress as a young footballer of local celebrity could be embarrassing ...' Cissie recalls how she improved Bobby's sprinting, having learned her trade from old Tanner. However, even when one senses some of Cissie's recollections might have been better left unsaid, Bobby dealt with her autobiography with the tact and diplomacy he was to display throughout his life. Bobby added that he realised coming from a famous football family accounted for this sometimes-misplaced passion, for he felt that she only ever wanted what was best for her son. Such skills of mediation have served Bobby well over the years, whether fronting a World Cup bid, starting a 10k race or launching a charity to clear landmines. Bobby Charlton is a highly skilled representative and diplomat.

My own mother was no Cissie Charlton. She came from a family background more used to classical music and gardening for leisure interests. She could not have helped me with football development any more than providing good nutrition and a word of encouragement, although these were always much appreciated. With Dad an absent parent too, I was used to playing without touchline encouragement, which probably explains why the coach, good or bad, was always such an important figure to me.

Continuing the string of spooky links to the Charlton family (in my own immature childhood mind at the time and obviously ignoring the considerable differences in our footballing abilities), like the two Charlton brothers, my own brother Gerry and I were opposites in terms of personality and preferences. My brother found my placid nature and obsession with football irritating. He liked to pull things apart (clocks, watches, bikes, anything really that ticked or moved) and then mend them. I saw no logic in this and just wanted things to work, all the time, never going wrong … because if they did, I could not mend them. Whereas my brother was the star pupil at school in woodwork and metalwork (as it was back then), I was spectacularly bad at these subjects. So, when I started to explore the Charlton family and what Bobby and Jack were really like, I was delighted to learn that they were brothers of very different natures, just as my own brother and I had been.

When Leo McKinstry published his well-researched account of the two brothers, *Jack and Bobby: A Story of Brothers in Conflict,* he painted a picture of siblings at odds in childhood, living under the same roof but with little else in common. It was exactly like that for my brother and me. Whilst both boys initially failed their 11-plus exams, Bobby later moved to the local grammar school under the review process, largely prompted by his forthright mother. The original grammar school chosen for Bobby (Morpeth Grammar) was a rugby-playing school and his mother pleaded his case to Northumberland County Council, thus triggering a move to a soccer-playing school, Bedlington Grammar School. In truth, Bobby's reputation was starting to precede him wherever he went in the Ashington area and beyond, and the school soon realised they had made a good decision to take

Bobby. It was clear that here was a boy who was going to play at a high level in football, whilst being a sport all-rounder, almost equally skilled at cricket. Academically, he was considerably brighter than Jack whilst never being a high-flyer in the more academic grammar school environment. Bobby often looked back and felt that he could have spent less time daydreaming about football and given more concentration to core academic subjects. I know that feeling too.

Bobby's academic ability was of little interest to me when I was 13 years old though, trying to learn how to play the game myself and watching him in United's first team. Then, he was this little pack of dynamite who wore the famous red shirt, tore into defences at will and made the game look so easy. He was also my idea of what a true sportsman should be like: supremely fit, focused on his game and generous in his comments about other players. As such, Bobby Charlton exerted a huge influence on my life growing up in Manchester. I saw in him everything that was good about the wonderful game of football, and he helped me shape my own life. Poor Bobby never had an inkling, of course, that he was doing this … but he did. I was never going to be a boat-rocker, more at home within a system I understood and liked rather than a scene of tension and argument.

Bobby Charlton, and Manchester United generally, were this huge family, not yet a global empire but growing rapidly and joyously by the mid-60s. I wanted to catch hold of their coat-tails and go along with them on that journey. Whether that was as a player or a fan was not the issue, just being a part of the Manchester United story was enough. Munich was behind us and the future was bright. Identifying with the surge of success and excitement that was Manchester United filled me with glee and optimism. When Bobby Charlton spoke in the 1960s about how he saw the club developing into a members' only, Real Madrid type of entity, I remember thinking that it would never happen. Clearly, Bobby was seeing something beyond the factory chimneys of Trafford Park, which were to me the constant framework in which I saw the club: provincial, working class, ambitious but never global. The certainty that youth brings is eventually replaced by the realisation of change, which now seems the only thing that can be accurately relied upon.

Bobby Charlton wasn't just a beacon of excellence for Manchester United and England, he became Bobby Charlton the national institution, the name indigenous populations remember in far-flung lands. Bobby Charlton the lifelong Red, Bobby Charlton the epitome of sportsmanship and grace – like modesty, two other qualities often so lacking in our new football world. Wilf McGuinness, so close to Bobby since they were teammates in the England Schools team back in the 50s, simply says of our best-loved knight: 'A bit special our Bobby.' What delicious understatement. Ryan Giggs is on record as saying that wherever he travelled around the world with United as a player, the person who often got the most attention was Bobby Charlton. It's an astonishing statement to make when you think of some of the wonderful United players of Giggs's day. Whilst my opinion counts for little I know, to me Bobby remains England's best-ever player and probably England's most-loved player.

When news of the sensational skills of Bobby Charlton eventually reached Matt Busby, he went to look for himself, watching Charlton play for England Schools. Entirely convinced by what he had seen on offer, Busby swooped quickly, aided hugely by the persuasive charms of Joe Armstrong. Most certainly, given the considerable presence of Cissie Charlton, it was indeed the mother in this instance who had to be won over; in this respect the charismatic Armstrong was able to convince Cissie and finally deliver the highly sought Charlton to Old Trafford.

Through 'that wonderful little man, Joe Armstrong', United won the race for his signature. Fast and skilful, Bobby had vision and tenacity. In Bobby's account of his youth-team upbringing at United, he acknowledges, like McGuinness, the huge debt he owes to Busby, Murphy and Whalley. He recalls how, in training, Murphy warned him about the dangers of long 30/40-yard passes and always wanting to dribble. Jimmy 'knocked the bad, schoolboy errors out of him', noting that the great players, such as in the 1953 Hungarian team, did the simple things well. It's a simple enough concept to grasp, yet for many lesser players an elusive one. Bobby started in United's fifth team in the Altrincham and District League. Only after a set period did a player move up to a higher team. When he reached the thirds, this was in the Manchester Amateur League against the tough factory and shipyard teams. Reaching the youth team was the next step up. Bobby, like many of the young players such as Bill Foulkes, who worked in a St Helens pit, took a local job and trained Tuesday and Thursday evenings at The Cliff. Here players collected their kit from a pile heaped on the changing room floor, a world away from the sponsored kit deals of today.

I have often pondered the fact that if Bobby Charlton says that he was not fit to lace the great Duncan's boots just how good was Duncan Edwards? It is the question that I have asked a hundred times yet shall never be able to answer. Like many fans of my vintage I suspect, one of the biggest regrets of my life is that I never saw Edwards play. Perhaps I had the next best thing in seeing the great Charlton play, so many times that I knew his every jink and shimmy, when the change of pace would happen and when he would shoot. And could he shoot!

Along with Edwards, in the 50s Bobby Charlton represented the crown jewels in Matt Busby's youthful treasure chest of talent. Most top clubs wanted to sign Bobby Charlton and those that didn't show interest obviously had not seen him play. He was such an irresistible force of youthful promise that it was hard to find any scout or schoolteacher who did not feel that Bobby was destined for the very top echelons of the game. His mother Cissie recalls that the house was so full of club scouts that on more than one occasion she had one in the kitchen while another was in the living room.

Wilf McGuinness is quick to point out that Charlton has sometimes been misunderstood and his natural reticence mistaken for aloofness. Whilst Jack took after his more outgoing mother, Bobby was quieter like his father. On the pitch, though, Bobby was more than capable of standing up for himself and was anything but quiet. McGuinness remembers one memorable moment in a match concerning whose responsibility it had been to call for the ball, resulting in a feisty on-field argument, where Charlton was certainly not afraid to air his views!

This incident reinforced a memory of my own, many years later, when refereeing a five-a-side game in which Bobby was playing during a corporate event. He challenged most of my decisions that afternoon, and initially I had to look twice to see that this was the nice Bobby Charlton, my boys' own hero, acting this way; but Bobby is a winner and even in a friendly game he had to make sure that he finished up on the winning team.

It was in the breeding ground for talent that was Manchester United in those glorious days of youth, where that winning instinct was honed and sharpened. With McGuinness and Colman both opening their homes to Bobby and his family, their friendships became more than purely professional. Noticeably, the word 'family' is used frequently in the autobiographical accounts of the players from the 50s and 60s, and arguably far less so in accounts of the following two decades. In the 60s, I grew up wondering how an institution like Manchester United could be so large and business-like and yet so normal and intimate. Clearly, something special was happening at the club for there to be such a carry-over into the private lives of these wonderfully talented young players.

Busby spotted problems before they grew, once calling out Eddie Colman who was fond of copying the Teddy Boy fashions of the day. Manchester was embracing rock and roll and for young men this meant suede shoes, long jackets and a practised look of attitude. Bill Haley had visited the city, and clubs like the Plaza and the Cromford had huge followings, with significant status too among the young, impressionable United players. Busby saw this as an unhelpful distraction for his young stars and advised Colman, in no uncertain terms, to drop the fashion.

In the late 50s, youth culture was changing fast amid the grit and grime of Manchester. As the United youngsters started to mature and look at what other pleasures the city had to offer, Busby again stepped in to warn against poor investments and inappropriate company. Coffee bars such as Lyons and the Kardomah were popular with the United players, as were the cinemas in town. Famous names such as the Bodega Jazz Club and Sale Locarno were places I also heard about as a youngster. They were, in my imagination, somewhere on the south side of Manchester, exotic and probably a little dangerous. My northern side of the city was old money, where change happened slowly, factory chimneys stood like sentry guards and chip shops closed at 10pm. But whether north, south, east or west in Manchester, Matt Busby knew the night scene and had a list of places where he did not want to see his young boys go.

Is there any wonder Bobby Charlton became a one-club man when the roots of his affinity to Manchester United were so well-founded? Perhaps there were times later in his career when the Madrid tanks were parked on the Old Trafford concourse and he thought about moving abroad; but where else would he have ever found so much talent, camaraderie and team spirit among fellow professionals? And such an adoring public. Paradise. Bliss. Family.

Tony Whelan remembers Bobby both as a senior player in his pomp and later in a coaching capacity:

'Bobby was obviously different [to Denis and George]. I didn't know Bobby too well. I was totally in awe of him, but then everybody was in awe of him, not just because of his prowess as a player but also because of his England role and what he had been through with Munich. If Sir Matt Busby was the Pope, Bobby was the Cardinal. He was always a little bit distant at that time. I got to know him better later on because I coached on his soccer schools for several years. I also had the privilege of going to Kenya with our academy team in 2004 when he was also there, and I found it a lot easier to get on with him then, later on, in our post-playing days. Bobby was wonderful with the young players in the soccer schools when he came out to coach. When he came out to Kenya he sat with the coaches at dinner, mixed in and was wonderful. It was a fantastic experience.'

Finally, they say you should never meet your heroes, but in my case it worked out well. In 1992 (the height of my PE school teacher days) I undertook a placement at Bobby's company, Bobby Charlton Enterprises (BCE), a sports firm specialising in youth coaching and soccer hospitality packages for businesses. In those days, BCE organised national and international multi-sport holidays for children, Bobby being one of the first former players to see the huge potential in large-scale, recreational soccer-coaching programmes.

Tony Whelan sums up the huge legacy left to youth football by the Bobby Charlton soccer schools:

'I don't think people understand how good his soccer schools were. I usually coached for him at The Armitage

Centre at Manchester University at Fallowfield, and it was fantastic. He had all sorts of sports: football, tennis, cricket and other sports. I don't think he always got the credit he deserved for this work as he had a lot of opposition from the FA, who were in competition with him. I think they threatened some coaches that they would not be allowed to coach for the FA if they coached for Bobby Charlton soccer schools. I cut my teeth as a coach at the Bobby Charlton soccer schools. There is no question about that. Really, he was the pioneer of soccer schools. Everything that followed was because of that. They weren't over-priced; the kids had a great time and learned a lot.'

David Beckham's emergence as the top performer at one of Bobby's soccer schools as an 11-year-old schoolboy in 1986 helped launch a spectacular career, of course, that hugely benefitted both Manchester United and England.

By the time of my somewhat less significant involvement in the schools in 1992, I had covered 18 years of teaching and, if truth be told, was ready for a break from the classroom. After two weeks placement at BCE, I knew I was looking for a more permanent break. The placement inspired me to coach at one of Bobby's schools at Hopwood Hall, Middleton, and also to develop my career further with my eventual move into higher education.

Also working for Bobby's company was David Sadler, who headed up BCE's Corporate Hospitality Division, arranging events such as Lunch with a Legend, which involved figures like the England cricketer Graham Gooch and football icon Eusébio. But Bobby's forages into an emerging sports market did not end there; a sports management division also existed, assisting players in terms of contract negotiation, product endorsement and the like. Coaching in schools and a sports clothing section rounded off the range of BCE's exciting new business ventures. After the placement, somehow the alternative of teaching 9G on a wet Tuesday afternoon seemed unattractive in comparison.

Working in BCE's Manchester offices, I spent the early part of the placement planning sports events, ascertaining schools' involvement, arranging first aid cover, overnight accommodation for staff and other vital tasks. In the second week of the placement I drove up to Stirling University for a corporate hospitality event with John Shiels, then the Sports Promotions Officer for BCE (now the Chief Executive of the Manchester United Foundation) with Bobby following on in his Jaguar.

When the event finally got underway, involving employees from a major insurance company, it was an education to see Bobby in action as he met the delegates and spoke to a large audience; so relaxed, so modest, so classy … so Bobby Charlton. The night before the actual football part of the event we had a fine dinner in the restaurant at the university. Suddenly, I found myself sitting opposite Bobby Charlton and David Sadler, two of the 1968 European Cup heroes, and, whilst calm and confident until that moment, I froze. Food seemed to get stuck in my throat and the idea of multitasking by eating and talking at the same time was hopelessly beyond me. Later John asked me why I had been so quiet at the meal, but I suspect the answer did not surprise him hugely. I was not the first to freeze in the presence of greatness.

Early the next morning, I travelled across the campus grounds with Bobby to the fields where soccer-skills tests had been set up for the corporate event. Now I was seriously freaking out, sitting alongside Bobby as we drove through the university grounds in his quintessentially English Jaguar. (What else would you expect Sir Bobby Charlton to drive?) I needn't have worried though. Bobby just chatted away so naturally, saying how cold it was for July but coming from the north-east he was used to it etc. Luckily, I couldn't get much of a word in edgeways, and the arrangement worked well for me. Bobby was equally relaxed talking to the large audience he faced when we got to the main field. I always think it is impressive when someone can be relaxed and genuine when public speaking and he certainly had that gift. Bobby spoke as naturally to the 60 or 70 delegates as he had to me back in the car.

It was during the formal soccer-skills tests that Bobby's talents really came alive though, and I got a close-up chance to appreciate how special this man's ability was. I recall one test where cones marked out three squares of different sizes about 30 yards away; players were awarded 50 points if they were able to chip the ball into the outer square, 75 points for the middle square and 100 for the smallest target. Each player had four attempts, hitting three with their stronger foot but the last one had to be lofted in using the weaker foot. In the afternoon, two Scottish international players arrived; their names escape me and, given the circumstances, I shall make no effort to ascertain that information. For when faced with their attempts, they both hit the first three balls well, as you would expect from international players. However, when required to use the weaker foot, the results were so embarrassingly poor that several delegates suddenly decided to look down and inspect the grass. The previous day I had seen Bobby demonstrate the skills test and score maximum point in all four hits … but then Bobby never really had a weaker foot, did he?

The second major event in my placement was very different: the Sega Sports Challenge staged at Leeds Polytechnic (or Leeds Metropolitan University as it is now known). Based at the famous Carnegie venue in Headingley, this was an all-schools event supported by Sega, then the major name in the emerging sports-gaming market. This gave me the opportunity to involve my own school, Falinge

Park High School, in something worthwhile. Falinge Park was a multicultural school with a high proportion of pupils from British Asian backgrounds, most of them Muslims. The catchment area was in a poorer part of Rochdale and a troubled region in terms of race relations. It felt good to involve children in a special occasion like this, and for many girls this was the first time that their parents had allowed them to participate in an out-of-school activity, let alone in a different city. The strict cultural traditions of these Muslim homes had hitherto forbidden this. It was testament to Bobby's impeccable reputation that some parents regarded this as a very special occasion and had allowed it to happen, simply because of one name: Bobby Charlton.

As we travelled home at around 7.15pm that night, it was a wonderful example of how sport can change lives in small ways. We did not even come close to winning the competition, but the children had really enjoyed performing at a top college venue, competing in sports such as softball, hockey, table tennis and football. We recorded the event on video, and for the kids meeting Bobby and other celebrities such as Henry Cooper, the boxer, was magical. For children raised in a town with more than its fair share of racial tensions, becoming a part of something like this was a helpful step towards improving community cohesion. For instance, one of our Muslim girls, Farzana, won the discus event even though it was the first time she had ever been allowed to compete in an inter-schools competition. When Sir Bobby looks back on his life, I wonder if he realises the enormous impact he has had, not just on the systems and the institutions he has helped and represented, but on the lives of ordinary individuals like Farzana … and me. Thank you, Sir Bobby.

Chapter 10

Denis Law: King!

AS a child, the names surrounding Manchester United always fascinated me. I knew the great players, of course, but also the ones who were attempting to break through in the reserves and A and B teams. I made it my business to know every name at the club from Bobby Charlton through to the groundsman; but then some names, especially the more peripheral actors in the Manchester United drama, were less obvious to me and sometimes I built up fanciful images of them. Willie Satinoff's name, for instance, intrigued me and I wondered just why he was onboard that plane as it tried to leave Munich airport? Willie Satinoff was a close friend of Matt Busby, tipped by some to become a club director, who had been invited to travel with the team to watch the game and who sadly perished in that fateful crash. Then there was Louis Rocca.

Again, an unusual name and I kept wondering how he fitted into the narrative? I found my answer much later in life, as my research started to go deeper into the club's history, and what an immense role this man played in the club's growth. But the intriguing, foreign-sounding name that resonated with me most back in the early 1960s, and which just sounded so exotic, was Gigi Peronace.

I did not know anyone in Middleton with a name like Gigi Peronace. The name was poetry to me. My pals had names like Dave, Mick, Stu and Kev. Gigi Peronace was such a cool name and represented a world beyond the factory-chimney horizons of north Manchester. When I learned that Gigi Peronace had been instrumental in bringing the sensational Denis Law to Manchester United, he took on a saintly persona to me. I saw him as a kindly old Italian in a sharp, double-breasted suit with slicked back hair and beatific smile: my imaginary Italian, Uncle Gigi. He ate at fancy Italian restaurants (naturally) where impeccably dressed waiters tended to his every need, and he holidayed on the island of Capri (which Gracie Fields had somehow found preferable to Rochdale).

In my world, on the rare occasions we did eat out, it was always the UCP, whilst I aspired towards the Berni Inn. Here the longed-for height of adult sophistication was a prawn cocktail with limp lettuce, a small piece of leathery steak with chips and a fluorescent knickerbocker glory to finish. No, Uncle Gigi's world was substantially different to that. Pure class. After all, this was the man who had brought someone mercurial to Old Trafford, a phenomenon, a player so sharp you could not blink when watching him in the six-yard box as you might miss his overhead kick, his scissor kick or his dust-up with a centre-half. It wasn't the time to sip a Bovril or sink your teeth into a pie, when the ball was in the opponents' six-yard box and Denis was playing. You had to have a heightened sense of the moment and sharp reflexes just to watch him. You needed to be physically fit to truly appreciate Denis Law.

Gigi Peronace was what we would now call a football agent/interpreter, a super-agent even, and had brought the magnificent John Charles to Juventus. Now, in 1961, he was returning to Britain to find the next gem. I imagined Gigi did all this work out of some philanthropic gesture, committed as he was to simply finding the best players in the world and then sending them to us at Manchester United. What an utter gentleman and what good taste he had to choose us. It never occurred to me that he might actually be paid to do this. However, Gigi's first acquaintance with Denis Law the footballer saw the Lawman heading the opposite way, with Peronace arranging the transfer from Manchester City to Torino. The maximum wage had just been abolished in England, with Johnny Haynes becoming the country's first £100 per week footballer. City had offered Denis £80 a week to stay, but the offer from Torino of a £110,000 transfer with huge bonuses persuaded the unsettled Law to head to the Azurri (Law, 1963; Law, 1979; MUTV, 2019). It was a move he soon came to bitterly regret.

But what had made Denis Law the footballer such a unique talent was not born in Turin but in the Scottish coastal city of Aberdeen. Denis was born into a family of seven children, with his father earning low wages as a trawlerman. He did not own a pair of proper shoes until he was 14 and walked to school in gym shoes, such was his family's poverty. When he received his first pair of Hotspur football boots around the same time, they had '... big ankle protectors and were as hard as a brick'. While poor diet and housing also gave Denis huge problems to overcome, his main obstacle was his eyesight; he had a very noticeable squint, with his right eye being badly crossed unless he wore corrective glasses. He was so self-conscious about his outward appearance that he kept the glasses on even when playing football, and they were smashed to pieces on several occasions. He suffered taunts from other children before this happened and certainly after such a calamity.

Scouted by Huddersfield Town, Law arrived at the large, draughty old Leeds Road stadium still awaiting the operation that would fix his eyesight problems. After a two-year wait he finally had the operation at Aberdeen General Hospital, and for the first time ever he could then open both eyes without having to look in two directions at the same time. Interestingly, Law marks this transformation and growth in self-confidence as the beginning of the swagger that later became his trademark. His sense of self-worth increased considerably the moment his bandages were removed and he stared at himself in the mirror.

Pushing his way through the junior teams under Andy Beattie's managership, Huddersfield drew Manchester United in the FA Youth Cup and the paths of Denis Law and Matt Busby crossed for the first time. United won the match 4-2, but Busby had seen something in the young Denis that he liked and immediately made an offer of £10,000 for him. Beattie refused to sell. In 1957 Beattie retired and a certain Bill Shankly took over the reins at Leeds Road, having been reserve-team coach up until then. While Beattie had been a quiet, thoughtful type, Shankly was just the opposite and players feasted on his enthusiasm and confidence. Law gives an inkling of the Shankly style when he recalls the often-told story of how Shankly (when later manager of Liverpool) would assess Manchester United prior to their match:

'Stepney – useless; Shay Brennan – can't kick, can't head; Dunne – can't kick with his right foot; Crerand – too slow; Foulkes – bad header; Stiles – the boy can't even see; George Best – not a bad little player but can't kick; Bobby Charlton – no use, get tight up on him ...'

The other classic Shankly story concerning his team talk before a match with United involves a similar withering analysis of the opponents, except he stops short of mentioning Best, Law and Charlton. There is a heavy silence in the dressing room before Ian Callaghan bravely asks about the missing three. Shankly replies, 'You're telling me you can't beat a team with just three players!'

Law also subscribes to many other players' accounts of Shankly insofar as injuries were concerned. Essentially, this might be summarised by saying that if a player got injured Shankly immediately crossed him off his Christmas card list. He was known to 'blank' players in the corridors as they passed him, choosing to whistle and stare up at the ceiling with no words spoken. Law recalls that the corridors were very narrow at Leeds Road and the interaction must have unnerved even the super-confident Denis.

In typical Busby style, the promising Law was remembered when Matt was appointed Scotland manager, and it was he who gave Denis his first international cap in 1958. When Denis was capped at 18 years 8 months, he was the youngest player to receive the honour since Bob McColl in 1899. It is an amazing fact that in 1958, England, Scotland and Wales were all managed by men with Manchester United affiliations, through Walter Winterbottom, Matt Busby and Jimmy Murphy. (It is also a little-mentioned fact that Winterbottom managed England for 16 years, from 1946–1962.)

However, in 1959 the ebullient Bill Shankly left Huddersfield to begin his reign as manager of underachieving Liverpool, with the restless Denis following him over the Pennines a few months later to sign for Manchester City in March 1960 for £55,000. Denis had thought he would be linking up again with Bill Shankly at Liverpool, but the club could not afford to sign him. Meeting Busby by chance in the Midland Hotel, Manchester (scene of so many football deals involving United), Busby explained that he was well placed for strikers at that moment in time. However, he left Denis with hope by saying, 'But, you never know'. Those words must have played in Denis's mind over the coming months when he failed to enjoy the training sessions at City, with endless lapping of the track replacing the ball work he had enjoyed under Shankly. After an underwhelming 1960/61 season in terms of results, Denis entered the radar of Inter Milan and soon signed a contract with them when approached in June 1961. Inter were looking for the next John Charles to emerge from Britain, the big Welshman having been such a success at Juventus.

Lured by the promise of a lot more money and with a youthful spirit of adventure, Italy looked a perfect fit for Denis. However, Gigi Peronace then appeared on the scene and suddenly it was not Inter that Law wanted to join but Torino, who Peronace was representing. Such was the persuasive demeanour of my imaginary uncle, that Denis signed his second Italian contract in a few days. Naturally, a stormy Italian legal battle then raged between Inter and Torino for some time afterwards, but Peronace's club eventually won out.

Piero Gai, spokesman for the Torino FC fan club, clearly articulates the effect the signing had on Torino: 'When he arrived at Torino it was like a revolution. Everyone knew Denis but we weren't expecting him to come to Torino. It was thanks to the agent Gigi Peronace, who managed to contact him and convinced him to play for our glorious team. Because Torino had an illustrious history. The tragedy at Supergra and five championships in a row.'

It is intriguing that Denis Law played for two football clubs that had suffered catastrophic plane crashes and, thankfully, he had avoided both. In 1949, all 31 people on board, including 18 Torino players, had died in the Italian crash. Torino were a huge club in those days and had won four post-war league titles; they were also leading the Italian league at the time of the crash. Returning from a match in Lisbon, the plane crashed at Supergra, a hill situated to the east of Turin on the south bank of the River Po. As had been the case at Manchester United, the effects of the crash were not just felt within the club but at international level too. In Torino's case, in one international match 10 of the 11 players on show had been from the club.

Having never recovered from the after-effects of the crash in terms of club stature, it was neighbours Juventus who were the top dogs in the city of Turin when Denis arrived. Financially, Torino were in dire straits, a fact Denis would later come to experience first-hand when payments were withheld. However, the astute Law had already won one of the early financial battles by refusing to kick a ball for the club unless he received one-half of his signing fee in advance. Despite great protests, the Italians reluctantly agreed. Denis admitted that when it came to contract disputes, he was indeed a fully paid-up member of the 'Denis Law Protective Society!'

Despite a disappointingly dowdy stadium, the reception in Turin was warm and Denis refers to it as 'a film-star welcome'. With Joe Baker, his Scottish teammate also signed, it was the name Gigi Peronace who again came to the fore when he assisted the players with interpreting. Neither Law nor Baker knew any Italian and at this point Peronace clearly became a great friend to the players; he was the channel through which the two men could speak with the club. While today the role of interpreter is replicated by all major clubs (Jose Mourinho once fulfilling the role for Bobby Robson at Barcelona) back in 1961, it would have been an even more vital lifeline for players, and both Law and Baker must have really valued Peronace's help. The wily Italian did all he could for the two players, whether it was outlining the trains they must catch, what the journeys to matches would be like, what time they must report for the team coach and other logistical issues.

When training was over, Law and Baker were holed up in a luxurious hotel, and certainly for Denis this was far removed from the humble beginnings he had known in his home life in Aberdeen. However, the hours were long and to venture outside of their surroundings meant a barrage of demonstrative if adoring fans and the pushy Italian press. For certain, both players had a rude awakening when asked to foot their own bills for their stays; in Denis's case this amounted to £400. Not for the first time was Peronace placed in the difficult intermediary position of supporting his British stars from the stringent demands of the club, which would have been termed unreasonable behaviour in the English game.

A turning point in Denis's Torino stay was the Christmas game with Palermo played in the Sicilian capital. In addition to some of the roughest tackling he had ever experienced, Denis had to dodge a barrage of broken bottles and fruit whenever he went to collect the ball for a throw-in, before one spectator spat in his face. The trip to Vicenza was little better when the players were spat at again and had rubbish thrown over them, as they sailed on a gondola under the Venetian bridges. Denis was very clear what he thought of this sort of treatment: 'Venice! What a dump! Give me the Manchester Ship Canal every time.'

Another well-documented experience for both players occurred one night when the car in which they were travelling, an upmarket Alfa Romeo Julietta Sprint, with Baker driving, took a roundabout the wrong way. While Law and his brother, who was also travelling with them, escaped with few injuries, Baker's were horrendous and included a broken nose, cheekbone and split palate. With his head encased in bandages, Baker was on the critical list for three days, with only his athletic fitness saving his life. The Italian press made a meal of the crash and presented it as a disgraceful, drunken incident, which was far from the truth. Baker had little experience of driving in Italy, the car was new, and a simple mistake had been made with frightening consequences.

More negative experiences followed in Law's brief stay in the Italian sunshine. He was sent off by his own coach for taking a throw-in during a game, against the coach's instructions. Peronace did not agree with the decision but was powerless to act, as so often in the problems facing Law and

Baker. As if this was not enough, Law was then banned from the ground for 14 days amid speculation that the sending-off had been orchestrated by the club to rid themselves of their Scottish star. Relying on Baker and Peronace to keep him informed of what was happening at the club, he was then instructed to travel to Lausanne where Torino had a friendly match planned. However, his journey was not about playing, rather it was a planned meeting about the sale of Law to Manchester United. Matt Busby was in town.

Busby picks up the story in a section called 'The Italian Job' in one of his early autobiographies, *Soccer at the Top: My Life in Football.* Busby was contacted by the Torino manager while in Majorca where he had gone for a tournament. By the time he had flown to Geneva the Italian press were across the story. No doubt seeing the similarity between this situation and the chase scene from the film *The Italian Job*, Matt said, 'A crowd of them waited for us, and to lose them we ran into a garage. Over the mountains we sped. It was getting more and more like a movie every minute. We arrived in Turin at 11pm.'

Aware that Juventus were interested in signing Denis and with the Torino officials no doubt inflating the numbers involved, Busby had no intention of going over £80,000. Now, long after midnight and unable to strike a deal, Law was ordered to return to Turin and was told his contract was being sold to Juventus for £160,000, a transaction that was legal in Italian football.

Given the volatile nature of the Torino fans, Denis did not fancy the idea of moving across town to play for the club's rivals. He was disgusted by his treatment and disillusioned with his Italian adventure in general. Denis returned home to Aberdeen and contacted the Professional Footballers' Association for support. Weeks passed before Gigi Peronace arranged to meet Law at Edinburgh airport. The Italian gave Law the news he wanted: the authority to sell him to

Manchester United had been arranged. Peronace was a good friend of Busby and clearly his role in Law's escape from Turin was central to the drama. The English press had dubbed Peronace 'The Italian Spy'. Busby paid a then-record fee of £115,000 for the tough-talking Scotsman, whose stubbornness had worn down the Italian club's pressure. From this amount, Manchester City were paid what Torino still owed them. Busby's long-game pursuit of Denis Law had been brought to fruition and he later claimed that bringing the Scotsman to United in 1962 was one of his best-ever signings. The fans on the terraces, like me, who were lucky enough to have seen Denis play would not argue with that. As for Joe Baker, he signed for Arsenal just a week after Law's departure from Turin, Denis winning a £5 wager the two players had made about who would leave the club first.

David Sadler recalls seeing Gigi Peronace around Old Trafford and speaks about the important role he played in bringing the Lawman to United: 'Gigi Peronace, his agent as we would call it now, was at Old Trafford a lot. I think he and Matt got on very well and he was right in the middle of Denis's transfer negotiations, so he knew him very well too. Buying Denis was such a shrewd piece of business.' The name of Gigi Peronace will forever be synonymous with that first wave of players from the English game who moved over to Italy to advance their careers. He was essentially the first football agent we had known in the British game. The Calabrian's list of clients is hugely impressive: John Charles (Leeds United to Juventus), Jimmy Greaves (Chelsea to AC Milan), Joe Baker (Hibernian to Torino), Denis Law (Manchester City to Torino, and Torino to Manchester United) and Liam Brady (Arsenal to Juventus).

Jimmy Greaves likens Peronace to a character from a Godfather novel, so charming, yet a person not to be crossed. In many ways he was the sort of character Matt Busby liked;

stylish and urbane, operating in a discrete, secretive world that Matt enjoyed sampling. There had been characters in Matt Busby's Manchester orbit that had a little of Peronace's strong presence, and it is easy to see why they became such good friends. In truth, Peronace was a very clever man, able to converse fluently in English and interested in finding out about the British way of life. He organised matches between the English and Italian troops during the war, and perhaps a comparison with Louis Rocca as a 'football Mr Fixit' is reasonable to see. Given that he was operating as a successful agent as early as 1957, when he arranged the move of Luton manager Alec Stock to AS Roma, his contribution to the global game of football cannot be underestimated. Certainly, in terms of delivering Denis Law to Manchester United, his name will always be an important part of the club's history. Luigi ('Gigi') Peronace became general manager of the Italian national team, working under Enzo Bearzot, before dying in 1980. He suffered a fatal heart attack and died in Bearzot's arms at the team hotel.

Quickly establishing himself at Manchester United, Denis clearly appreciated the opportunity afforded to him by Matt Busby. He says, 'It was an exciting time to join Manchester United. Sir Matt was rejuvenating the team. It was the 60s and it was buzzing. Everyone was getting over the war and now it's the swinging 60s: George Best, The Beatles, Carnaby Street. The music was great.' As well as the new attacking dimension he brought to the team, among his teammates Denis was modest, friendly and approachable. However, that said, he left players in no doubt what he expected if they were on his side in practice games, as Tony Whelan discovered:

'Denis was just an absolute whirlwind. I idolised him as a player when I was a kid, that arm in the air, that impishness, that cheekiness. He was such a phenomenal presence on the field, his heading ability, his gymnastic ability, his athleticism. You just couldn't help being attracted to him as a player. As a human being he was always joking, always up to something. I remember as an apprentice none of us had cars and we were always trying to cadge lifts to Old Trafford from older players who had cars. The senior players were the only ones who had cars then. Even the junior pros didn't have cars. But I remember everyone wanted to get a lift from Denis. He had a Jag and he would always give lifts. In the car he was always chatting away about something, he was a great personality. He was just a wonderfully warm, smiling, jovial, mischievous guy. That's what I remember about him. He was always approachable, always fun, but if you went in the five-a-sides with him you'd better be playing! If you were on his side then he didn't take any prisoners and would think nothing of telling you off, telling you that you had to play properly. He was always quickly down to business when he was playing.'

Whilst preferring to play deeper at times, Denis says that Sir Matt Busby made clear that he never wanted to see him in his own half. Incredibly, and maybe just a little tongue-in-cheek, Denis says, 'I was never a striker really!' But the name of Denis Law is synonymous with one particular thing: goals. If the Barcelona fans had christened Gary Lineker 'Gary Goals', we had 'Denis Goals' two decades earlier. The nature of his goals was so memorable. Whilst he scored more than just about any other striker in the country from short range, he also scored many from outside the area. For headers he would soar like an upside down bungee jumper, whilst his execution of overhead kicks and 'scissor' goals was just stunning. The newspapers of the day confirm this. Leading with the headline: 'Three-goal Law But Reds Lose in Seven-goal Humdinger' for the league match with Leicester City in 1963, the *Manchester Evening News* continued: 'Stiles gave him possession as Law was standing with his back to goal. Law slipped on to his back and scored with an overhead kick which had Banks completely baffled – hardly surprising.' (*MEN*, 16 April 1963)

The thing about Denis, though, when you study his goals looking back, is the vast range of finishes. Some were scored after a stunning dribble, many after the goalkeeper had parried or after a cross came in; left foot, right foot, headers, scissor kicks, overhead kicks, back-heels … he just did the lot. He potted them in the corner like Hurricane Higgins playing snooker, a deft flick of the head or a cute side-footer. He smashed them in either of the top corners. He rounded the keeper, going to the left just as comfortably as the right. Memorably, when a cross came in and the ball was just behind him, he was somehow able to turn, spin and smash the ball into the net in one electrifying burst. He caressed them in, he blasted them at the goalkeeper's head, he scored on lush pitches, on hard, bare surfaces, on ice, in mud, big important matches, less significant matches … just anywhere, on any type of surface.

He must also be the cheekiest and best back-heeler of all time, which included the famous goal for City on the day the Reds were relegated in 1974. Denis was quick to point out, though, that it was not his goal that had sent United down, but the fact that Birmingham beat Norwich on the same day. The moment when he halted his raised-arm salute, which was to him automatic, is still to me the most enduring, significant non-goal celebration. Like a lover who had moved on but still had deep feeling for an ex, Denis's heart was on his sleeve that day. It is surely one of the most poignant Old Trafford moments ever.

Matt Busby recalls Denis's unique goal celebrations, saying that he was the first British player to salute the crowd, adding, 'Early on at Old Trafford, the multitudes cheered him and he soon became what the crowd called him – "The King".' When you examine the quality and scope of his finishes, though, it might be asked why goal celebrations these days have got so very silly. Here's the man who could score any type of goal, expertly, consistently and you just got the same, simple celebration ... every time. The one that always worked best for me, though, was when he scored a special goal right in front of the Stretford End, maybe on a big European night or during a tense FA Cup game. Then row after row of fans cascaded forwards in a huge wave of humanity, inching to get just a little closer to the player who had saved the day.

He was the Lawman, the gunslinger, the wild-west hero who had saved the town from destruction when evil forces from the dark side of Manchester or Merseyside threatened. He also fronted foreign opposition in classic blood-and-guts encounters, as with Estudiantes in 1968, when both Stiles and Best were dismissed in a game long remembered for its controversy. With Denis it was all raw aggression allied to sublime skill and determination, and the crowd adored him. As Cliff Butler says, Denis was, 'the Stretford End's lads' lad.' Or, in the words of Tony Whelan, '*What* a player!'

For these crucial goals, sometimes when his temper was frayed after last-ditch, unscrupulous defending, he accentuated the salute with a few air-punches to the Stretford End, as if he was smacking a big, mean centre-half on the nose. Sometimes, however, he actually did just that, and Jimmy Ryan vividly recalls such moments, which often occurred during the marvellously atmospheric European nights:

'I remember on a few of those big European nights at Old Trafford, with the Manchester fog drifting around the ground and the ball would be up the far end, and you would suddenly hear a massive roar from the Stretford End. What had happened was that Denis had smacked one of their players off the ball! The Stretford End loved him and there was no doubt that when he won that European Player of the Year, he was the most exciting player in Europe. No doubt at all. Everything he did was so alive, and you always knew something was going to happen with him. I loved the European nights and how the ground always had fog around it because of Trafford Park, then you had the floodlights shining through it. You just felt something was going to happen and much of the time it was Denis who would find a gap and smash it in.'

In today's VAR world of elite football, such moments are now filmed and punished, but back then it was just wonderful live theatre, over in a moment and remembered forever if you saw it. At one end of the pitch you had a football match going on and at the other a three-second boxing contest. If you missed the off-the-ball punch-up there was a loud, communal cry of, 'What's 'appened?' The response was usually, 'Denis just belted 'im!' followed by hearty laughter. I remember someone saying once, 'Good lad Denis, he'd been askin' for it!' The crowd lapped it up. Nobby Stiles also did a nice line in unnoticed 'take-outs', with Amancio of Real Madrid being perhaps his most famous victim, in the first minute of the second half during the 1968 European Cup semi-final at the Bernabéu. As Paddy Crerand later pointed out, Amancio's impact during the rest of the match was then somewhat minimal.

A fiercely proud Scotsman, Denis was overwhelmed to be given the Freedom of Aberdeen by the city. When playing for Scotland against England, it was always the year 1314 and he was Robert the Bruce, at Bannockburn, routing the English foe. Not that Denis was a big man either. If ever a man fitted the saying 'it's not the size of the dog in the fight, it's the size of the fight in the dog that matters' it was Denis Law. Jimmy Ryan rightly calls Denis the 'sword-carrier' for the team, the one who, with true fighting spirit, led the team astonishingly bravely from the front. He just frightened defenders to death, illogically so when players like Jack Charlton, Ron Yeats and Charley Hurley towered above him and were almost twice his width. The slim, ball-playing defenders of the Alan Hansen era had still to arrive. Centre-halves in Denis's days looked like heavyweight boxers and never trained in snoods.

The significance of Law's arrival at Old Trafford is a fact confirmed in the autobiographies of his colleagues at United. Bill Foulkes says that his was the transfer '… which really galvanised Manchester United' in the 1960s. Law scored 29 goals in his first season, despite the fact that United very narrowly avoided relegation. Foulkes recalls how: 'His fabulous talent – not only for scoring spectacular goals, but for creating them too – allied to ferocious bravery, unquenchable enthusiasm and sheer charisma turned the club upside down.' On another occasion when facing Law during his earlier Manchester City days, Foulkes remembers how he suddenly caught sight of Denis flying in to clatter him, showing complete disregard for the ball. He tells how the evasive action probably saved his career. He adds, 'I have never seen anyone more fearless, no matter what the size of his opponent.'

Denis Law always punched way above his weight in every sense and his teammates knew it. John Fitzpatrick says of Denis, ' He could score goals, make goals and could look after himself as well!' George Best remarked that, 'He headed a ball as hard as other players kicked it.' Bobby Charlton says, 'Denis Law was like lightning', whilst Pat Crerand adds that no United signing was ever better than Denis Law's. To Sir Alex Ferguson, Denis was, 'The best Scottish player of all time.' Denis Law was the signing that sparked the fightback to glory after the horrors of Munich.

What many fans of the time probably never realised was the extent of Denis's injury problems whilst at United. The fact that he missed the European Cup Final, of course, is famously documented, but there were many other occasions where he suffered debilitating knee pain and yet still performed amazingly well. David Sadler recalls:

'Denis struggled with injuries a lot of the time at United. I think he came back from Italy with an injury or injuries, and when you look at Denis's career he probably wasn't at his best as a player at United, but he brought so much else. Denis was so sharp, and he played where it hurt, so he was always going to get injuries. He didn't score the spectacular goals like Bobby. There weren't many 25-yard screamers, but he had some incredible things that he used to do. His heading ability was amazing, he had no height to him and was never even into double figures in weight, probably, nine and a half stone soaking wet. The height he got when heading, though, was ridiculous. He put the fear of God into defenders and his purchase was fantastic.'

Jimmy Ryan gives an idea of the status that Denis Law held at Manchester United when he describes the first time his brother met the Lawman:

'At the 50th anniversary of the 1968 European Cup Final in London, I took my brother along, who is a huge Denis Law fan. He was his idol. When we were on the way back north, we got off the train at Stockport as Nicky Butt was going to give us a lift home. And then Denis got off. I said, "Denis, I have to introduce you to my brother because you have been his idol." My brother was shaking hands with him and he just couldn't believe it. By then, of course, Denis wasn't the Denis from his prime, but my brother just thought it was unbelievable to be meeting Denis Law. "I shook hands with Denis Law!" he kept telling me when we got home!' Style was another Denis Law trademark: 'He would grab hold of his cuff and raise his arm. It was so Denis! His trademark. Maybe he got the idea from Italy. He did like Italy but not the football club, which was too strict. But for United he was brilliant, for us he was an icon. The goal celebration, the raised arm, the cuffs being held, you always knew it was Denis. That was definitely Denis!'

John Cooke, too, recalls his style: 'Denis always walked with a straight back, an unbelievable player and what a nice fellow. He was super confident, not arrogant but very confident. He used to wear this dark blue overcoat with raglan sleeves. Denis was always immaculately dressed. He had that Cantona touch, or maybe Cantona had that touch of Denis! Like Bobby and George, he just gave you total encouragement. A brilliant person.'

Denis clearly had a certain panache that was being noticed at Old Trafford. His boots in particular created much envy among the younger players. Jimmy Ryan says:

'Denis Law had these black, hand-made Italian leather boots and they had everything you ever dreamed about in a football boot. We had trouble even getting boots from United because they were so tight! "We've got some boots for you" they would say, "you've been asking for the last three weeks." But they were antiques! Denis had these boots to die for, just taking them off his peg was an experience. The leather was right, the shape of the boot was right, the weight, everything right. They were fantastic even compared with Adidas or Puma, which were the ones I later wore most of my career, but they were nothing compared to the boots that Denis had.

'I remember I wore a pair of Puma boots that were paper thin, but as soon as someone stood on them the leather ripped! Adidas and Puma were just making standard boots. When you picked Denis's boots up, you just looked at them, the style, the cut, even the laces and no one had the nerve to even try them on! He had them made in Italy, in Turin I suspect. Denis looked so Italian-cool. Players like Denis were just "up there", a level above us and I would never speak to him first unless he spoke to me. I didn't speak to Bobby either, they were just in a different league to me.'

What is clear, though, was that 'big-time Charlies' (as Wilf McGuinness puts it) were not allowed to strut around Old

Trafford in the Busby era and the rule applied to everyone. But for Denis Law this was never an issue anyway, for there was a generosity of spirit and genuine humility that defined the man. Jimmy Ryan speaks for many others when he gives just a glimpse of the way ordinary people still feel about Denis:

'Denis used to say to me that whenever he goes to Stirling, he always calls at the Golden Lion for an overnight stay to break the journey to Aberdeen; and as soon as he walks in, the guy behind the bar has a pint of lager pulled for him! The next day he would drive on to Aberdeen. People remember Denis Law!'

They do indeed. Long live The King.

Chapter 11

Manchester's Fifth Beatle

THAT Manchester United were able to rebuild within ten years of the Munich disaster and win the European Cup in 1968 is remarkable and speaks volumes for the key signings and skilled youth development programme of that period. However, we know far more about the effects of the major signings (Law, Crerand, Stepney et al.) than we do about what was happening at youth level. What we do know for certain is that, amazingly, eight of the players who played in that 1968 final were products of the United youth system: Brennan, Foulkes, Sadler, Stiles, Charlton, Aston, Kidd and Best. David Sadler and George Best signed professional forms for United as 17-year-olds so Busby rightly included them in this group. Of these eight players, four hailed from the Greater Manchester area: Foulkes, Stiles, Aston and Kidd. What is also certain is that the vision for youth development remained strong at Manchester United despite the tragedy the club had experienced in Germany. The scarlet thread survived in the face of horrific circumstances. This much is demonstrated by the fact that Manchester United won the FA Cup in 1963, the FA Youth Cup in 1964, the Swiss Blue Stars tournament six times during the 1960s, the First Division in 1965 and 1967, and the European Cup in 1968. Clearly, massively successful signings like Law were made, but the role of youth development in the early to mid-60s was also very significant, a point emphasised by David Sadler:

'Things were now starting to gel a little because the club had bought Law, Crerand, Herd, Cantwell, Setters, and there were also these players coming through in the more normal, home-grown fashion. Even players like John Fitzpatrick, who came from Scotland was just a kid, so we were mostly home-grown. George was different because he was an established player and there was no holding him back. He had been the real prize.'

From that 1964 Youth Cup-winning team came several young players who contributed greatly to the resurgence of the Reds, including Jimmy Rimmer, John Fitzpatrick, David Sadler, John Aston Jr and the incomparable Best. Few texts deal as directly with the effects of the youth policy at Manchester United in the early years following the Munich disaster as Colin Shindler's delightfully left-field book, *George Best and 21 Others*. Clearly the renewal of success in the 1960s was not down to marquee signings alone, magnificent though they were.

There was a crop of youngsters coming through in 1964 that restored pride in the scarlet thread that linked generations of young, home-grown talent. The youth influence would have been even greater too, had the wonderfully gifted full-back Bobby Noble not been so badly injured in a road traffic accident at the peak of his career. The feeling within the club before his accident was that Noble was a player who would go on to spend the next ten years as both a first-team and international defender. Noble was the sort of full-back Jimmy

Murphy naturally liked, insofar as when he tackled opponents they stayed tackled.

But, inevitably, we turn to the stand-out figure from that most famous of Youth Cup games: George Best and the Youth Cup semi-final between Manchester United and Manchester City on 8 April 1964. Amazingly, 29,706 spectators watched the first leg of the semi-final at Old Trafford and around 50,000 over both legs. For David Sadler the memories remain sharp:

'We had a good youth team taking shape and we went on to win it in 1964. Jimmy Rimmer, the goalkeeper, went on to play many games for United. Bobby Noble, the full-back, was the defender who was going to whizz into the first team, along with George. He was captain of the youth side and looked set to play for United and England for ten years or so. However, he had a motor car accident and it more or less finished his career. One or two others, like John Fitzpatrick and John Aston, and myself, were all talked about as potential first-team players. This was the first time since Munich that a good batch of players came through, similar if you like to the class of '92 players later on. We did the same, winning the Youth Cup, and things were looking good. The Youth Cup crowds were really amazing and reserve-team matches were well attended too. The semi-final of the Youth Cup, though, in 1964 was unbelievable. I can remember George was playing for Ireland and so he didn't play in all the youth-team games. There was that one week, though, when he played Saturday at 3pm, then on a Monday (the first semi-final leg), then on the Wednesday for Northern Ireland, then on the Thursday in the second leg of the Youth Cup and then on the Saturday again! It was just a given that he would play. George would much rather play than train, so he was just doing what he loved doing.

'And it wasn't that easy moving around in those days either, just getting over to Ireland wasn't straightforward. He loved playing, he just loved it all, and the rivalry with City was tremendous. City were growing and they had some top players like Glyn Pardoe, who I knew from England Schoolboys days. He scored a lot of goals just like I did as a kid. Glyn and I became very good friends and have remained so. When I got that hat-trick in the 1964 final it was probably the quickest hat-trick I ever scored. For the last goal, George beat just about everybody, passed to me and I drove it home from about three yards. George was just terrific, a full international playing in the youth team.'

Fast-forward 41 years and on the Saturday after the death of George Best (25 November 2005) I was in Altrincham, shopping with my wife, Cathy. Even though continuously threatened by the industrial-scale commerce of the nearby Trafford Centre, the town was busy as people bustled past, with mothers starting their Christmas shopping and children pointing out the gifts they wanted. On the news, I had heard that a makeshift shrine was growing steadily outside Old Trafford and it crossed my mind whether I should go and 'pay my respects'. Now, you may disagree, but I just have a thing about outpourings of grief on street corners. I acknowledge that it works for some, but to me grief is a private thing and I had already shed a few tears alone after George's passing. However, against all my reservations and to the utter astonishment of Cathy, I announced that I was going to catch the Metro down to Old Trafford and see what was happening, presenting it more as sociological research than personal sadness.

The packed tram slid into the station behind the cricket ground and I made my way slowly down Brian Statham Way, past Lancashire cricket ground, carrying on into Warwick Road. By the time I had reached Sir Matt Busby Way my eyes were stinging with tears, and I was blowing my nose and trying to pass it off as a bad cold. I needn't have bothered, there were lots of other 50-somethings who were beyond stifling their grief. George's passing had not only been a part of our own youth disappearing but also the loss of a family member, the United family, and a third of the glorious trio we had all grown up watching. After a while, I realised that had anyone not been shedding tears they would have looked so out of place. It was that sort of day.

The weather was typically Manchester, grey and drizzly, but the little area beneath the famous Trinity statue was surrounded with love, colour and admiration. There were fathers explaining to their sons and daughters about the genius we had lost. The older ones like me knew we had witnessed genius and felt blessed just to have seen it. Along with the Manchester men there, I wondered how many of George's former girlfriends had attended the shrine too … but then that is all part of the George Best story, isn't it? How did one small boy who was too homesick to even finish his trial at United grow to command such love and respect among so many people worldwide? At George's Old Trafford shrine, people spoke mostly about how lucky they felt just to have seen him play. Strangers were talking to each other, taking photos and offering to send them on to other people they had met there. ('If you just give me your email address, I'll send it on to you …') Everyone needed to talk and share.

I had always thought of us 'owning' George in Manchester. He had that great honour bestowed upon him, like Sir Matt Busby, Sir Bobby Charlton, Paddy Crerand, Denis Law et al., of being an adopted Mancunian. And yet, when I saw the way in which Belfast responded to his death, I felt so incredibly stupid. Why indeed would they not intensely mourn their own son? Manchester and Belfast shared most of George Best's life on this earth and both cities, therefore, have that special connection. George may have travelled the world and spent much time in the US particularly, but these two cities were his special places.

George Best's story began at 16 Burren Way, a council house on the Cregagh estate in East Belfast. Parents Annie and Dickie had their names down for some time on the Housing Trust register and moved in there when George was two and a half years old, and sister Carol 15 months. It was a friendly street where Catholics and Protestants mixed well, a fact sister Barbara later recalled in her moving story of *Our George*. George was the first-born child. He had four sisters and one brother, Ian. Rent was 14 shillings a week and Annie and Dickie moved in with one table, four chairs, one bed and cots for George and Carol. Annie and Dickie were very caring parents and the children were brought up strictly but lovingly.

At 11 years old, George, who was an academically capable boy, passed the entrance exam for the prestigious Grosvenor Grammar School in Belfast. Two things impeded his progress there. Firstly, he had to pass through a predominantly Catholic area to reach it and suffered sectarian taunts on the journey. Secondly, it was a rugby not soccer school, and George had fallen in love with the round not oval ball. Truancy followed and poor academic reports. A move to nearby Lisnasharragh High School, where football was the main sport, was amicable to all parties when it came.

In 1961 United's renowned scout in Belfast, Bob Bishop, famously sent a telegram to Matt Busby saying, 'I think I've found you a genius.' So, aged just 15, George and another Belfast boy, Eric McMordie, caught the ferry to Liverpool heading for trials with Manchester United. But then, in atypical United style, the club contact didn't appear and the potential genius and his pal finished up taking a train to Manchester and taxi to Old Trafford. How homesick they must have felt after that poor welcome, alone in a big city. Perhaps not surprisingly, the next day both boys returned to Belfast. The story about how Best came back to Old Trafford has been retold and elaborated upon at times. The reality according to Busby was that the following week, after George's return, he wrote to Dickie Best saying George was always welcome to try again at United. 'Three weeks later' Dickie wrote back to Busby and accepted the offer. Of course, whereas all this could have been quickly arranged in an email conversation or video call these days, the process was much slower in 1961.

Old Trafford then was a spartan affair compared to today's high-tech magnificence. It had been improved significantly since the bombs had fallen on it during the Second World War, but it was still mostly standing room only with primitive facilities for fans. Next to the ground was Trafford Park Industrial Estate, the largest of its kind in Europe. In 1941 several of Hitler's intended bombs had missed this massive hub of production and hit the football ground instead. But with the help of their neighbours City, who loaned United their pitch for 'home' games, the ground was eventually reopened in 1949. Matt Busby was acutely aware of the social significance of the industrial estate. He had come from a hard, working-class mining community and insisted that United should play entertaining football to give Trafford Park workers something to shout about come Saturday. In the 60s, Trafford Park was a huge, sprawling network of sheds, yards, mills, tunnels, waterways and railway lines. It was a dirty, noisy, dangerous, 24/7 operation. Almost an afterthought from the Industrial Revolution of the century before, the complex flanked the club. Rooted in this ugly, industrial landscape, many United fans were Trafford Park workers. Mixing in the Stretford End in the early 60s was to stand next to a worker who had finished a 6am–2pm shift dressed in overalls and a donkey jacket. Pies, or fish and chips were the pre-match meal for these fans, with a couple of pints of Boddington's bitter to wash it down (and not a prawn cocktail or executive box in sight).

How these social layers of football support have changed though. On the rail journey back to Crewe from Manchester after watching the 1999 Treble homecoming, I could only catch the slow train, which stopped at most of the stations south of the city, before passing into Cheshire. I was interested to watch how few fans alighted at the more modest towns on the outskirts of Stockport; whereas, when the affluent Cheshire villages like Wilmslow and Alderley Edge were reached, the exodus was, by comparison, huge. It spoke volumes about how the fan base had changed since those gritty Trafford Park days, when the football ground was filled with people from poorer, working-class areas.

As we walked through Trafford Park for a night match in the 60s, the menacing darkness masked the tall chimneys and ugly gable ends, as the smell of diesel and oil assaulted our nostrils. But these were often the most memorable nights, particularly in European Cup games when the excitement on the pitch was at its greatest. It was interesting and humbling to discover that the sense of anticipation was present in the United dressing room too. With enormous modesty and sharp recall of these famous nights, David Sadler says:

'Thinking about the putting together of that group of players, there were some of us who were fortunate to be there. What I mean is, there were any number of players who could have played where I played, or where Shay played, and maybe Bill, but there were then the others, the ones you couldn't possibly replace: Best, Law and Charlton, of course, but also Paddy Crerand, Nobby Stiles, Tony Dunne. They were all special in their own way.

'I've spoken to a lot of people about those days and they all say they just couldn't wait to get there, because you never knew quite what was going to happen. You always knew something was going to happen though. It must have been fantastic to have that anticipation when you are going to a match. All the players have talked about the European nights. They were so special. It's daft but I always talked about the grass being greener, but they were special nights and the grass did seem greener because of the lights. You could hear people because of the roars, but could you see them? Not really. There were just these great waves of people behind you and they were all for you. It was incredible.'

That the sense of anticipation of the unexpected was being transmitted to the players involved in the drama perhaps accounts for the gloriously exciting, live theatre that followed on the pitch. And these big European games always seemed to bring out something special in the Best, Law, Charlton triumvirate.

For the away ties, the places where United travelled to always intrigued me. Indeed, like many kids I guess, my geography skills were enhanced by recognising the positioning of football grounds on a map. This began with English grounds, of course, but then spread to European knowledge. By the mid-60s, having never been abroad, places like Madrid and Milan just sounded so darned cool and were a part of the Manchester United world. I never considered that if you supported a less successful team, your club would probably never travel further than Filbert Street or the Hawthorns. I just took it for granted that most seasons there would be European nights for us, whilst for other supporters of less successful teams this was icing on a cake they would never taste.

The 1968 European Cup journey introduced me to places I knew precious little about. They sounded very East European, film noir places where shady looking men in long gaberdine raincoats flicked their cigarettes into the gutter, put on a pair of dark sunglasses and started to follow you. When I eventually saw supporters from Yugoslavia (as it then was) and Poland they were, unsurprisingly, nothing like my perceptions of them had been. They bought Bovril and ate pies too. Nevertheless, these teams caused me to look at an atlas and I owed most of my early geographical knowledge to European football. But then, overseas travel had not really been opened up to the masses and package holidays to Majorca were regarded as exotic. Even for footballers like David Sadler, moving around in between games was not always easy:

'In 1968, on the way to the final, we travelled to places like Sarajevo and Górnik Zabrze. We didn't have phones in those days and just getting to these places was a challenge. Everything had to be set in stone from leaving Manchester. How do you explain how travel was in those days? We were told this, that and the other, but communication wasn't the best by any means.

'When you look back at that particular European run, United and Real Madrid have always had this tie-up. It has to go back to the early 50s, even possibly before that. Madrid made such an impression on Matt and Jimmy. (You always have to talk about Matt and Jimmy as the same unit.) Real Madrid had arrived in our front rooms after that final in Glasgow in 1960, when they beat Eintracht Frankfurt 7-3. I do remember that final and they looked so magnificent, in all white and with the black boots. But how fantastic was Di Stefano? He was just majestic, unbelievable. Then there was Puskas, who just strutted about the place and yet still scored four! Unbelievable.'

Names like Puskas, Di Stefano and, later, Amancio and Eusébio were just immense draws for United fans like me who craved not only foreign competition, but a broadening of horizons that travel can bring.

The arrival of George Best into the Manchester United narrative began in an insignificant enough fashion. The *Manchester Evening News* of 23 April 1963 recorded his youth-team debut thus: 'Manchester United's youth team for the fourth round of the FA Youth Cup tie with Newcastle United will have three newcomers – goalkeeper David Ikin, centre-forward David Sadler and outside-left George Best.' Jimmy Ryan recalls the arrival of George Best at Old Trafford:

'Where I grew up in Scotland, a mining village, everybody played football and there were two types of players: people who could dribble and people who were tough and tried to stop the dribblers. Every mining village in Scotland was probably the same, and you always wanted to be like Jimmy Johnstone, Jim Baxter, beating people like they did. It was the Scottish way. When I first saw George, and this might sound a funny thing to say, he looked like any other kid dribbler I had seen in Scotland in the village or the park; with George I was impressed yes, but more impressed with Willie Anderson who had an absolute rocket of a right foot and was such a strong runner. Willie was a typical English player to me. He could run and cross, not so much individual dribbles like I was doing.

'But then when I kept looking at the dribbles by George, I suddenly realised that he was very rarely losing the ball when he was dribbling. George was always much better than the people who dribbled in my village. George was a genius. It's one thing to play in the street like that, but George went in the first team and he played exactly the same way! George and I both made our debuts against West Brom. I was the year after him though, against the same full-back Graham Williams.'

Whilst George's progress at United was spectacular and he was undoubtedly being 'fast-tracked' through the club sides towards the first team, he was living an extremely sedate life at this early stage. John Cooke recalls how Best's talented feet remained planted firmly on the ground:

'George was a one off, unbelievable. But he wasn't put on any sort of pedestal at the club, he was just one of the lads. When I signed schoolboy forms, I remember the club put me into some digs in Stretford and I was only around the corner from George. In those days most digs were close to the ground.

'Even though you trained at The Cliff, the young players had to meet at Old Trafford. I stayed at Mrs Cropper's at Stretford with Jimmy Nicholson and Denis Walker. Sometimes they took me to the bowling alley at Stretford. George lived more or less opposite the alley, at Mrs Fullaway's house, and he used to go in there most nights. George once told me to come and have a go at bowling. I had never even seen a bowling alley before! George was a natural, strike after strike he got, no effort, but then he would have been outstanding at any game that involved a ball.'

Best's arrival in the first team five months later underscores the rapid progress he had made. To have seen George Best make his first-team debut on 14 September 1963 was to have witnessed history. The old story of the senior journalist advising the rookie sitting alongside him springs to mind: 'Son, don't bother recording the scoreline today, just make a note of the date.' George Best had arrived. However, George was by no means coming into a successful Manchester United team. The season before they had narrowly escaped relegation and patience was wearing thin, despite the FA Cup win. Best, like Sadler, benefitted from the fact that Busby had to react to the Charity Shield thrashing by Everton, but both players were ready for the step up.

I was ten years old when I saw George Best's debut. The day had started much like any other Saturday in the McGuire household. I had played a school match in the morning, made my way home on the 59 bus and was eating my dinner, prior to leaving for the United game against West Bromwich Albion at Old Trafford. There was no rush, and my mother and I then caught the double-decker, number-17 bus into Manchester. Going past the Embassy Club (a 'rites of passage' venue for many young people in north Manchester back in those days, including myself in my late teens) and then the cemetery just north of Cheetham Hill, I gazed out at a small park as

I always did; the reason being, this was where a murder had been committed some years previously. A young woman had been strangled there. Whereas such an event is now an almost weekly occurrence, back then it was rare and the sight of the scene always shocked me.

Passing over Piccadilly, we walked briskly to Chorlton Street to catch the onward bus to Old Trafford. When we got there, the queue was long, and the wait caused us to miss the connection. There would be another bus along in a minute or two, but we decided to walk as it was a fine day, with the weather still deciding whether to hang on to summer or morph into autumn. We never had enough money for taxis in those days, so we set off walking, down to Deansgate and then the mile and half along the Chester Road to Old Trafford. Having not done this before, we misjudged the time it would take and soon everything seemed to be a rush on this particular day. Going past the White City dog track, we could hear the different sounds coming from the crowd, telling us the game had already started. By the time we reached the end of the queue to get into the Stretford End, the match was almost ten minutes old.

A match against West Brom was not particularly special in those days and most fans regarded it as simply a necessary hurdle to get over, to obtain two points and propel us up the table. I certainly had no idea that it would be a game I would later look back on and speak to others about as an 'I was there' moment. The reason for the special nature of the occasion was being confirmed, even before we reached the top of the terrace steps and started to push our way through the massed crowd, to try to reach our favoured viewing position. The game was about 15 minutes old by then, and suddenly I heard a huge roar from the crowd, even though I could not see over the burly dockers blocking my way. 'What's happened?' I asked the old fellow who always saved a little space for us on the tall step immediately to the side of the Stretford End tunnel. Lending me his arm and hooking me up onto the step, he replied, 'It's that little number 7. George Best they call him. He's just skinned the full-back!'

I looked across the pitch to see a slender, dark-haired lad who looked so relaxed as if he was just playing with his mates in the schoolyard. The next time he got the ball, he showed it to the full-back, Graham Williams (a tough, seasoned professional and international player), and then whipped it inside of him. Williams tried his best to intimidate the youngster, but the slightly built Best was significantly faster and more skilful than his opponent. It was like a bullfighter, coolly sweeping his cape left and right as the 17-year-old reduced the veteran to crude, desperate lunges. How pleased I was to have seen that debut and to have been a part of that 50,453 crowd.

With typical incisiveness, Bobby Charlton summarised the scale of Best's achievement that day when he recalled the embarrassment he felt seeing a fellow professional and international player being beaten so repeatedly by a boy who looked far younger than his 17 years. In a more colourful, later recollection, Charlton said of Best's annihilation of Williams, 'He twisted his blood.' Matt Busby said that Best had sat impassively in the dressing room reading a programme before the game, whilst other players went through their well-rehearsed, nervy rituals. And then, as Busby later recalled, 'The match began and almost immediately the little whipper-snapper had taken the game by the scruff of the neck and was cheekily beating his man as if he had been in the First Division for ten years.'

In my own junior school world, I was a big lad for my age and long strides easily took me past other kids in school matches. I foraged forwards in straight lines, with just a little change of direction when another player got close.

Skill didn't really come into it, just size and athleticism. But seeing Best play that day unnerved me and made me realise that size may not matter as much as I had thought. He looked like a child playing in a man's game, but his skill made him look like an adult dominating a youth match. The twists and turns, the shimmies left and right, the dropped shoulders and a blistering turn of pace. Here I was watching the same game played in a different way. As an aspiring footballer, Best's debut was a revelation, but the sight frightened me too as it made me realise exactly where I was in terms of ability. 'How could I ever be as good as that lad?' I remember thinking.

On the way home from the match, we travelled aboard the packed, double-decker bus back into the centre of Manchester, being forced to sit on the top deck with the smokers, always something we tried hard to avoid. It is difficult to convey to young people of today the extent to which cigarette smoke filled the buses, trains and public places back in those days. Frequently, if you sat at the back on the top deck it would be impossible to see the front window, so dense was the acrid cloud. However, I did not mind the smoke that day, content to be a part of the excitement felt by fans who talked only about the Irish kid who had made his debut on the wing.

It says everything about the way in which Busby and Murphy nurtured their talented youngsters that Best was not selected for the next match, despite his audacious debut. But it wasn't long before Busby realised that Bob Bishop's assessment of the outrageously confident, eight-stone boy from Belfast was correct: George Best was indeed touched by genius. They had sensed this in training, of course, when he made old pros like Maurice Setters and Noel Cantwell look pedestrian, but this game was the absolute realisation that the transition to senior football would, for George Best, be a breeze. A walk in the Trafford Park.

By the mid-60s, Best had established himself at the fulcrum of the team, along with the other established greats, Law and Charlton. The club was starting to put the misery of Munich behind them, with the uttermost dream of the European Cup now starting to come into focus. George had arrived at a club only three years after the fateful Munich air crash, and to a manager almost broken in health. For the club to now be back in contention for Europe by the mid-60s, this was astonishing progress.

By 1965 George was the predominant name in British football. In the 60s he had seven separate soccer annuals devoted to him, a unique feat in those days. If you look at other books from that period, George is shown or referenced in almost every one. He was the face of football and more copies of any book or periodical would be sold if it included a picture of George Best. Breathtaking displays for United were followed up by virtuoso performances for Northern Ireland. George was the pin-up boy of English football, gaining as much attention for his looks as for his performances. Everything he touched seemed to turn to gold and he was loved and admired hugely, both within and outside the game. David Sadler was well placed to watch George develop some of his business interests outside the game:

'Later in his career, I was there when George opened the boutique in Manchester and the one he had already opened in Sale too. These were almost unknown things, footballers didn't do that type of thing then. Very early in his career he was doing a lot of advertising and off-field stuff. There had been one or two who had done a bit of this kind of thing, but nothing like George was doing. I think maybe Bobby and Denis and a few others might have had agent-type people before, but George was really the first in a serious way. His attitude to this type of work was not always the best though. I remember this agent came over from Ireland and booked George to front some Irish folk bands in about a dozen dance halls over in Ireland. We always knew where we would be with the usual match times, so George was to fly over, go to the gig on the Saturday night and if he wanted to come back to Manchester on the Sunday morning, that was fine. He would get paid for doing this, I think it was £500 for each one. Well, he did the first two and when the next match was finished I said, "You're off are you?" George said, "No, I don't fancy going." I said, "You'd better go." He said "No, I've been to the first couple." And that's how he became, he didn't always have the utmost respect for things on the outside of the game. Put him with footballers and he was fine, but not all the other stuff.

'I used to think, "Why are you not doing that? £500 is an enormous amount of money." I guess even for him that was a huge sum of money. We never discussed wages though, and I never knew what he earned, even though we were in digs and roomed together. I know we were all getting paid decent money and that was good enough. The football was the important thing. That was the thing we discussed, things like advertising sausages didn't matter. He loved his cars but he had no respect for them. If someone said the E Type was a great car he would buy one, but he was also quite happy to take a bus or taxi. It didn't bother him to have these possessions.'

From my own point of view, by the time I was 12 years old, in 1965, I was interested in anything that I perceived as being 'cool'. Obviously, The Beatles were cool, as were The Hollies and Herman's Hermits. TV programmes also gave a lot of guidance. Eliot Ness in *The Untouchables* was incredibly cool because he was good-looking, dressed well and stopped mobsters ruling Chicago. McGill, *The Man in the Suitcase*, was also cool; he solved complex criminal cases within an hour, never got flustered and, again, dressed impeccably. Certain footballers were cool. Jimmy Ryan was cool with his Mod haircut, dark hair parted at the side and long sideburns. The only United player who had longer sideburns (from what I could see from the Stretford End) was full-back Frank Kopel. He had Tom Jones-style sidepieces down to his jawbone. Embarrassingly now looking back, I declared at the time that this too was cool and examined my own paltry, facial hair in the mirror on a regular basis. Willie Anderson was definitely cool. He had long, dark hair and wore Beatles jackets. However, as the 60s wore on, the King of Cool was George Best. The dark hair, the confident smile, the well-fitting sweaters and jackets; he was the ultimate clothes horse for any garment. George Best was the epitome of 60s style and girls swooned when they saw him; cool, cool, cool. Uber cool.

A one-time youth player with Best at United, Barry Fry estimated that George could put 10,000 extra girls on the gate at Old Trafford. That's an exaggerated figure perhaps, but certainly many girls and young women became interested in the game through George rather than the football. In the mid-60s, the sounds of teenage girls was more akin to a pop concert than a soccer match. Their shrill screams were a counterpoint to the throaty roar of dockers, factory workers and railwaymen. Football had now fully emerged from the post-war period into a time of relative prosperity in the 1960s, and George Best was at the forefront of that social revolution.

The maximum wage had been abolished in 1961. Televised games increased and in 1964 *Match of the Day* was first screened, watched by 20,000 viewers. By 1966, and the World Cup Final, the figure had increased to 30 million. The media was expanding dramatically and George's explosion into the game coincided with this new phenomenon. With his sublime soccer skills and film-star looks, George was a media dream. Significantly, there was no provision at this time within football clubs to formally educate young players, and the Manchester that Best was seeing in the 1960s was not the austere, post-war city that Charlton, Edwards and Coleman had experienced in the 1950s. With training over, he had time on his hands and a new world opening before him, as football and popular youth culture collided head on.

During the mid-60s, Manchester had a burgeoning club scene, with dozens of new nightclubs having opened. So, a trip to the Gaumont cinema on Deansgate and back to digs to listen to Sinatra LPs that had sufficed for the Babes a few years earlier, was far behind what George was now being offered. The city was big, bustling and brash. The dirty rivers and canals, alongside the grubby mills, started to be flanked by trendy cafes, wine bars, bespoke fashion houses, modern hair salons and continental restaurants. Gambling dens flourished and drinking houses grew rapidly.

The sober ways of the Busby Babes and the restraints of the post-war 50s were now a long way off. By the mid-60s, Manchester was partying and so was George. Hairstyles and fashion were paramount, of course, and the Beatles mop-cut was a style copied by George and other prominent soccer stars of the day; George became the main Manchester celebrity to fuse these elements of youth culture. In the Manchester clubs, the impresarios and DJs of the Busby Babes era a few years earlier, like Jimmy Saville, were now being replaced by younger, competitive rivals in a regenerating city.

Probably George's defining moment on the field, though, will always be that memorable, heart-warming game in 1968 when Manchester United beat the mighty Portuguese champions Benfica 4-1 to win the European Cup. Prior to the game, Best and Sadler, still in digs at Mrs Fullaway's house on Aycliffe Avenue let us not forget, had been going through the match ahead. With typical youthful bravado and spirit, Best had been telling Sadler what he intended to do in the game. This amounted to how he would beat four players, nutmeg the last defender and send the keeper the wrong way as he walked the ball around him. When he reached the goal line, he would then stop, kneel down and head the ball over the line. Amazingly, the grainy clips on YouTube suggest that he was not a million miles away from executing that plan. What a goal!

A huge 60-yard punt upfield from Stepney is flicked on by Brian Kidd. Best nonchalantly collects the ball and, with his first touch, using his right foot, nutmegs the Benfica defender, whose leg swing connects only with the polluted air of north London. Best touches it with his right foot again, now heading diagonally across the face of the goal. The goalkeeper, José Henrique, sees where he is headed and swoops to drop on the ball. He has done everything correctly as, to all intents and purposes, Best is going to take the ball around him to his right and the keeper's left. Just as his hands prepare to drop on to the orange ball, Best cuts it back inside him, again using his right foot. The keeper is hopelessly committed now and made to look foolish, pouncing on thin air. He had been on an errand to collect the ball and the task looked straightforward enough. Now he is suddenly involved in damage limitation. Behind him, Best seems bored by his succession of three right touches and finishes off the move by cutting the ball inside and to goal, using his left foot this time. As it bobbles, tantalisingly, over the line, Henrique is now chasing it frantically. To his credit, he chases so hard that he slides over the goal line and finishes up embroiled in the back of the net. He now looks like a giant tuna fish caught off the Lisbon coast. Paddy Crerand used to joke with Best, over the years that followed, that the keeper was still chasing that ball. Only in his dreams did he ever get there in time.

After the goal, Best turns and raises his right arm as he runs back to the centre circle. Long before he reaches it, though, the arm has dropped and the celebration is over, as for all the players. Indeed, Best now looks almost subdued. This is an elite professional football team, the score is only

2-1, and 28 minutes of extra time remain. When George Best played that night, as for all Manchester United players in that game, he was the consummate professional. They still had a huge job to do with the likes of Eusébio on the field. However, further goals from Kidd and Charlton sealed the historic victory. When Busby embraces Best at the end of the game, it resembles a father greeting his son who has come back from the war. For both men there could never be a better moment.

When Manchester United won the European Cup in 1968, Matt Busby's dream had been realised, incredibly only ten years after Munich. George was the jewel in a glittering array of talent within the United team. But in 1968 George was only 22 years old, yet to reach full maturity in either his personal or professional life. Players such as Charlton, Foulkes, Law, Crerand and Stiles were coming towards the end of their careers. The team failed to kick on after the European win and the decade petered out, with established greats retiring and players of far lesser quality replacing them. David Sadler reflects:

'The team were allowed to get to the point where there were a lot of players looking ready to call it a day. George and I were still young, both of us only 22 years old. However, the likes of Bill, Bobby, Paddy and Denis were really struggling with injuries and these were big, important players. We weren't going to get a lot more out of them. That was the thing. They had been so critical to the team winning the league and the European Cup. Once those things were over, that team as a unit never played together again and were never likely to. There were just so many toppling over an age when they had to finish … and what better way to finish?

'Then there were players like Tony Dunne, who was for two or three years clearly the best full-back in Europe. Tony was great; we used to say he was a curler, he could never hit a straight pass, he always had some curl on it! And Shay on the other side, or Francis Burns (that was the way they split that position up), he was never a kicker. And Bill, he maximised what he had. He was the best of that team for doing that, making the most of the ability he had. Bill wouldn't fit in now, but in terms of the big games you remember, he was just so important to us.'

George could not cope with performing with lesser players, when before it had been the likes of Denis Law, Nobby Stiles, Paddy Crerand and Bobby Charlton. Individually, George's career peaked in 1968 when he became the European Player of the Year. What is indisputable, though, is that Best was a part of a remarkable team hosting three European Players of the Year. Even now such a glorious trio of players is unheard of, with perhaps only Messi, Suárez and Neymar having come somewhere close to enjoying an equivalent status.

The George Best his teammates remember was generous, modest and dedicated to football. Tony Whelan recalls an experience during his US career:

'We were training in pre-season and you were responsible for your own lunch. Maybe four or five of us would go for lunch with George to a place around the corner called Denny's, and we would just get a light pancake or similar for lunch. And George would never let you pay. By the third or fourth day one lad had had enough, so up he goes to pay and George had already put a tab on for that week and the next. That generosity is what I remember George for. He would do it quietly too. When he passed away, obviously some years later, I got a call from one of the lads and the first thing he said was about going to Denny's and George not letting us pay. That's exactly what George was like. I had the privilege of telling his son that story about a year ago when I bumped into him here.

'George was just lovely and I have the warmest regard for him. Obviously, his football talent was immense, I've never seen anybody take the ball like him, and a generous footballer in terms of the praise he gave other players and how he rarely criticised others. A thoroughly decent human being, a warm-hearted man. He was a terrific trainer, too. Always in the top three in running. I just remember thinking, "Wow, George Best, look at his fitness, look at his physique", and what a work ethic he had. George was very respectful, too. Once I was left in charge of eight players who were injured and in rehab, whilst the team were away playing a match. George was among them. He just got on with his work without any complaint doing his running, press-ups, sit-ups, not a problem.'

On the day of George's funeral, an estimated 500,000 mourners lined the way as the coffin was driven through the streets of East Belfast. On the way to Stormont, a large, paramilitary wall mural was covered up as a sign of respect, with seemingly every section of society united in grief. The funeral car was bombarded with flowers and scarves, as the Belfast Boy made his final journey, to be buried in the same grave as his mother, Annie.

George was often described as a 'flawed genius' and, for some observers, a serious personality flaw is essential to fit their definition of the term genius. Personally, I don't agree with the analysis. We have never had Roger Federer around for dinner, but he seems the perfect sportsman and his tennis achievements the best in living memory. Whatever the merits of the argument, it is fair to say that the concept of genius is difficult to define, and also that it is perhaps more usually associated with the mind rather than the body. I simply know that in my seven decades on this earth I have seen only one genius in the flesh. He usually wore either number 7 or 11 on a bright-red shirt, had long hair and did things on a football field that no one else has done since he played his last game for Manchester United.

Mozart was only 35 when he died. He was once dismissed from his position at the Salzburg court and was touted around

Europe as a child protégé by his father. Yet neither of these facts are what people remember most about Mozart, they remember only his music. And, in a similar fashion, respect should be shown for the football genius who was George Best. Predicting his legacy, George once said, 'They'll forget all the rubbish when I've gone and they'll remember the football.' Rest assured, dear George, anyone who saw you play and who loves the game of football, whatever their club affiliations, will always have that uppermost in their minds.

Chapter 12
Time Passages

7 May 1968: Truth will out

Three weeks before Manchester United's 1968 European Cup Final victory, my mother decided to educate me about something I already knew: no child could legitimately have so many uncles. Even excluding my imaginary Uncle Gigi, I still seemed to have more uncles than a person ever needed. In addition to my insanely handsome, flamboyant Uncle Tommy, I had other more ordinary uncles who would come over from Ireland from time to time. 'What are the chances?' I used to think when pondering why I had more uncles than those of all my friends put together.

The oldest was Uncle Willie, who was many years senior to my dad and probably in his late 70s when I knew him. He was short, kind, humorous, walked with a limp and always had a drop of blackcurrant in his half pint of Guinness. He was not a big drinker and I liked that since I knew he would not cause trouble. Kind and sober worked well for me (and still does). He just enjoyed a tipple from time to time. Then there was Uncle Ted, who was frequently referred to as Ned, causing my young children to grow up thinking these were two separate

people. He was far younger than Willie: a vigorous, happy soul who chain-smoked, drank Jameson whiskey and worked the family farm in County Mayo. Ted seemed to have an amazing capacity for consuming drink, but I never saw him drunk. I guess he had been weaned on pocheen made on the family farm. Ted's wife, Eileen, who was a nurse, cooked and cared for Willie who lived with them for many years.

I liked Ted and Willie, but whenever they visited us in Manchester it was hard for me to work out the relationship that both men had with my dad; Willie was impassive, while Ted seemed to want little to do with him. As with Tommy, there seemed to be resentment from the past, something that had happened in Ireland before my dad had started his English adventures. Sometimes arguments about the family farm in Mayo would crop up. The farm and land were originally of modest value, but in the Celtic Tiger period they later came to represent very valuable real estate. However, the resentmen
was about something even greater than this, I concluded
could never have asked my dad outright what the reasons w
we did not have that type of relationship.

Both Ted and Willie spoke with heavy, west of Ir
accents which I always found interesting. Their voices
to rise and fall rhythmically with every sentence a
was looking for the humour in any given situation
recounting a story about the intellectual abili
compared to donkeys or describing the poor food
ride across the Irish Sea. However, as soon as m
in any conversation, their humour seemed to
it was meant for the others in the room but n
sorry for him when this happened.

Having an excess of uncles wasn't
gig, since they often arrived with smal
important contributions to the McGui
when times were hard, which they freq

just when I thought I was in danger of becoming 'The Man From Uncle', shortly before the trip to Wembley for the European Cup Final in 1968, this exceptional number of uncles was explained.

This long story (which certainly wasn't the first concerning my dad) began with my mum outlining the early years of my dad's life before he began his tour of England. After his expulsion from the Catholic Brothers' school, his Republican adventures in the 1916 Easter uprising and resulting skirmishes with the Black and Tans, Dad had married his first wife in the 1920s, with whom he had five children. I never knew that and listened intensely. When his wife died young, instead of facing up to the reality of the situation, he abandoned his five young children, caught the ferry to Liverpool and interchanged the names Maguire and McGuire when it suited his ends. He did not want to be found. Each child went to a different home, except Ted who stayed on the family farm to be raised by Willie, Dad's brother. Whiskey helped Dad to forget the past, although he never told me that in 'the living years', like so many other things in his life.

Thus, the resentment felt towards my dad which I could sense from family members was perfectly understandable, and with all five children from that first marriage (my half-siblings) now passed, maybe some of that ill feeling remained with them all until the end. I hope not, but who could blame them if it did? This was rural Ireland in the 1920s when he walked out, and the taking-in of five hungry children would ave been beyond the capability of any one family. In truth, ealing with the needs of five young children by himself must ave been a terrifying thought too. Certainly, it was more an he wanted to cope with. Ireland then was an extremely or country and help would have been very limited. Thus, children were placed here and there, with one finishing iving with a family in a lighthouse. Sadly all of them knew

little about either their birth mother or father. Life must have been extremely difficult for each one of them.

It was this situation that my dad had been running from all his life. From trying to drink his way out of the problem, through to his 'marriage' to my mum and beyond, he could never outrun his past though, and his last days were characterised by poor health and bitter regrets. One day I walked into his bedroom to find him kneeling at his bedside with his rosary beads in his hands, crying and praying. It wasn't the colourful, ebullient dad I had known all those years.

From my point of view, I probably got the best deal of all his children. His drink problem was the most I ever had to face and for the most time he was a kind father, even if he never did any of the traditional father-son things. Certainly not football. I would have remembered that. The police never pursued the bigamy charges against him any further. Now, after this latest revelation, suddenly I had a more believable number of uncles; I also now had four half-brothers and a half-sister.

To be quite honest, though, approaching the age of 15, with the European Cup Final beckoning and having got used to expecting the unexpected in our family, this new discovery disturbed me very little. As a child, I had benefitted from having a terrific team of decent, dependable others around me. I was progressing well with my football and had become quite a confident young man. Teams and community were important to me then, and still are. Manchester United and their sensational Trinity had certainly helped too.

Also, the anticipated excitement of that May evening in the capital city, and a momentous victory, was all-consuming. I was seriously into pop music, too, and the charts were full of fabulous tracks like 'Jennifer Eccles' by The Hollies, 'Can't Take My Eyes Off You' by the uber-cool Andy Williams, 'Lazy Sunday' by The Small Faces and the superlative 'What a Wonderful World' by Louis Armstrong at number one. Little did I know that on 28 May 1968 Matt Busby would be serenading his players and their families with that song, at the victory celebration at London's Russell Hotel. What I would have given to have witnessed the old man crooning those lyrics; I think I would probably have traded my match ticket for that, since I knew from the outset we would win. I was nearly 15, with the world before me. We were Manchester United and we had Best, Law and Charlton. We would win, even without the Lawman who, sadly, was injured. It just had to be. As David Sadler said, 'It was written.'

7 July 1984: Mending bridges

The look of utter shock on my dad's face told me that death was not what he had expected on this fine Saturday morning. Later, I was given the contents of his suit pockets, which amounted to a crisp white handkerchief, some house keys, two Uncle Joe's and £7.25 in loose change. He was on his way from the pub to catch a taxi when he dropped down dead in the street. Had he caught the taxi he would have had under a fiver on him, all the money he possessed in the world. No savings, no endowments, no occupational pension, no insurance policies, not even a wallet. Money went straight into his pocket and straight out again, usually to the bartender of the Lever's Arms and other local watering holes. One pub put a plaque up on the wall in his honour; they owed him that for he certainly improved their takings each week. Despite money constantly being a problem for him, he always wore a good suit, a smart pair of shoes and a clean white shirt and tie, with a fancy tiepin. He never had money but showed plenty of style. I liked that about him.

The week before his death, Gerry and I had taken him back to his County Mayo roots. He had met three of his abandoned sons and put to bed at least some of the resentment from the past. Enough at least for civility, cordial handshakes and a shared drink or two. He was too old by now for trouble and his demeanour begged empathy not condemnation. He had Parkinson's disease, advanced prostate cancer and a world-weary look in his eyes. They sparkled a little after a glass or two of sweet Irish whiskey and overall he enjoyed the trip, but his zest for life had gone and the stress of the awkward reunions had weakened him. It was his time.

One day we visited Cong, the village where the cult movie *The Quiet Man,* starring John Wayne (Dad's favourite actor), was shot in 1952. The village was, endearingly, still living in the past and we did the usual tourist thing of buying posters and other memorabilia. We walked around the imposing, nearby Ashford Castle where my mother and father had visited on their honeymoon. On another day we drove to Croagh Patrick, a Catholic Pilgrimage mountain site, overlooking beautiful Clew Bay and Clare Island. As the sun set, he rested his stick and leaned on the iron gates at the bottom of the hill, puffing away on a cigarette whilst watching me climb the slope. He may have looked far younger than his 47 years when he married, but he looked much older now than his 81 years, at the end of his life. His appetite was poor and even his capacity for drink had faded.

The crossing of the Irish Sea had been rough on the way home. Earlier in his life the challenge would have been met with a couple of pints of Guinness and a full Irish breakfast, but not this time. He lay in his cabin and seemed to feel the jolts of each of the harsh waves in turn. On the Thursday, two days before his death, we said our goodbyes as we dropped him off at his beloved 'little shack' on Oldham Road. I kissed him on his stubbly cheek as he flicked the ash from his cigarette into a saucer and thanked us for taking him on his final journey 'home', to Ireland. He meant it. It was the last time I saw him alive.

He would never arrive home drunk again, never upset our mother again and never spend all the family money on drink. But he would also not bring sweets home on a Thursday night again, he wouldn't play 'Danny Boy' on the mouth organ, he would never paint our lightbulbs again and I wouldn't feel the rough bristles on his chin as I kissed him goodnight. I often think of my dad and the way in which drink changed what he thought, what he did, who he was. What had once been a friend had become a master. I loved my dad but hated what alcohol had done to him. I could perhaps understand a little of George Best's sad ending, having seen the effect drink had on my own father. I hated, too, the burden of guilt my dad had always carried and what it had done to him.

4 February 1995: 'No Georgie Best there …'

I took my mum to her last-ever game at Old Trafford on this day. It was a present for her 65th birthday. United played Aston Villa and ground out a hard-fought 1-0 victory with a goal from Andy Cole. The previous time she had watched the Reds play was the European Cup Final at Wembley in 1968, although her last visit to Old Trafford was in 1965.

For this birthday treat, we had good seats kindly arranged for us by Billy Garton, another ex-United player (from the 80s) who I had been teaching on a physical education teacher training course. So, the gap in terms of watching United at Old Trafford, from my mum's point of view, was nearly 30 years. We were seated in the North Stand as it was then, or the Sir Alex Ferguson Stand as it is now known. Back in my mum's mind, though, were the shallow terrace steps and a little later the state-of-the-art 'Cantilever Stand'. The seats were excellent, directly opposite the halfway line and close to the front. Looking around the stadium, I could see her mind thinking back to when the pie seller used to walk around the cinder track, which enclosed the field of play. The ground was now 'of the time' she said approvingly, whilst I sensed a little sadness when she looked over to the Stretford End and remembered those swaying masses, the white wooden fencing and Ronny the dodgy ticket man.

When the match commenced, she studied the play carefully before making her shrewd observations, comparing what she was seeing in a then-developing United team with the majesty of the Trinity days. After one powder-puff shot (to use David Meek's classic line) barely trickled through to the Villa keeper, she opined, 'Well … he's no Bobby Charlton is he!' On another occasion a looped cross begged to be met by a powerful header. When it wasn't, she exclaimed in a voice loud enough for the first three rows to hear, 'Denis Law would have got that!'

At the end of the game we walked down the steep steps and out into the cold winter night. She marvelled at how quickly the stadium emptied and how civilised the crowd was, compared to the mid-60s. The Warwick Road of her memory was somewhat edgier, with the crowd more boisterous and probably a little drunker. The fan base was more middle-class now, she concluded. She was right. We walked on and on until we reached the car park at Old Trafford Cricket Ground. (The idea of her now walking the length of even Sir Matt Busby Way is unthinkable, let alone to the home of Lancashire cricket.) She had loved the birthday treat but I could tell it wasn't the same excitement for her as 'back in the day'. Summing up the occasion, she said tartly, 'There's no Georgie Best there is there?' We hadn't caught the Reds on a good night for sure, and the great Treble side of 1999 was some way off, but then in another sense she was right wasn't she, there isn't another Georgie Best anywhere is there?

21 November 2018: 'Oh … David Sadler'

I was coming towards the end of my weekly visit to see my mum in the residential home where she now lives, high above

Middleton town centre. The library where she met my dad is 100 yards below the home, and the statue of Samuel Bamford is 200 yards away, facing out towards St Peter's Field and the Old Trafford floodlights. I started to gather my belongings together, ensuring that I had given her everything she needed until my next visit: the Nobby Stiles autobiography *After the Ball*, a jar of Manuka honey and three bags of sweets. Still a devoted 60s United fan, she had earlier read and enjoyed *Cissie*, and Sir Bobby's *My Manchester United Years*.

She forgets one or two things these days, but not worryingly so, and we always laugh through the situation. It's never awkward. If I ring and ask what she had for lunch, she pauses, then usually says, 'I can't remember.' She then always adds, 'I had something.' I usually say in mock anger, 'I know you had something, but what?' and she will laugh. This time, just as I was walking towards the door, I remembered something I knew she would want to know. 'By the way,' I said, '… next Monday I am going to interview David Sadler for the book.' As quick as a flash, she replied, 'Oh … David Sadler. I liked him! He was a good clean player.' She struggled to remember what she had for lunch three hours ago, but could be back in the swaying, boozy, smoky, friendly, sweary, uproarious Stretford End of 1965 in an instant.

The wooden scoreboard is opposite. The 'Kilvert's Pure Lard' sign is in the distance beyond. Bobby has just let fly with a thunderbolt. Denis has defied gravity to hang menacingly still in the damp Manchester air, before rocketing home a header. George has just left a full-back longing for early retirement. 'Great days,' she says, 'great days.' They were indeed.

Chapter 13

Playing Memories and Legacy

THE term 'legends' is much over-used these days and its worth devalued. But if ever the term fitted any players, it would be the United Trinity of George Best, Denis Law and Bobby Charlton. Magnificent to watch, exemplary performers for young players to study, and hugely impressive as personalities, their legacy will last for all time. Perhaps, though, always listing them as 'Best, Law and Charlton' suggests that a rank order is implied. Nothing could be further from the truth. All were wonderful, virtuoso performers, with unique yet complementary talents. Deliberately mixing the order of quotes a little here, I asked their contemporaries from Manchester United to recall their own favourite memories of the unique trio:

DAVID SADLER:

DENIS

'I don't think I was fortunate enough to play with Denis in his prime. I think that must have come either at his City spell after

Huddersfield or at Torino. But he just had this phenomenal nose for goal and the opposition absolutely hated playing against him. They knew they were in for a physical afternoon, but why would they think that? He was only nine and a half stone! But they were right. Physically, he could intimidate people. He would just go out and score, getting ten a season from three or four yards because he was the quickest one to react. He would do that every season. It wasn't luck, he just had something special. There were times when Denis wanted to move away from being a striker; I know he wanted to play deeper. There's one goal where he picks it up just outside our box from the keeper, an attacker comes in and he goes this way, another comes in and he goes that way, and then, as he's getting near to the tacklers, he plays a quick pass and he's suddenly ten yards past the defender yelling for the ball. He then knocks it in and yet it had started from way back. I have listened to people who have known Denis for longer than me and they say when he was 17 or 18, at Huddersfield, and he wasn't just the goalscorer, he was the complete footballer.'

BOBBY

'Look at what Bobby had been through with Munich. He was a quiet, reserved guy who expressed all he wanted to do through his football. He didn't make a big fuss of you as a new lad, even when he was the captain. He didn't come over and say, "Do this" or "Do that". He was quite difficult to get to know in the early days, but then we were years apart in age. We were in different parts of our lives. We were just starting out and he had lived the lives of I don't know how many people. He walked out of an aeroplane crash for goodness sake, just incredible things he had been through in his life, even by 1963.

'In training, he was first out and last back, not always literally but often. If Alex wanted to do some crosses, Bobby would be there saying, "Let me do it. I'll knock the crosses in." Different types of crosses, he would just do them all. At United, Bobby and George were real athletes. George was the same in many ways as Bobby, a great trainer.

'In terms of being two-footed, Bobby would be the best in that category as he would score as many 30 yarders with his left as with his right. He just struck the ball so perfectly. Phenomenal. Jimmy Murphy didn't talk about anything other than football, and when speaking about Bobby he would always talk about how smoothly he moved around the pitch.'

GEORGE

'George wasn't in the team at the start of the 1963/64 season, but he was showing enough in training, it was just a matter of time. He was pretty frail compared to most, but there was never a moment's doubt about his ability. You knew that first-team and then international football would happen, but there was just that doubt about his build, whether he could take the physical side. However, as soon as he played in the reserves it was very clear there wasn't going to be a problem. I think the way I progressed was fairly normal, getting the odd game here and there, getting tougher and stronger. With George it was a question of how quickly he would progress. He got left out the odd game, but he pretty much flew on from there. You just couldn't stop him.

'With George, I think it was the first week I was there, Jimmy Murphy said in this gruff voice, "I've seen some things ... but in this last few weeks I've seen something new. George plays two-touch and he knows you're coming in and he knocks the ball against you, and the ball drops over there, and he runs on to that ... he's playing two-touch on his own! I've never, ever seen anything like this!" George was in with Bill Foulkes, Maurice Setters and Noel Cantwell, all big old pros, who had been around and didn't want any of that going on. He would beat Maurice, as he lumbered about, and I'm sure George must have run underneath his legs sometimes! It was such fun to watch, incredible.

'As for the goals, I remember one at Arsenal where George took it past just about everyone, and I was at his shoulder and simply knocked it in. He wasn't very happy about that as he had done all the hard work, running the length of the field with the ball! He scored some incredible goals. It became where you just never thought that something wasn't possible because he could do anything, even though what you had just seen two seconds ago wasn't realistic. I could score in all the levels on the way up, but at that very top level I couldn't do it. But I was fortunate enough that people stuck with me and I could play somewhere else, which I could do competently enough. But with George, he was the best player in every position, I think. He could have done as well as Tony Dunne did at full-back, for example.

'You could not intimidate Denis, Bobby or George and they had their own ways of sorting out things. George's way was to have this arrogance, particularly with people who just knew no better than to try and kick lumps out of him. There were a number of players who earned livings out of playing football like that, which is really no way to play. George liked nothing better than to turn around and go past them again, he loved taunting them. He was the matador with the cape all over again. "You think you can get it? Come on then!" He would take it away from them and ask, "Can you get it now?" George was so two-footed, as all the greats are.

'You couldn't injure him, he wouldn't let you know you'd hurt him; he wouldn't scream or shout or go down. If you kicked him and knocked his feet from under him, he would just bounce straight back up in the blink of an eye. And if you thought you'd got the ball, you hadn't, because in the next second he was up and he had got the ball back and then he would taunt you. What could we defenders do? The ball had gone and he'd gone! He was two or three yards the other side of us now and he made us look like idiots. He was just phenomenal.

'Then there was George's debut when he was up against the West Brom full-back, Gareth Williams, who was as wide as he was tall! An unbelievable debut. And then George against Benfica: incredible, just incredible. You look at it now and you think, "How could he do that? How could he do stuff like that?" He made top-quality players look silly. Of course, by 1968 things had really started to change with George, but what a player he was. It's hard to make people believe how good he was, there's so little footage around and it is just little bits and pieces of the same film.'

JOHN COOKE:

DENIS

'I remember one game against Spurs involving Denis, who was always on the edge of being offside. Alex Stepney volleyed the ball upfield to Denis, who had just gone offside. The linesman flagged, and Denis caught the ball and turned around to Pat Jennings. Denis suddenly volleyed it from his hands into the goal. Obviously, no goal, but what a showman. The crowd loved it. The swagger and the goal celebrations. The raised arm, holding his sleeve. And, of course, that goal for City. The first non-goal celebration really. I still see Denis through the Old Boys' Association. What a player he was. No one better in the air than Denis. He used to have this great spring, the way he used to hang in the air. Then there were some of the goals he scored for Scotland. Unbelievable.'

BOBBY

'Bobby, what a player! Two wonderful feet, a rocket shot in both. What a player. What a trio: Best, Law and Charlton.

You couldn't wish for three better players, or three better men or better role models. Three European Players of the Year in one team at the same time. You just can't beat that. What a special time.'

GEORGE

'A training ground we used in those so-called glory days of the 60s was the Ship Canal pitch. When this was used, all the senior players would get changed at Old Trafford, and a couple of selected apprentices would serve them with tie-ups, plasters and Vaseline and whatever else they needed prior to the sessions. One day it was my turn to wait on the first-team players along with another apprentice, Brian Kidd. The morning began by helping Jack Crompton get all the kit out for the players. While we waited for the players to return from the Ship Canal pitch, we headed up to the top of the main stand, where there was enough space to sharpen our skills with some head tennis and other games we played like "Wally". [Here the aim was to make the ball hit the wall at a such a speed or angle that it made your opponent's subsequent shot difficult to return.] There were no hospitality boxes in those days, just a concrete passageway and girders supporting the roof. At around 11.30am, Kiddo and I would go back downstairs to make two pots of tea for the returning senior players.

'On one such occasion George said to us, "Cookie, Kiddo, get two bags of balls and come out on the pitch with me." Down the old tunnel we went, under what is now the South Stand, and turned left for the Stretford End. George told us to stand behind the goals and fag [return] the balls for him. We had 20 balls, 10 in each bag. George then proceeded to hit inswinging corners with his right foot from the corner where the "new" tunnel is now, but what was then the Stretford End Paddock. They were going in like rockets, one after the other, until all 20 had found the net. Not content with such perfection, George then walked to the other corner flag and started hitting the other 20 balls with his left foot. Twenty more inswinging corners found their way into the back of the net. Whenever I meet Kiddo, he often starts the conversation by asking whether I am still telling the inswinging corners story! One Saturday, following such a routine the day before, I went to watch the first team play at West Brom away from home, where Best repeated the feat, bending a corner into the net with two minutes to go. After the ball had rocketed into the top corner of the net, Jimmy Hill said on TV that it was a "fluke goal from George Best". However, there was no luck about it.

'George would be a sensational player in today's game, or any other era, whilst fitting into the Brazilian style of play particularly well. I remember another game, during the Docherty era, when George was making a comeback, playing on the left wing at Old Trafford. Even in that condition George was still outstanding, a different type of player, without the long, mazy dribbles but still able to cross immaculately and use the ball creatively. The press did not always help George. I just remember him only as the nicest of people, modest, friendly and sensational as a player. But that could be said of all three of them: George, Denis or Bobby.

'Of course, when George got dressed up there was no one like him. I used to see George's latest haircut and think, "Wow. He looks good. We're going to win tonight!" We used to stand up at the back of the stand, me and Kiddo, and watch. I remember one game when George was just out of this world. Every time he got the ball the girls and women used to scream, a loud, shrill noise. It was like a pop star was playing! I used to think, "What on earth is going on here?" So sad that we did not have the knowledge to protect George then, because of course we had never seen a player like him. But there is so much rubbish written about George and people should just remember him for the football. What a player he would have been had he gone to a World Cup.'

CLIFF BUTLER:

DENIS

'Denis Law ... well, from day one there was just something about him! He just looked the part, he looked different to other players. There weren't a lot of blond-haired players for one thing. I always remember when he first signed for us. There's a famous photo of him in training and his boots are completely different to anybody else's, they've got no marks on them anywhere and they were obviously Italian. He did bring a lot of swagger back with him from Italy and it made him into a world star. There was just something about Denis, the way he held his cuffs, he was just different. He wasn't a big man either, quite slight, but with his tenacity and speed, what a wonderful player. By a street, a motorway even, he was my favourite player!'

BOBBY

'Bobby, of course, had come through things with Munich, but really all three of them were completely different characters. Bobby was especially liked by the older fans, many of whom had grown up with him over the Munich period. Bobby, Denis and George were all unbelievable. Nearly every match was magical if those three were playing.'

GEORGE

'George Best ... well, in my humble opinion, the greatest player of all time. Absolutely incredible footballer and one of the nicest people you could ever hope to meet, so humble, so decent, softly spoken. I met him two or three times, only briefly, but a beautiful man. With a football at his feet, he just twisted the defender's blood, so wonderfully talented. In the European Cup Final in '68 his socks were down to his ankles, just a terrific player. With George, until Barcelona and Manchester City came on the scene in recent years, most people thought the 1970s team that Brazil took to the World Cup probably had the best 11 players: Pele, Rivelino, Jairzinho and so on. But if George Best had been in that team they wouldn't have noticed anyone else. He *was* Brazilian in his own way. I was at a reserves game at Northampton pre-season and talking to a lad in the press box. I realised he was a similar age to me. I said to him, "You were there in '69 weren't you?" He said, "Was I there? Here's the team," and he reeled off all the names. "What a day that was, what a player he was," he said to me. You should have seen the pitch that day, it was like the Somme. We both agreed he was the greatest player that ever lived, George scoring six that day in an 8-2 win. What would George have done on these pitches nowadays? It doesn't bear thinking about.'

JIMMY RYAN:

DENIS

'I do remember playing indoors with Denis at The Cliff and thinking how he used to play one-touch often, quick as a flash, playing the ball and then moving straight away. He was so sharp. He was so brave and so very quick-thinking. You had to be just as sharp to play with him and give him the return balls to run on to. He was so aggressive and with anybody, Bobby Moore, whoever, it didn't matter. Bobby must have been four or five inches taller, but Denis was so aggressive, however big they were. The first time I saw Denis, he came down to Old Trafford the first week I was there. I was down there to clean the boots. Some of the first-teamers were still there and I saw

Denis hammering balls against these double doors, the ones that led out on to the pitch from the tunnel. Someone was throwing the balls to him and he's absolutely walloping them: bang, bang, bang! He was like lightning. After about five or six of these rockets hitting the door every time, the ball popped! I could hear the air coming out and they weren't old balls either. I remember thinking, "I don't think my shooting has this kind of power!" That was the first time I had seen him, and it was enough for me.'

BOBBY

'Bobby had great acceleration and power. He had this way of stopping and then accelerating powerfully, leaving the defender for dead. He was so smooth. I used to try and copy what he did, as I did with Denis. Bobby as a player was as smooth as treacle. His shooting was explosive and he was such a hard runner. When we used to have these 40-yard races he was off the mark so quickly, as were Denis and George too. Bobby was a bit reserved, but he had been through such a lot with Munich; I got on terrifically well with him. I mean, the Busby Babes were like gods to me.

'These young kids playing in the first team, winning the league. They were all legends to me. Bobby, Harry Gregg, Billy Foulkes, they had all been through the same things. Bobby never spoke much about it, but I remember once flying to Australia on tour and on the way into Perth it was very bumpy. I could see Bobby from where I was sitting, and he was shaken.

'I had a great experience with Bobby and Nobby Stiles. They were both fantastic with me. Nobby was like a big brother. One day Bobby said to me, "I'm playing golf tomorrow. Do you want to come and caddy for us?" I thought, "It's a lovely day and I'm not doing anything here. Why not?" Then he introduces me to the most famous batsman who has ever lived, Sir Donald

Bradman! I didn't know the first thing about cricket, but I was thinking, "Wow. Sir Donald Bradman!" Bobby, Nobby, Shay, they were older than me, a different generation, but they were looking after me. Here I am caddying in a four-ball between Bobby, Nobby, Shay and Sir Donald Bradman! Bobby, Nobby and Shay were like the Three Cavaliers, they just bounced off each other. On the way to New Zealand we had a ten-hour stopover and I went down to the beach. I didn't put any suntan lotion on and got sunburnt. I was in absolute agony. In the hotel I was sharing a room with Nobby, and after about an hour in comes Nobby with a bottle of something, blue stuff that went powdery. He had been to the chemist. He made me take a couple of aspirins and then he puts this stuff all over my back. I'd played about six games for United and he'd won the World Cup. I just thought it was amazing. He didn't have to do that. What can you say? There was definitely affection in the club at that time. It was like a family.'

GEORGE

'What separated George from the other dribblers I had seen as kids was that George could do it at any level. George was very dedicated, he trained so hard. In fact, I should have picked it up from him! Training exhausted me and I wasn't going to be racing up the front. George was at the front of the line. Occasionally, George would nutmeg you and sometimes I would think he's a bit like a Scottish player, Eddie Gray or Jim Baxter maybe. The village where I lived was largely divided into Protestant and Catholic, and my village had a Boys' Brigade team. Rangers buses would come to one village and Celtic buses to another. That way I saw some good games.

'I subbed for George once or twice and for Denis at least once, but it never bothered me what the crowd thought of not seeing them, as I was just intent on getting through the game.

I think having George there to get past maybe did affect my career, but it's not something I regret. I probably regret a lot more that I did not train as hard as I could have done. I never really thought, "George is keeping me out here." It was only later on at Luton that I trained really hard as the penny had dropped.

'Playing against George in the US, his girlfriend introduced herself to me and then I spoke with George. I said to him, "We'll meet up in Dallas, I'll come and see you at your hotel." I drove down to the hotel the night before the game, which was scheduled for the afternoon of the next day. I went in and asked for "Mr Best". The receptionist called George's room. There was no answer. It was about 7pm. I looked all round the hotel before walking down these stairs and there's a table there, with all the Los Angeles players drinking. Bobby McAlinden was there sitting beside George. Back home, we used to meet the City lads like Bobby McAlinden in town in the 60s. I was maybe with Bobby Smith or Alan Wardle or George then. Bobby wasn't drinking but all the rest of the team were. I said to George, "George, you know it's hot here in Dallas." He said, "It's hot in Los Angeles too." He didn't realise that the Dallas heat is so different to Los Angeles. We even had to take our drinks in the shade. I said, "George, it's *really* hot here!" Come the game and in 15 minutes we were 3-0 up! The drinking the night before just wrecked the team, but even then George scored two goals before he tired towards the end of the game!'

WILF MCGUINNESS:

DENIS

'Denis didn't say a lot, he just got his job done. He was a goalscorer. He cost a lot of money but even he had to learn the United way. He had that certain style too, where he used to hold his cuffs. What a great buy he was. Denis could kick you if he had to. He could give you a whack!'

BOBBY

'Bobby's parents would come and stay at our house in Blackley, and sometimes I went to stay with Bobby up in Northumberland. They were special days and Bobby was such a great player. When we were playing for England Boys at Wembley, aged 15 years, it was just terrific. When Bobby played in that youth team we all knew he was going to be special. He had such a powerful shot, never great in the air, but could he hit a ball! He didn't have to head it! Bobby was special. He played out wide for England Boys then. When he got to United, he had David Pegg in front of him, who was an amazing player, able to go past players on the inside or outside. Bobby did National Service and he was always very correct, very quietly spoken. Bobby would come to our house and he would just sit in the corner and read the paper. He was so shy. Bobby was a star and had already promised United he would sign. Bobby was the best player in the England Schools team, but I was the second best! I've always had confidence! Bobby was a star, a relative of the Milburn footballing family, of course.

'I always expected Bobby to be a great player, but then I expected to be one too! I had captained England Boys after all. He was better than me, of course he was, but I was still captain! Bobby would just drop his shoulder and do the body swerve, and he would go this way and the defender went that way. He was class, just class. He was two-footed. He was not a great tackler, I had to do that for him! Seriously, Bobby was a terrific player and we were great friends. We always thought Bobby would blossom into a great player and he did. He could run with it at speed, turn with it, finish with a tremendous shot; he had everything you would ever want in a player. He might be England's best-ever player, but he wouldn't like you saying that.

'We used to go on holiday to Pontins holiday camp at Prestatyn. Can you imagine that happening now? People say Bobby can be a bit aloof, but he couldn't afford to be with the other players and all the mickey taking. No, Bobby was good fun and it was a great time.'

GEORGE

'George was just a genius. I remember him coming as a kid. We had brought him over from Ireland and you could tell he was going to make it. I had finished playing then after breaking my leg. I remember thinking, "We've got a special one here!" so perhaps it was as well I had retired before facing him! He never had any nerves, or at least he never showed them. But he was as quiet as could be. Stories went around about George later on that just weren't true. What a player he was. What a dribbler.

'The coaches didn't mess with his style either. They knew to leave that alone and not tinker with it. Every goal he scored was special. Every opponent was frightened of him. He took a dip in form for a while and then he blossomed. He was the star, but he never behaved like a big shot. It wouldn't have been allowed at United.'

TONY WHELAN:

DENIS

'As a young player I always admired Jimmy Greaves, but I thought Denis was amazing too, the sharpness of his finishing. He was sheer class. His heading was immense. Pele was probably the first foreign player I really watched and admired. Then there was Puskas. But in the 60s, I saw Denis Law and just thought, "Wow!" I always remember him scoring the goal in the '63 Cup Final and then I remember going to Old Trafford and him scoring a goal on the far post. He just used to hang in the air. And the way he celebrated his goals, he was unique. He was just immensely inspirational with a mischievous personality, which I loved! I remember he was on the treatment table a lot because I knew him towards the end of his career, but when he was fit he was brilliant. I don't think I really saw him in his prime. I always remember him scoring an amazing goal for Scotland against England at Hampden. As a kid at school, Denis was my hero even though I was a City fan.'

BOBBY

'I happen to think that the best goal I have ever seen was Bobby's in the '66 World Cup against Mexico. He picks it up in his own half, the way he turns, slaloms and glides down the pitch before hitting the ball sublimely into the top corner – staggering! In the circumstances, too, it was so important. It's the second game and England haven't scored yet, and then he scores a goal like that. I don't think I've ever seen a better goal. Bobby Charlton was completely unselfish; he just gave everything for the team and the club. I think that's the thing that marks him out. Not just in terms of his football, but also in terms of what he had to overcome. He understood United and the highest of standards required at the club. Bobby symbolised, indeed embodied, the club's greatness.'

GEORGE

'Even on the tours, George would say, "Well done" or "Good pass that" and you'd think, "Wow, George Best just said that to me!" You don't need a coach to reinforce it if George said that. So I always had a lot of time for George. I thought he was lovely, and when I played with him at Fort Lauderdale Strikers in 1978 he hadn't changed in that sense. In terms of the football, we had a goalkeeper called Arnie Mauser who played for the US national team, quite a big guy, about six foot two. Well, he did the Beckham chip on him (years before Beckham) and he wasn't that far off his line. The goals weren't full size because it was only a three-quarter pitch. And George chips him from the halfway line and everyone is going, "Wow!" but George is so nonchalant, as if to say, "It's just what I do." No arrogance about him at all. We restarted the game (a scrimmage they called it in America) and within five minutes he'd done it again! To his eternal credit, the coach Dave Chadwick just said, "That's it, we've finished the game," saying you just couldn't carry on playing after seeing that. And I always remember that nobody went in. Everyone was just standing there talking about what they had seen, asking George about what he had done. It was one of the most fantastic things I had ever seen in my football career.'

THE UNITED TRINITY : THE LEGACY

We all remember Best, Law and Charlton for their footballing abilities. I was probably a bit quirky as a child in terms of also seeing personality traits in my heroes, which may or may not have been present and with no accurate way of ever truly finding out. That was just me, whilst the fantasy definitely helped me get through childhood and develop into a (reasonably) sane human being.

In terms of evaluating their playing legacy, during my research I found it heartening to know that there is still, in our modern football world, a continuing attempt being made to learn from these three giants of the game: George Best, Denis Law and Bobby Charlton. Tony Whelan's words sum up the treasures that these greats left behind at Manchester United:

'I think the thing about those three players is that they are inter-generational. They have qualities that cross generations. They have human qualities that endure and abide; it's what they gave to a public audience at that time, a Manchester public and also an international public. They all had a wonderful gift and they each expressed it in their own way. The fact that all three were different and had different gifts is wonderful. You can take a little bit of each one and sprinkle it on everybody. We would want all of our players to have something of all three of them within themselves. Certainly, the self-expression is the thing about them that I would want to give to young players, the way they expressed their personalities through their football. The way Bobby played, said, "I'm Bobby Charlton." The way Denis played said, "I'm Denis Law." When Denis Law strutted on to the pitch he was saying, "I'm Denis Law, this is me!" When Bobby came out of the tunnel he was saying, "This is me, this is the way I play." With George, he just said, "This is the way I play football." Wow!

'And I think that is what you want to convey to young players, to express themselves and flourish in their own way. And I think the wonderful thing for those three players was that they had an environment, created by Matt Busby and Jimmy Murphy, that allowed them to do just that. That was the magic and the genius of Busby and Murphy, that they created an environment where those players could thrive and express themselves as players in their own way. It wasn't a dictatorial thing. And it was like this too for the other players before them, who sadly died. They were also encouraged to express themselves; David Pegg, Duncan Edwards, Liam Whelan, all those players talk about what a great club it was and how it was fun to play, to socialise together. Wilf talks about that, how they went to town together, to the pictures together, to

Switzerland together. It was fun, it was joyous, and everyone was singing from the same sheet together and dying for the same cause.

'If you're a better footballer individually you would be a better player for the team. They shared everything, weren't selfish and just did everything for the team. We use our own gifts for the benefit of the team, finding out where our gifts fitted in. I think that's pretty much the story of Matt Busby's career, creating that environment where people could retain their own identity within the framework of the team. And that's not easy to do, is it? Sir Matt had great human qualities and I think Sir Alex was the same. It's not all about process is it? In today's world a lot of it is about procedures, policies, process and structures. Sometimes we miss our way and forget that these human qualities bring out the best in people.'

For me, whenever I watched George Best, Denis Law and Bobby Charlton play, I was always lifted to a different plane and inspired to fulfil whatever potential I possessed. Once I had entered Old Trafford and climbed the steps to the Stretford End, I knew that I was going to experience an electrifying magic show where anything was possible. The world suddenly became a place of opportunity. Through that inspiration, and the kindness of friends and family, I had a vibrant, happy childhood that I would not have traded.

Those special Manchester United games, the big FA Cup ties, the foggy European nights, and, of course, the first, momentous European Cup win will always hold a certain place in my heart. The memories are a part of who I am, and I'm pleased I have them. In the 1960s, walking through Trafford Park Industrial Estate might not have been pretty. The refreshments at the ground certainly could have been better, and I never, ever experienced the luxury of sitting to watch a game. But you know what? I miss those days. They were okay. They were more than okay.

Acknowledgements

I AM immensely grateful for the kindness and encouragement shown by a great number of people. Paul and Jane Camillin at Pitch Publishing were always most helpful and efficient throughout the different stages of publication, and I would like to thank them for taking a chance on me as a first-time author. I must also thank Duncan Olner at Pitch for the stunning front cover. Tony Whelan facilitated the interviews undertaken at Manchester United and was a constant source of expert knowledge and advice, always delivered in a most friendly, professional manner. Paul McGuinness was also most helpful in arranging the interview with his father, Wilf McGuinness. Tony Whelan and William Cooper helped me enormously with drafts of the book at key stages and gave honest, invaluable advice. I could not have wished for more interesting and insightful contributors to the book and am forever grateful to Cliff Butler, John Cooke, Wilf McGuinness, Jimmy Ryan, David Sadler and Tony Whelan. They gave of their time graciously, and it was humbling to see how much they enjoyed reliving their own memories of this golden era. Thanks too are due to Alan Wardle, Secretary of the Association of Former Manchester United Players, for good cooperation. The staff at Central Library, Middleton

Library (both Manchester) and Manchester Metropolitan University Library (Manchester and Cheshire campuses) were always helpful and a credit to their profession. Overall, the help and encouragement I was given by everyone left me with the feeling that we all shared something very important: each of us had fondly remembered the Best, Law and Charlton years at Manchester United. More than anything, I hope I have been able to reflect a little of this warmth, respect and nostalgia in the text. Finally, a special thank you to my wife, Cathy, who has patiently endured my obsession with a 1960s world during the writing of this book.

Picture Acknowledgements

My thanks go to Jeremy Parrett at Manchester Metropolitan University Library, Visual Resources Centre, who was exceptionally supportive in supplying me with the wonderful images of 1960s Manchester. Staff at Chethams Library, Manchester, were also most accommodating in terms of allowing access to their fascinating Belle Vue Collection of photographs. Alex Jackson, at the National Football Museum (NFM) in Manchester, also provided excellent cooperation in allowing access to the museum's brilliant collections. I am also thankful to Neil Smith for his daytime photographs of Manchester and the NFM. Finally, my thanks to Helen Tse for photographs of her famous family restaurants.

Bibliography

Arthur, M., *The Busby Babes: Men of Magic* (Edinburgh: Mainstream Publishing Company, 2008)

Bennett, A., *Keeping On, Keeping On* (London, Faber & Faber, 2016)

Best, G., and Wright, G., *Where do I go from here? George Best: an autobiography* (London: McDonald and Co./Queen Anne Press, 1981)

Bracknell, D., *Cup Fever* (film) (Manchester, Children's Film Foundation, 1965)

Bret, D., *Brit Girls of the Sixties, Volume 1* (Kobo website: https://www.kobo.com/gb/en/David Bret, 2010)

Busby, M., and Jack, D., *Matt Busby: My Story* (London: Souvenir Press, 1957)

Busby, M., *Soccer at the Top: My Life in Football* (London: Weidenfeld and Nicholson, 1973)

Charlton, B., *Sir Bobby Charlton, The Autobiography. My Manchester United Years* (London: Headline, 2007)

Charlton, C., and Gledhill, V., *Cissie: Football's Most Famous Mother Tells Her Story* (Morpeth: Bridge Studios, 1988)

Clayton, D., *Manchester Stories* (Ayr: Fort Publishing, 2013)

Crolla, A., and McGuinness., D., *Million Dollar Crolla: Good Guys Can Win* (Durrington: Pitch Publishing, 2017)

Daily Express, *Survivors Speak; United Players Tell How They Escaped* (London: Daily Express Publications, 1958)

Davies, R.D., *Dedicated Follower of Fashion* (London: Pye Records, 1966)

Dunphy, E., *Sir Matt Busby and Manchester United, A Strange Kind of Glory* (London: Heinemann, 1991)

Ferris, K., *Manchester United in Europe* (Edinburgh: Mainstream, 2004)

Gibb, B., Gibb, R., and Gibb, M., *Massachusetts* (Song) (London: Polydor, 1967)

Green, G., *There's Only One United, The Official History of Manchester United* (London: Hodder and Stoughton, 1978)

Henderson, J., *The Last Champion: The Life of Fred Perry* (London: Yellow Jersey Press, 2009)

Hopcroft, A., *The Football Man* (London: Aurum Press, 2006)

i newspaper, *Marcus Rashford – How People Reacted to the Bombing Made Me Proud To Be A Mancunian.* (London: Johnston Publications Ltd, 23 May 2018)

Kes, *Film, based on the book A Kestrel for a Knave by Barry Hines* (London: Woodfall Film Productions, 1969)

Imlach, G., *My Father and Other Working Class Football Heroes* (London: Yellow Jersey Press, 2006)

Law, D., *Denis Law, Manchester United and Scotland, Living for Kicks* (London: Stanley Paul & Co, 1963)

Law, D., *Denis Law, An Autobiography* (London: Queen Anne Press, 1978)

Leigh, M., *Peterloo* (film) (Manchester: Film 4 Productions/ British Film Institute/Thin Man Films, 2018)

Leighton, J., *Duncan Edwards, The Greatest* (London: Simon and Schuster, 2012)

Manchester Evening News, *Youth Team Debuts* (Manchester: Manchester Evening News, 1963)

Manchester Evening News, *Recap: The IRA Bomb in Manchester ... What Happened on June 15, 1996* (MEN, 15 June 2006)

Manchester Evening News, *Town Mourns As The Boss Dies* (Website) (https://www.manchestereveningnews.co.uk/

news/local-news/town-mourns-as-the-boss-dies-1014762, 2007, accessed 13 August 2018)

Manchester Evening News, *Phil Lynott's Mother Recalls Exciting Days in Manchester* (Website) (https://www.manchestereveningnews.co.uk/news/greater-manchester-news/phil-lynotts-mother-recalls-exciting-855110, 2011, accessed 20 July 2018)

Manchester Evening News, *Munich Remembered: Manchester United Tragedy in Quotes* (Website) (https://www.manchestereveningnews.co.uk/sport/football/football-news/munich-remembered-manchester-united-tragedy-8585706, 2015, accessed 27 November 2018)

Manchester Evening News, *This Is What Love Looks Like* (Manchester: MEN, 23 May 2018)

Manchesterhistory, *Underground Manchester: The Tunnels, Tube Station, Shops Hidden Beneath the City's Streets,* (Website)
(http://manchesterhistory.net/manchester/tours/tour4/area4page13.html, 2018, accessed 24 August 2018)

McCartney, I., *Manchester United 1958–68: Rising From the Wreckage* (Gloucester: Amberley Publishing, 2013)

McGuinness, W., *Wilf McGuinness: Manchester United Man and Babe* (Warwickshire: Know the Score, 2008)

McKinstry, L., *Jack and Bobby: a Story of Brothers in Conflict* (London: Harper Collins, 2002)

Murphy, J., *Matt, United and Me* (London: Souvenir Press, 1968)

MUTV, *Denis Law: Made in Aberdeen* (Manchester: MUTV, 2019)

Parkinson, M., *Best: An Intimate Biography* (London: Hutchinson and Co, 1975)

Phillips, D., *Twisted Wheel Memories by the Original in the Crowd* (Website) (https://www.soul-source.co.uk/articles/soul-articles/twisted-wheel-memories-by-the-original-in-crowd-r183/, 2018, accessed 24 May 2018)

Poole, R., (Ed) 'What don't we know about Peterloo? in *Return to Peterloo* pp. 1-19 (Manchester: Manchester Centre for Regional History, 2014)

Poole, R., 'The Middleston Peterloo Banner' in *Return to Peterloo,* pp. 159-173 (Manchester: Manchester Centre for Regional History, 2014)

Rea, A., *Ancoats, Little Italy* (Website) (http://www.ancoatslittleitaly.com/, 2010, accessed 22 June 2018)

Retrowow., *60s Mods*, (Website) (https://www.retrowow.co.uk/retro_style/60s/60s_mods.html, accessed 30 July 2018)

Roberts, J., *The Team That Wouldn't Die, The Story of The Busby Babes* (London: Arthur Barker, 1975)

Shindler, C., *Fathers, Sons and Football* (London: Headline, 2001)

Shindler, C., *George Best and 21 Others* (London: Headline, 2004)

Shorrocks, A., *Winners and Champions* (London: Arthur Barker, 1985)

Stiles, N., *After the Ball* (London: Hodder and Stoughton, 2003)

Thescooterist.com. (Website) (http://www.thescooterist.com/2012/08/youth-culture-mods-rockers-1960s-1970s.html, 2012, accessed 30 July 2018)

Tse, H., *Sweet Mandarin* (London: Ebury Press, 2007)

Weight, R., *Mod: A Very British Style* (London: The Bodley Head, 2013)

Whelan, T., *Birth of the Babes, Manchester United Youth Policy 1950–1957* (Manchester: Empire Publications, 2005)

Yorkshire Evening Post, *31 March 1965, Manchester United 0 Leeds United 1,* (Website) (http://www.mightyleeds.co.uk/matches/19650331.htm, 1965, accessed 24 August 2018)